# A Web of New Words

ENGLISH CORPUS LINGUISTICS

Thomas Kohnen / Joybrato Mukherjee (eds.)

VOLUME 15

PETER LANG EDITION

Daphné Kerremans

# A Web of New Words

## A Corpus-Based Study of the Conventionalization Process of English Neologisms

PETER LANG
EDITION

**Bibliographic Information published by the Deutsche Nationalbibliothek**
The Deutsche Nationalbibliothek lists this publication in the Deutsche Nationalbibliografie; detailed bibliographic data is available in the internet at http://dnb.d-nb.de.

Zugl.: München, Univ., Diss., 2012

D 19
ISSN 1610-868X
ISBN 978-3-631-65578-8 (Print)
E-ISBN 978-3-653-04788-2 (E-Book)
DOI 10.3726/978-3-653-04788-2


Peter Lang Edition is an Imprint of Peter Lang GmbH.

Peter Lang – Frankfurt am Main · Bern · Bruxelles · New York · Oxford · Warszawa · Wien



This publication has been peer reviewed.

www.peterlang.com

*To Charlie, the sweetest innovation of all*

# Acknowledgements

This book presents the updated and thoroughly revised version of my doctoral dissertation submitted to and accepted by the Ludwig-Maximilians-University Munich in 2012. As far as I know, currently no neologism exists capable of succinctly expressing my thanks to all the people that have been involved in the realization of this project in many different ways. First and foremost I would like to thank Prof. Dr. Hans-Jörg Schmid, who acted as my dissertation advisor at the Ludwig-Maximilians-University Munich, for giving me free rein to develop my ideas that lead to the present study. His support, confidence and advice have been priceless. I also owe a big thank you to Prof. Dr. Stephanie Hackert, who kept my table clear off other tasks, which allowed me to focus entirely on my research.

Special thanks I owe to Susanne Stegmayr, now Grandmontagne, whose tireless efforts in developing, programming and nurturing our NeoCrawler have made the entire enterprise possible in the first place. Most of all, however, I would like to thank her for her equally tireless support and friendship.

Many thanks also go to Dr. Thomas Hawes for his meticulous proofreading and invaluable encouragement in countless other ways. Special thanks go to Dr. Sandra Handl, Dr. Susanne Handl and Dr. Ron Kuzar, with whom I discussed several parts of this work and whose critical comments have been of major help.

I am greatly indebted to Dr. Kathryn Allan for her hospitality during the experiments at University College London. I would also like to thank Johanna Brandt and Shuai Shao from the statistics department at the Ludwig-Maximilians-University Munich for their expertise and help with the statistical analysis.

I also owe special thanks to my parents, who have been a source of silent support and confidence during the entire project, and to Fleur and Pippa, for teaching me the one or the other new word.

Above all, I thank my husband Marc for being genuinely interested in my work and unfailingly encouraging me in everything I do.

# Contents

# List of figures and tables

# 1. Introduction

## 1.1. General introduction

Neologisms are like casting show winners. A minority of them become established singers, some are one-hit wonders and others almost instantaneously disappear into oblivion. The commercial framework of TV shows, gigs and record deals provides a supportive context for initially and instantaneously acquiring a high degree of popularity. As soon as the winner and runners-up have been crowned, however, attention quickly dwindles and independent careers take off or do not take off. Some winners might still score a hit with their finale song before vanishing from the public stage, others do manage to outlive the initial hype. Occasionally, a contestant does not even have to win to embark on a successful career. There does not seem to exist a recipe for success, nor a foolproof system that predicts who will make it and who will not. After all, many pop- and rockstars do not even need a casting show to become famous. In language, similar processes continuously take place. Of the many new words that enter the English language at a given point in time, some just happen to blend into it almost unnoticedly, whereas others stand out, receive a good deal of attention as ephemeral fashion words only to disappear after the hype has settled down. Although the following study is not intended to develop a linguistically-programmed crystal ball that would prophesy which novel words will become established in the English language, the underlying question is the same as for the casting show winners: which factors determine or influence, and to what degree, whether a novel formation diffuses through the speech community and possibly becomes a permanent addition to the language?

Prior to discussing the scope and aims of the present work in 1.2, it is necessary to briefly sketch the etymological origin and development of the word *neologism*, because it is partially responsible for the vagueness with which it is applied in linguistics (see 2.1.1) and its study in the realm of lexicography rather than in more theoretically-oriented branches, leaving the central question in the previous paragraph largely unanswered. Thus, simply put, a neologism is a new word, from Greek *neo-* 'new' and *logos* 'word'. Following this definition, neologisms as sources of lexical enrichment are intrinsic parts of dynamic language use and development, both from a synchronic and diachronic perspective. Perhaps surprisingly, the word *neology* and its subsequently emerging lexical family did not appear in English until the Enlightenment in the 18th century as a borrowing from French (cf. Clauzure 2003: 208)[1]. In French, the interest in neologisms had been awakened earlier by the Pléiade poets in the 16th century, who claimed that the more words a language has, the more perfect it becomes and therefore introduced many novel formations and borrowings in their works and the language at large (cf. Alaoui 2003: 150-156). Not until the 18th century, however, did the concept gain a strong foothold in the French language and become lexicalized as *néologique* in 1725 (when the *Dictionnaire néologique* appeared as the first of many new word collections to reflect technological developments and political ideas), *néologisme* in 1734 and *néologie* in 1759 (cf. Alaoui 2003: 163-172). In English, the first use of *neological* in 1754, borrowed from French, is attributed to Lord Chesterfield, who envisioned a dictionary for the elite, "a genteel *neological* dictionary, containing those polite [...] words and phrases, commonly used by the beau monde" (quoted in Clauzure 2003: 208). Such dictionaries of hard words had already existed since the 17th century, for instance, Robert Cawdrey's *Table Alphabeticall* from 1604, but were concerned with borrowings from Latin, Greek etc., which were of course new in English, rather than novel English coinages per se.

Towards the end of the 18th century, possibly influenced by a similar development in French, *neological* acquired a second, slightly more negative sense (cf. Clauzure 2003: 209), as illustrated by another quote by Lord Chesterfield (in Clauzure 2003: 208): "the affected, the refined, the *neological*, or new and fashionable style, are at present too much in vogue in Paris". Such objections fit the general spirit of 18th century England, in which language purity and reform were high on the agenda (cf. Baugh and Cable 2002: 274-288). Although Clauzure (cf. 2003: 218) claims that the same negative connotation affects *neologism*, again transferred from French (cf. Sablayrolles 2000: 55), on the basis of the quotations or illustrations in dictionaries, not all of the examples from the *Oxford English Dictionary* (OED) support this claim[2]. Moreover, *neologism* seems to have entered the English earlier than assumed. Clauzure mentions 1800 or afterwards (cf. 2003: 208, 211), but the OED lists an attestation from 1772[3].

1 For a review of the development of the concept in French, see Sablayrolles (2000: 22ff.).

2 See for instance "Since that day neologisms have fertilised the barrenness of our Saxon" from 1841 and "The class which, to use a modern neologism, 'formulates' the ideas [etc.]" from 1875 (cf. OED entry for *neologism*).

3 "Observations on this Neologism... I thought indeed I was intirely [sic] done with this Canon when I came to the explication of the last word Hecaterogenosem.", Jean

In view of its origins in a time when the language was seen as in need of protection from, rather than embellishment with, instances of lexical innovation, it is not astonishing that "[t]he history of English lexicography begins with the study of neology", as remarked by John Algeo, neologist pur sang (1993: 281) and neology has remained somewhat neglected in theoretical linguistics. He lists an impressive chronology of dictionaries, word lists and popular books devoted to neologisms from Cawdrey's 1604 publication until the end of the 20th century (cf. 1993: 282-282). In recent years, these print records have been and are being supplemented with online collections such as the periodical *Word trends and new words* blog from the OED[4], MacMillan's *Open Dictionary* and *BuzzWord* column[5], Webster's *New Words and Slang* section of their *Open Dictionary*[6] and various private word-watching websites among which Paul McFedries' *WordSpy*[7] and Michael Quinion's *World Wide Words*[8] are the most acclaimed.

In spite of a common interest in neologisms, lexicographers, word spies and neolinguists have different goals and work within different theoretical paradigms. Whereas lexicographers continually face the difficult challenge of collecting new words and deciding which ones to include in their dictionaries, neolophilical word-watchers simply amass novel coinages, predominantly conspicuous vogue words that frequently turn out to be one-hit wonders, and provide a rudimentary profile of meaning and use. Neolinguists occupy an intermediate position. In addition to tracking new words, they are profoundly interested in their linguistic behavior and relation to other linguistic phenomena, which necessarily transcends a mere description of form and meaning. However, since their concerns are purely theoretical in nature, they do not need to evaluate the linguistic and extralinguistic durability in order to justify inclusion in dictionaries. Nevertheless, the question of why certain words become established and others become obsolete periodically arises here too. Partly due to the fact that neologisms have seemed to belong in the realm of lexicography and partly due to the lack of

---

Nicolas Jouin de Sauseuil. 1772. *An analysis of the French orthography* or *The true principles of the French pronunciation, exhibited in several easy schemes and tables* (cf. OED entry for *neologism*).

4 blog.oxforddictionaries.com/category/word-trends-and-new-words/.

5 macmillandictionary.com/.

6 nws.merriam-webster.com/opendictionary/.

7 wordspy.com.

8 worldwidewords.org.

adequate empirical tools, this question has largely remained unanswered[9]. Crystal even claims that "there is never any way of telling which neologisms will stay and which will go" (1995: 132). Rather than taking this statement at face value, in the present study, I will provide a tentative answer to the unanswered question by empirically investigating several linguistic and extralinguistic factors that affect the conventionalization process, i.e. the process by means of which neologisms become established in the language and the speech community, to varying degrees.

## 1.2. Research questions

In view of the importance of language as a communication device in everyday human interaction, the need for new words arises perpetually "as they are required" (Aitchison 1991: 118). Most conspicuously, this need emerges when new objects or concepts are introduced in society or when objects or concepts change and their original names have become inept (cf. Aitchison 1991: 118). The social need is frequently intertwined with a semantic need in the language, i.e. to fill a lexical gap (cf. Bauer 1983: 43; Aitchison 1994: 158; Kjellmer 2000: 221). The coinage of new words is not necessarily motivated by naming requirements in society. Stylistic concerns or the need to be succinct play a role too, particularly in formal and creative writing (cf. Bauer 1983: 43; Aitchison 1994: 158). Thus, one major German bookseller praised their new recommendations as "unputdownable books"[10]. 'Unputdownable' can hardly be characterized as a new concept and it is doubtful whether this particular lexical gap needs to be filled. Rather, *unputdownable* condenses an entire syntactic phrase ('difficult/hard/impossible to put down') into one novel coinage, which saves space and catches the attention of the reader. Often, however, speakers create novel words with less

---

9 In her unpublished PhD dissertation Boulanger (1997) approaches the matter of establishment of neologisms from a similar perspective, which differs from the one adopted in one important aspect. She investigates the potential influence of a selection of linguistic and social factors post facto and measures the success of establishment of a new word as inclusion in a general-purpose reference dictionary at one point in time rather than longitudinally tracking the diffusion through the speech community in terms of frequency of occurrence. Since dictionary inclusion is a slightly artificial criterion for establishment, based on the decisions of editors and lexicographic committees and not always accurately reflects the actual state of establishment, I have adopted a dynamic, process-based approach and refrain from statements of success or failure of neologisms.

10 From the Hugendubel magazine *Büchermenschen* (February-March 2012: 22).

conscious effort because they cannot instantaneously recall the established word in a conversation or because the lexicon does not provide an adequate expression (cf. Bauer 1983: 43). These instances of conversational need are individual, small-scale innovations that typically quickly disappear or remain restricted to the vocabulary of the conversation partners.

Despite the ubiquity of new word coinage processes, their products predominantly make transient appearances. Algeo observed that 58% of the new words collected in the *Britannica Book of the Year* between 1944 and 1976 were not rewarded with a dictionary entry, which represents evidence of their non-establishment or obsolescence (cf. 1993: 281, 283). Whereas he focused on a classificatory description of the extinct words and offers socio-functional explanations for their "desuetude" (Algeo 1993: 281) or death, other authors have concentrated on their birth and suggested several diffusion-inhibiting or -promoting factors. Unfortunately, many of these claims have never been investigated empirically, nor systematically, for instance, only with regard to a small selection of neologisms and restricted to specific genres (see 2.1 for an overview). The present work presents a large-scale, usage-based approach to these claims and attempts to provide a solid scientific basis for studying the diffusion of English neologisms.

In his entertaining book *Predicting New Words*, for instance, Allan Metcalf proposes to assess the failure or success rate of neologisms according to the "FUDGE factors" (2002: 152). He says that "the success or failure of new words is not entirely random. Some factors evidently make for success, while others hinder it." (2002: 149). His FUDGE collection consists of linguistic and extralinguistic components. In his opinion, "unobtrusiveness" (2002: 155) is particularly significant (cf. 2002: 144, 167, 185); new words should "fl[y] under the radar" and "camouflage[...]" themselves, because "[o]ur minds are inclined to reject a conspicuous new word; it has to blend into the familiar landscape (or wordscape) before we can let it in" (2002: 156). In linguistic terms, this means that a novel lexeme should be phonologically, morphologically, semantically and orthographically consistent with established patterns in English (cf. Kjellmer 2000: 206, 208-216[11]). Moreover, it should be formally and functionally-semantically unambiguous, because of the requirements of successful communication. Since new words are by definition not or at best minimally familiar to the reader or

11 Although Kjellmer is not concerned with the establishment of new words, but with the probability that they might be coined in their particular form with their particular meaning, I assume that formal acceptability is not only a requirement for a word to be created, but also for it to become conventionalized.

hearer, the intentions of the writer or speaker can only be transferred unproblematically if the meaning is straightforward, i.e. not competing with other senses that are equally new. As a corollary of the unobtrusiveness factor, neologisms stand a better chance of becoming conventionalized when they are not the topic of metalinguistic discourse (cf. Metcalf 2002: 185). Metalinguistic discourse involves readers or writers, speakers or hearers commenting on the coinage, existence, emergence or formal shape of a neologism or providing explanations and definitions, e.g. *I thought "bromance"*[12] *was a very clever term, the first time I heard it*[13]. These instances are commentarial-evaluative meta-uses; the word itself becomes the center of attention, but is not used with a new class of referents as in objectlinguistic use in the example *Is this gay or bromance? I'm confused:(?*, introducing a passage on an instance of a complicated intense male friendship[14]. Although initially, diffusion might be promoted by metalinguistic usage, reflected in an increase in frequency, it is debatable whether such metalinguistic discourse will also propel the active-objectlinguistic use of the neologism forward[15]. The unobtrusiveness criterion yields the two following negative hypotheses to be presently investigated:

- H1: Semantic ambiguity, and/or
- H2: Dominant or disproportionally high use in metalinguistic mode inhibits conventionalization.

From a socio-pragmatic perspective, a positive influence is to be expected when the neologism is used in more formal types of sources like newspapers and large Internet portals, because they guarantee a large readership that in turn can diffuse the neologism further in ever expanding circles (cf. Kjellmer 2000: 224-225; Fischer 1998: 16; Schmid 2011a: 75, Paradowski and Jonak 2012: 56). Since new words spread through individuals' speech and writing, the size and social structure of the audience plays an important role in the potential diffusion process. Moreover, new words appearing in newspapers tend to be coined by professionals or prestigious persons. As Kjellmer notes, many newspapers and media

12 "Intimate and affectionate friendship between men; a relationship between two men which is characterized by this" (from OED entry for *bromance*, entered in June 2013).

13 Facebook page of *Upworthy*, Sept 12, 2013, facebook.com/Upworthy/posts/628073293900199.

14 *Yahoo answers*, unknown date, answers.yahoo.com/question/index?qid=20110716083501AABOFsO.

15 In Schmid (cf. 2011: 75) metalinguistic discourse is assumed to have a positive effect on the conventionalization.

broadcasters have special experts that invent new words for new concepts and supervise the use of these in the publications (cf. 2000: 224). Whenever such a word appears, the authority or prestige of the coiner and/or user appeals to the reader-speaker and enhances its adoption into the lexicon of the individuals (cf. Bauer 1983: 43; Aitchison 1994: 157). Chesley (2011), for instance, found out that the degree of knowledge of AAVE hip hop vocabulary is determined by the degree of popularity of the artists. A special case in point is provided by the many websites with Bushisms and Palinisms, where people collect the idiosyncratic uses or coinages of these politicians in a mocking way. These social and socio-pragmatic aspects result in the following hypotheses:

- H3: A first or frequent use in more formal types of source and/or
- H4: The authority or prominence of the coiner and first users promotes conventionalization.

The fifth hypothesis to be investigated is motivated by extralinguistic reception concerns. When a new word appears in a language, not only its structural, i.e. phonological, orthographical and semantic attractiveness is gauged, but also its usefulness for communicative purposes. This phenomenon has been studied in linguistics as "nameworthiness" (Downing 1979: 838; cf. "usefulness" in Aitchison 1994: 157) from the perspective of the concept or "semantic need" (Kjellmer 2000: 221) from the perspective of the coiner. Thus, when a novel formation fills a lexical gap or denotes a nameworthy concept, it stands a better chance of becoming conventionalized, because its linguistic existence meets a communicative demand that has arisen in discourse and society (cf. Kastovsky 1982: 159; Große and Neubert 1982: 13; Lipka 1992: 110; Kjellmer 2000: 221-224; Schmid 2011a: 75)[16]. These assumptions underlie the following hypothesis:

- H5: The nameworthiness of the represented concept or its salience in society promotes conventionalization.

The final factor of influence that will be investigated is the existence of collocational syntagmatic networks in which the neologism is embedded. I assume that these collocational patterns function as cotextual anchoring points (cf. Baayen

16 Metcalf on the other hand acknowledges the durability of the concept as a promoting factor, but claims, in his rather programmatical chapter "The myth of gaps" (2002: 63-77), that "[w]hether a new word survives does not depend on whether it fills a perceived gap in our vocabulary, and not even on whether it is useful, since the landfill of discarded new coinages has an ample supply of useful terms." (2002: 76-77).

of linguistic innovation, because it is the prime medium of innovation and its propagation in the 21st century and also relatively uncomplicated and cheap to access.

In order to be able to use the Internet as a linguistic data pond a custom-tailored webcrawler was built by Susanne Grandmontagne, Hans-Jörg Schmid and me at the Ludwig-Maximilians-University Munich. The NeoCrawler scoured the Web in weekly intervals to retrieve and process occurrences of all of the 44 neologisms selected for the study. Each of these pages was then manually classified according to a set of socio-pragmatic features with the purpose of compiling a social and linguistic profile of the neologism under consideration. These usage-based profiles served as the basis for the statistical model supplying quantitative evidence for the degree to which each of the selected factors influences the diffusion process. The study thus relies on data reflecting changes in real time and provides an innovative in-vitro perspective on lexical change in the fastest growing and changing medium that the Internet is. Although the use of the Internet as a data source for linguistic study is not entirely problematic, as discussed in chapter 3, it offers a unique way to closely observe language innovation and change. As I will show, the use of state-of-the-art technology propels linguistic research forward and sheds light on processes previously out of reach such as fast and immediate lexical innovation, which in turn supplements the existing theoretical frameworks with more detailed insights.

## 1.3. Outline

In the next chapter I will provide a detailed discussion of the nature of neologisms and their establishment process, first within the traditional framework of structural linguistics and lexicography (section 2.1). I will focus on their not unproblematic definition in 2.1.1, the theoretical aspects of lexicalization and institutionalization in 2.1.2 and discuss two empirical studies that have investigated the latter in 2.1.3. In section 2.2 cognitive-linguistic aspects of neologisms are presented. Three of these aspects, co(n)text (2.2.1), exposure (2.2.2) and transparency (2.2.3) are highlighted, because of their importance during comprehension and lexical retrieval. The theoretical chapter concludes with an introduction to the conventionalization process in 2.3.

Chapter 3 is devoted to the innovative methodology with which the neologisms under consideration have been collected and monitored on the Internet. Since the use of the Internet in linguistics is currently hotly debated, this chapter starts with an overview of general problems pertaining to this issue in 3.1.1 and presents technological tools and methods that make the Web accessible to linguistic research in sections 3.1.2 and 3.1.3. In 3.2 I will introduce a new tool that was developed for the present purpose, the NeoCrawler. The NeoCrawler consists of two compatible components: the Discoverer, responsible for detecting novel formations in online language (3.2.1) and the Observer (in section 3.2.2), which is in charge of periodically crawling the Internet and downloading novel instances of the neologisms. The Observer is furthermore equipped with an integrated socio-pragmatic classification system that enables an in-depth investigation of the abovementioned hypotheses 2, 3 and 4. This classification system is presented in detail in 3.3.2. In 3.3.1 I discuss the selection criteria for the 44 neologisms under consideration. The methodological chapter concludes with a note on the operationalization of the nameworthiness factor, which was tested in a small-scale experiment (3.3.3).

The results of the present study are discussed in chapter 4. The first research question, concerned with the stages in conventionalization processes observed for the neologisms in the sample, is answered in section 4.1 and shows that four different stages were found: non-conventionalization (4.1.1), transitional conventionalization (4.1.2), recurrent semi-conventionalization (4.1.3) and advanced conventionalization (4.1.4). I should like to point out that the assigned stages along the conventionalization reflect the developments observed until January 2011 and might not present the actual status at the time of publication. In 4.2 I discuss the influence of the various factors discussed above with the help of a generalized binomial regression model.

The final chapter presents the results obtained regarding the emergence of syntagmatic lexical networks. A brief theoretical overview of the concept of collocation in 5.1 is followed by a detailed discussion of two routes of emergence, gradual development in 5.2.1 and instantaneous emergence in 5.2.2. Other syntagmatic patterns of variable strength are discussed in 5.2.3. The last section, 5.3, is concerned with the linguistic origin of the collocates, discussed in the light of their function as cotextual anchoring points, and concludes with a note on their role during conventionalization. A conclusion, summarizing the main findings, is found in chapter 6.

# 2. Neologisms in linguistics

Before giving an overview of previous neologism studies in linguistics, I will discuss the various definitions that have been suggested by word-formation experts, lexicologists and lexicographers (section 2.1.1). It will become clear that the concept of neologism, though ubiquitous in the literature, is far from straightforward. Since neologisms are not only a subject of interest to theoretically-oriented linguistic disciplines, but also play a significant role in the compilation process of dictionaries, section 2.1.1 will start with an overview of lexicographers' definitions and practices. The remainder of section 2.1. will proceed with a discussion of the establishment process of neologisms in lexical theory (2.1.2) and present recent empirical work by Hohenhaus (2005) and Fischer (1998). In section 2.2. I will describe various psycholinguistic studies that have been concerned with the mental processing of neologisms before introducing the socio-cognitive framework of entrenchment and conventionalization that theoretically underpins the present study (2.3).

## 2.1. Lexicographical and lexicological approaches

### 2.1.1. What are neologisms?

Standard reference dictionary compilers aim to provide the most accurate, complete and inclusive record of vocabulary. When new words massively influx the language, as has been observed by many lexicographers in the last 50 years (cf. *Collins English Dictionary,* 3rd edition, [3]CED 1992: viii, *Preface* to the 2nd edition of the *Oxford English Dictionary*, [2]OED 1989), decisions have to be made on whether these neologisms will be included at some point in time or not. In dictionaries, neologisms are often defined, if the term is used or defined at all, as "new words" or "new senses or usages of existing words" (cf. Berg 1993: 159, [3]CED 1992: vii, *Random House Webster's Unabridged Dictionary,* 2nd edition 1993: x, *Webster's Third* 1976). Since reference dictionaries would become unmanageable if all these new words were added, lexicographers face the difficult challenge of selecting which words will be included and which ones will remain undocumented. Graeme Diamond, current Editorial Content Director at the OED, admits that it is a highly complicated task to assess a word's durability and distinguish ephemera from lasting contributions to the language. The group therefore tracks and monitors potential candidates and their life-cycle via reading programs and the Oxford English Corpus. He compares lexicographers to "19th century gold panners: they must sift, and sift again to find the true gold" (December 2006 new words update[19]). According to the *Concise Oxford Dictionary* (COD) 70% do not make it into the dictionary because of their short-lived career in language (COD 11th edition 2008: 5). Recently, new word editors have also embraced the Internet in their task, albeit with mixed feelings. Despite being a wealthy source of language and offering uncomplicated access to it, the Internet also poses challenges to modern lexicography in the field of neology. On the one hand, it acts as the prime medium of linguistic innovation, with many lexemes sprouting up online before anywhere else (cf. Gleick 2006: 8; Hargraves 2007: 139), on the other hand, the vast array of online databases and resources makes it difficult for lexicographers to select the most appropriate ones for finding neologisms and evaluating their behavior prior to any decisions on inclusion (cf. Barnhart 2007: 133). Nevertheless, as Hargraves remarks, lexicographers are increasingly relying on the Internet because of its up-to-dateness, unmirrored range of forms of communication and the linguistic varieties used in all these situations (cf. 2007: 139-140, Gleick 2006: 12).

In order to find the "true gold", lexicographers have established a set of heterogenous inclusion criteria. Continued frequency over a longer period, defined by the OED and the *Third Barnhart Dictionary of New English* as a decade[20], is one of three criteria dictionaries like the OED, CED and Random House apply before a new word merits an entry. New words thus need to have made a lasting contribution to the vocabulary and acquired an established foundation, which filters out transitory vogue words or ephemera (cf. *Preface* to the 2nd edition of the OED 1989, [3]CED 1992: ix; Barnhart 2007: 135). However, the online editions of the major dictionaries attempt to follow the rapid pace of lexical innovation more closely and loosen the ten year period of attestation (cf. OED *Online*[21]). Thus, *selfie*, defined as a 'photographic self-portrait; esp. one taken with a smartphone or webcam and shared via social media', was added to the OED *Online*, 3rd edition in June 2014 (OED *What's New*, June 2014[22]) and *retweet*, to pass on a tweet on Twitter, will be included in the twelfth edition of the COD

19 oed.com/news/updates/newwords0612.html

20 From the statement made in December 2009 at the release of new words, see oed.com. However, Gleick (2006: 6) reports that continued use over five years is sufficient.

21 oxforddictionaries.com/page/newword

22 public.oed.com/whats-new/

(OxfordWords blog November 2011[23]), although they have not been in general use for an entire decade yet[24]. Similarly, Merriam-Webster runs an online *Open Dictionary*, where users can add new words with definitions. They do reserve the right to delete transitory or less useful words (cf. Merriam-Webster's *Open Dictionary* guidelines[25]). Secondly, the word or new sense needs to have entered the common, general and globally-used English vocabulary and occur in a wider range of contexts than purely scientific or technical use (cf. *Supplement to the* OED 1972: v, ³CED 1992: viii, Barnhart 2007: 135). Both *Webster's Third* and the OED (1972: v) moreover consider the usefulness of the new word. Usefulness is defined as being likely of interest to the user or likely to be looked up. This criterion tallies well with the nameworthiness of concepts and events, which is studied in the present investigation as a potential factor of influence on the conventionalization process of English neologisms (see sections 2.1.2 and 3.3.3). Unfortunately, the editors do not describe in detail how usefulness is assessed.

Like lexicographers, many linguists do not precisely define neologisms. It is striking that given the substantial body of research in word-formation and lexicology, the concept of neologism has been taken for granted as self-explanatory. Marchand (cf. 1960: 367-370) and Stein (cf. 1973: 276-288) devote a whole chapter to neologisms, but do not explain the term. Most text books list *neologism* in the index, but cross-checking the referenced page(s) reveals that a definition or clarification is often missing (cf. Kastovsky 1982; Katamba 1994; Lipka 2002). Bauer's first reference under *neologism,* for instance, leads to a passage in which new words are classified as loans or nonce-formations. The latter he explains as "new complex word[s] coined on the spur of the moment" (1983: 42). Where does the neologism fit in: is it a general term that covers both possibilities, or is it used as a synonym for *nonce-formation*?

The distinction between neologism and nonce-formation is indeed important. As early as 1906 Henry W. and Francis G. Fowler, founders of the *Concise Oxford English Dictionary* (COED), were concerned with the use of neologisms in written English. In their prescriptive style book *The King's English* (1906, 1954: 28-30), which dedicates a brief chapter to the appropriate use of neologisms in writing, they distinguish between words that refer to new objects and

---

23 blog.oxforddictionaries.com/2011/11/reports-of-the-death-of-the-cassette-tape-are-greatly-exaggerated/

24 The first attestation of *selfie* dates from an Australian Internet forum in 2002, fulfilling the decade-principle. The word did however not gain general currency until the beginning of the second decade of the 21st century.

25 nws.merriam-webster.com/opendictionary/guide.php

become part and parcel of the lexicon of the speech community and the majority of its members.

In the following section I will sketch previous research on the socio-pragmatic process by means of which neologisms become established in the speech community, i.e. the *institutionalization* process, and discuss the establishment with regard to various formal issues neologisms are affected by, known as *lexicalization*. In addition, cognitive aspects will be addressed as a preamble to the theoretical framework of entrenchment and conventionalization, which is presented in 2.3.

### 2.1.2. The establishment of neologisms: Lexicalization, institutionalization and hypostatization

The diachronic, gradual and individual process by means of which novel lexemes and lexical units become a permanent addition to the lexicon of speakers and the language community is labeled *establishment* (Schmid 2011a: 71). Traditionally, this process has been studied from a structural and socio-pragmatic perspective. The former is commonly referred to as *lexicalization* (Lipka 1977: 156, 1992: 101, 107, 2002: 113, Lipka et al. 2004: 3; Hohenhaus 2005: 353; Fischer 1998; Schmid 2005: 73, 2008: 3-4, 2011a: 71), the latter as *institutionalization* (Lipka 1992: 107, 2002: 112, Lipka et al. 2004: 7; Hohenhaus 2005: 359; Fischer 1998; 15 Schmid 2005: 73, 2008: 3, 2011a: 71). However, Bauer (cf. 1983: 45ff.) uses these terms to describe the stages in and not the linguistic perspectives on the establishment process. In his terminology, the first stage reflects the coinage moment, when a nonce-formation is used for the first time. The second step is the institutionalization stage. The new lexeme, semantically unambiguous and lexically transparent becomes item-familiar to the speakers. The last stage is formed by the lexicalization. Formal changes resulting from systematic changes in the language, for instance, certain suffixes like *-th* in *warmth* or *-ment* in *government* becoming unproductive, affect the lexeme. A similar definition is found in Quirk (cf. 1985: 1515). An overview of the characteristics of the establishment process from the different linguistic and cognitive perspectives is found in Table 1 on page 29 (cf. Schmid 2008, 2011a: 71). In the following, these perspectives will be discussed in detail.

Lexicalization[31] denotes the process in which a complex new lexeme or lexical unit undergoes semantic and formal changes, causing its syntagma character to

31 In Lyons, the term "fossilization" is used (1977: 547). Leech prefers "petrification" and "idiomatization" (1974: 226).

be gradually lost to a greater or lesser extent and its structurally and semantically unitary character strengthened. As a result, the meaning cannot be derived from the semantic sum of its constituents nor from the meaning of the underlying word-formation process (cf. Lipka 1977: 155, 1992: 101, 107; cf. Kastovsky 1982: 164-165). Whereas in many cases of lexicalization the lexeme is only affected by minor changes, such as the full vowel reduction of /æ/ to /ə/ in *postman* or the addition of the semantic feature [+ PROFESSIONAL] or [+ HABITUAL] in *-er* nominalizations like *writer* or *teacher* (cf. Lipka 1992: 108), more extreme effects of lexicalization will lead to demotivation and idiomaticity of the lexemes involved. A word like *holiday*, for instance, has become both phonologically and semantically opaque or demotivated, since the first component is no longer pronounced identically to the adjective *holy* ([həʊli] vs. [hɒli]) nor is the meaning of the entire compound transparent or compositional. A *holiday* is not merely a 'holy day', but 'a day or an extended period of recreation, often away from home' (cf. Lipka 1992: 108). Demotivation and idiomatization have different linguistic and extralinguistic causes (cf. Lipka 1992: 108-109). As in the example of *holiday* or *postman*, phonological changes are responsible for the structural connection to the free morphemes {man} and {holy} to be obscured. Graphemic adjustments too, as in *tuppence,* can lead to increased demotivation. If the first syllable cannot be recognized any longer as *two*, the entire compound becomes non-compositional and opaque. Non-compositionality and semantic opaqueness also arise through semantic change. Semantic features can be lost or added as illustrated in the example of *writer* above, or the lexeme can be subjected to metaphorical shifts as in *ladykiller*[32] or metonymical meaning shifts as in *redbreast*[33]. Some cases do not result from linguistic, but from extralinguistic changes. Despite the replacement of blackboards by objects with a green surface or more recently whiteboards, the former term continues to exist as a generic name for the object that is placed at the front of a class room and used by teachers and pupils to write on. Thus, a

32 The earliest citations in the OED *Online* entry for *ladykiller* evidence a quite literal meaning for the second element, with references to death or intense sorrow ([...] *leaves her, as he thinks, to die of a broken heart* or and [...] *to have a woman kill herself out of love for him!*), instead of the more modern meaning of a man who likes to seduce women.

33 Similar to the metaphorical shift in *ladykiller*, the metonymic shift in *redbreast* may be indiscernible from a synchronic point of view. From a taxonomic perspective however, *redbreast* is currently used as a synonym for *robin* and refers to the European or American robin, whereas other birds in the redbreast family exist, e.g. linnets and bullfinches (cf. The Royal Society for the Protection of Birds).

change in the composition, material or conception of the extralinguistic referent, i.e. a denotational change, can also cause a language-internal process of demotivation. Naturally, a combination of the various linguistic and extralinguistic causes also occurs, as the *holiday* example shows. However, it should be noted that the absence of motivation or transparency is not only caused by diachronic developments, but can affect the lexeme from the moment of coinage (cf. Lipka 1981: 122; Blank 2001: 1597-1599; Schmid 2008: 4, 2011a: 78).

Lexicalization has also been described with a different set of terms, particularly in the context of language change[34]. In an attempt to provide a structured classification of the various linguistic changes that result in the loss of formal autonomy of constituents (lexemes and morphemes) during lexicalization, Brinton and Traugott (cf. 2005a: 47-57) distinguish between different types of "fusion" (2005a: 47, 2005b: 4-5), depending on the formal outcome of the process. Despite the semantic, morphological and/or phonological changes, the individual constituents might still be recognized as such and be distinguished from the other constituents. This happens on the one hand when larger syntactic constructions fuse into single or multiword lexemes, which is called "univerbation" (Brinton and Traugott 2005a: 48-50)[35]. The degree of opacity depends on the age. Older phrases are typically more opaque than younger phrases. Thus, words like *handicap*, from *hand-in-cap* and *goodbye* from *God be with you*, are less morphologically transparent than *mother-in-law*, where the single lexemes are clearly identifiable as such (cf. Brinton and Traugott 2005a: 48-50). A second subtype on the other hand consists of affixes that have developed diachronically from independent compound constituents. The present adverbial *-ly* suffix (as in *normally, typically*) is derived from the Old English free lexeme *lice*, which had the meaning of 'body, likeness' (cf. Brinton and Traugott 2005a: 50-52). What causes such complex lexemes to be reduced to simplexes (lexemes or bound morphemes) is that some word-formation processes have become unproductive or words have become obsolete. The simplification of complex lexemes can also obscure their formal autonomy to the extent that the elements are not recognized

34 An overview of the various usages of lexicalization can be found in Brinton and Traugott (2005: 18-22).

35 Surprisingly, in a publication from the same year, Brinton and Traugott use a different terminology (2005b). In this article, they distinguish between univerbation or fusion, bonding for changes that result in the loss of morphological boundaries, and coalescence, which is reserved for changes that result in the loss of phonological structure (cf. 2005b: 4-5). As mentioned above, in their monograph they treat univerbation as a special case of fusion.

synchronically as such anymore. The indistinguishability of historically independent lexemes and morphemes in present-day simplexes presents the second type of fusion. Examples of this type are on the one hand words like *mermaid*, in which the first element is a reduction of the obsolete Old English *mere* 'sea', and *husband* from Old English *hus* ('house') + *bōndi* ('dweller') (cf. Brinton and Traugott 2005a: 50-52). A second subtype is "demorphologization" (Joseph and Janda 1988: 198-202; cf. also Brinton and Traugott 2005a: 52) or "phonogenesis" (Hopper 1994: 31; cf. also Brinton and Traugott 2005a: 52). In such processes, the changes only affect the morpheme's "grammatical-semantic contribution to the word, while retaining part of its original phonological substance" (Brinton and Traugott 2005a: 52), as illustrated by *alone* from *all* + *one* and the *sw-* sequence in *swine* or *swill*, which can be traced back to PIE **sū*, 'pig' (cf. Brinton and Traugott 2005a: 52-54). Furthermore, Brinton and Traugott introduce a reverse effect of lexicalization: the increase in, instead of loss of, autonomy (cf. 2005a: 57-60). On the one hand this involves clitics that develop into independent words; however, most cases of "declitization" (Brinton and Traugott 2005a: 58) are controversial (cf. Brinton and Traugott 2005a: 58-59). On the other hand, much less controversial, are cases of "syntactization" (Brinton and Traugott 2005a: 60), in which a (bound) morpheme becomes an autonomous lexical unit, as in the recent examples of *ology* 'subject of study' and *ism* 'doctrine, theory, practice' from the suffixes in *biology* and *capitalism* or *ex* (as in *my ex was a disaster*) from the prefix in *ex-wife*/*ex-husband* (cf. Brinton and Traugott 2005a: 60).

Returning to the establishment process, in which the different types of lexicalization mentioned above can be observed, the establishment process can be divided into three stages: creation, consolidation and establishment (cf. Schmid 2005: 73ff., 2008: 3, 2011a: 73-82) that gradually segue into each other. These stages together with their main characteristics are summarized in Table 1 on page 40. It is important to note that not every neologism will pass through these phases to the same degree. Since not every novel coinage is semantically ambiguous, for instance, its meaning might already be evident without the necessary contextual and cotextual anchoring typical for the creation stage. Similarly, particularly with highly frequent and salient lexemes, the transition from creation to consolidation phase in the institutionalization process cannot always be empirically attested. When Scott, the hygienic household necessities manufacturer, released *tube-free toilet paper* in October 2010, the phrase experienced a sudden and speedy diffusion into the speech community. Many of these pages contain reports with the purpose of marketing the product or first consumers' tests. However, the original coinage event, probably by marketing experts at the Scott headquarters, is not documented. It therefore remains unclear when the lexeme passed from its creation into its consolidation stage. The example moreover shows that the degree of initial semantic ambiguity can be rather low, since the meaning of *tube-free toiletpaper* can be neatly deduced from its part as 'toiletpaper without, i.e. not rolled on, a tube'.

Turning to the discussion of the three stages, from the point of view of lexicalization, the creation stage involves the formation of a new lexeme via established word-formation processes or borrowings, or the development of a new lexical unit by means of semantic transfer. The ad-hoc formation thus consists of novel combinations of morphemes (or morpheme-like elements). These combinations, or more rarely also the morphemes involved, were not previously encountered in language by hearers/readers. Given the many semantic relationships[36] that can be conveyed by the configuration of morphemes, the meaning of the novel combination is often highly ambiguous and thus depends on the con- and cotext for a correct interpretation as intended by the coiner. The importance of context and cotext will be discussed in detail in section 2.2.1. During the next stage, the consolidation stage, as described in Table 1 on p. 40, the semantic ambiguity is gradually reduced and the context-dependence consequently loosened. This reduction of ambiguity and contextual emancipation is caused by the repeated occurrence in the supporting con- and cotext strengthening the association of one particular meaning to one or more formal variants. Formally, orthographic alternatives will also tend to disappear, but not necessarily to the same degree as the semantic ambiguity, because the spelling of a lexeme is not as decisive for successful communication as its meaning. As Schmid (cf. 2011a: 76) notes, even a highly established word like *email* is still found in the spellings *e-mail*, *email* and *E-mail*. Finally, a lexeme is said to be established or lexicalized when the reduction of semantic ambiguity and context-dependence is followed by the addition of semantic, phonological or orthographical features that obscure the

36 When asked for the meaning of the non-lexicalized *pea-princess*, informants in a study carried out by Downing (cf. 1977: 820) produced a wide range of interpretations. Some selected the place/occupation reading and defined *pea-princess* as a princess of pea people/the Pea kingdom. Others referred to the famous fairy-tale "The Princess and the Pea" by Hans Christian Andersen, in which the princesshood of an alleged princess is assessed through her ability to feel a pea under 20 mattresses, both literally and metaphorically. The latter group defined the word as a sensitive person. Again others interpreted the compound exocentrically and defined it as a princess with a head or body like a pea, of the color or size of a pea. Lastly, some informants also selected a partially metaphorical understanding and described the meaning as "a daughter of a pea magnate" (Downing 1977: 840).

structural connection to its components. This in turn might lead to demotivation and idiomatization as described above.

From a socio-pragmatic perspective, a neologism might start diffusing through the language and subsequently become part of the common vocabulary of individual speakers and the speech community at large. This process has been termed *institutionalization* and has been defined by Lipka as "the integration of a lexical item, with a particular form and meaning, into the existing stock of words as a generally acceptable and current lexeme" (Lipka 1990: 95, 1992: 107, 2002: 112, cf. Lipka et al. 2004: 7; cf. Schmid 2005: 73, 2008: 3-4, 2011a: 71; cf. Hohenhaus 2005, cf. Fischer 1998: 15). In the first phase of institutionalization, a lexeme is newly formed by a speaker and uttered or written down for the first time; it is therefore a nonce-formation. The reasons for speakers/writers' creating previously non-existing words are multifarious. Frequently, users will need to instantaneously and largely unconsciously assemble a new lexeme in order to overcome certain problems, either because the correct word does not automatically spring to mind, or because the existing word stock is not adequate to capture a particular concept or message. More conscious are coinages for humorous, stylistic or creative reasons. Poets, for instance, often create unusual words in order to express their idiosyncratic needs, science-fiction writers to accurately name and refer to non-existing objects and ideas (cf. Hohenhaus 1996) and journalists to succinctly describe complex matters in a structurally simple manner. In terms of familiarity, hearers or readers may not know the precise meaning, but they are familiar with the word-formation process by means of which the word has been assembled and can infer general semantic characteristics from this process. At this stage the word is said to be *type-familiar* (cf. Lipka 2002: 112; cf. Schmid 2011a: 74). The possibility exists for almost every newly coined nonce-formation to start diffusing through the speech community and become item-familiar (cf. Lipka 2002: 112; cf. Schmid 2011a: 74) until the final phase of the establishment process has been reached and the once new lexeme is familiar to and used by the majority of the speech community or its subcommunities. Save for the small-scale study by Hohenhaus (2006), the consolidation stage, in which the diffusion process is focused on, has not been investigated in detail. As mentioned in chapter 1, I will try to fill this gap with the present work.

Of the factors discussed in the introduction, many linguists assume nameworthiness to be the primary influence on the diffusion process. Lipka, for instance, claims that the degree to which a lexeme becomes institutionalized depends on the nameworthiness of the category it expresses; *snowman,* for instance, is unlikely to be firmly institutionalized in Africa (cf. Lipka 1992: 110, cf. Lipka et al. 2004: 10; cf. Kastovsky 1982: 159). Thus, the cultural and societal need for a given lexeme or lexical unit to refer to a nameworthy entity or concept motivates the linguistic process of institutionalization. As mentioned above, it is my aim to empirically investigate this naming need factor and its influence on the diffusion of neologisms. However, Lipka (cf. 1992: 110) also recognizes the unpredictability of nameworthiness needs. Some lexemes have not become institutionalized in spite of the nameworthiness of their extralinguistic phenomena and objects. Non-institutionalized examples from a modern, technologically innovative and evolving world include *whisper jet* 'a particularly quiet plane', which Boeing introduced in 1964[37] (cf. Lipka 1992: 110). Although lexemes or lexical units can be said to be institutionalized when they are familiar to and used by the majority of speakers, this status can be reversed. When the denotatum loses its salience and topicality (defined below in 2.1.3), or altogether disappears, the lexeme may very well become de-institutionalized (cf. Lipka et al. 2004: 11). If de-institutionalization is measured strictly in terms of frequency in contemporary discourse, words like *millennium bug* or *Y2K*[38], which were in vogue towards the end of 1999 but have lost their naming need and do not (or hardly) occur in current language[39], would belong to this category. However, due to the hype and worry surrounding the turn of the millennium, it is probable these words have left traces in the lexicon of speakers and societies. The example illustrates the need to introduce a cognitive perspective on neology, as proposed by Schmid (cf. 2005, 2008, 2011a: 71-82; see also Lipka 1977).

As Table 1 on page 40 shows, the cognitive description of the establishment process of neologisms is on the one hand concerned with the degree to which a new lexeme or lexical unit is accessed and activated as a single unit in the mental lexicon of the speakers, i.e. *entrenchment* (cf. Langacker 1987: 59, 100; cf. Schmid 2003: 82, 2007: 118-119, 2008: 20-22, 25, 2011a: 71, 80), and on the other hand with the cognitive status of the underlying concept, i.e. *hypostatization*[40] (cf. Lipka 1977: 161; cf. Schmid 2003: 78, 2008: 5-10, 27-30). From the former perspective, a new lexeme is typically accessed and processed from its parts rather than holistically. Immediately upon creation, the lexeme thus functions as

37 georgiaencyclopedia.org/nge/Multimedia.jsp?id=m-3576.

38 Example from Lipka et al. 2004: 11.

39 In the OEC, a total of 169 occurrences were found, 61 of them in sources from 2000. If the unclassified tokens are discounted (44), the tokens from 2000 account for almost 50% of the word's occurrence between 2000 and 2010.

40 In the second revised and translated edition of his 2005 textbook, Schmid abandons the hypostatization effect and incorporates it into the entrenchment aspect. Since these two terms describe different but interrelated effects, I retain the distinct terms.

a so-called "pseudo-concept" (Schmid 2011a: 74) that cannot be activated as a whole yet, but through its formal realization as one lexeme nevertheless seems to suggest the existence of one conceptual unit in the brain. This suggestion is derived from the hypostatizing effect of words or their power to call up categories and form concepts (cf. Leech 1975: 35, 37). Therefore Lipka describes hypostatization as the phenomenon whereby the existence of a linguistic sign presupposes the existence of the denotatum in the real-world (cf. 1977: 161; cf. Schmid 2008: 5) or more precisely a class of denotata (cf. Hohenhaus 1996: 317). Although hypostatization affects all content words, its effect has been observed more strongly in nouns than in adjectives and within the noun category most remarkably for abstract nouns, which do not have tangible, real-world denotata. As Schmid (cf. 2008: 6-7) remarks, this cline is determined by the very fact that nouns profile stable and delineable objects and events, whereas adjectives profile qualities that appear and disappear in time (cf. Bolinger 1980: 79). Therefore, nouns are said to have a higher reification potential and consequently invoke a static class of objects more swiftly than adjectives (cf. Schmid 2008: 6-7). Moreover, within the noun class, concrete nouns by definition refer to a class of tangible objects that have already existed before, but have not been named yet and thus seem to be inherently hypostatizing. The effect is more significant for event or action and abstract nouns like *booze-cruise* and *infomania* (cf. Schmid 2008: 7). Schmid claims that "the nouns carve an apparently neatly bounded segment from the constant flux of events going on in the world [...]" (2008: 8). Unlike for concrete nouns, the concepts represented by event/action and abstract nouns will not have been naturally perceived as a distinct category prior to their linguistic realization. Speakers might have known about the existence of these events or ideas, but it remains doubtful whether they have thought of them as one holistic conceptual gestalt that is recurrently automatically activated. This gradual development into one concept where the unit becomes more salient than its parts happens during the establishment process. The conceptual status changes from a pseudo-concept into a gestalt, whose meaning is not computed from the sum of its parts, but holistically as one unit that has acquired additional conceptual substance (cf. Schmid 2011a: 76). This process takes places through repeated encounters in the consolidation stage and is completed in the establishment phase.

Concomitantly, the lexeme receives an entry in the mental lexicon as a result of which its retrieval, activation and processing will become automatized. After creation, the lexeme is not yet listed as a distinct addition to the mental stock of words, but assembled from its parts. With each recurrence, a temporary entry is created and etched deeper into the mental lexicon. Furthermore, these traces are strengthened by the paradigmatic and syntagmatic lexical, semantic and syntactic connections the lexeme starts to develop within the mental network (cf. Schmid 2011a: 76). As mentioned in the previous paragraph, frequency is a prerequisite for gestalt formation. The firm establishment of novel lexemes in the mental lexicon too is determined by frequency. The more frequently a speaker encounters a particular lexeme, the more probable it will be listed under a separate entry and become entrenched (cf. Langacker 1987: 59, 100; Schmid 2008: 19-20, 24-26, 2011a: 80, 2007:). A summary of the three perspectives and the stages in the establishment process of neologisms is presented in Table 1 (cf. Schmid 2008: 3).

*Table 1: The establishment process from three perspectives (adapted from Schmid 2008: 3)*

| **Perspectives**<br>**Stages** | **Lexicalization** | **Institutionalization and conventionalization** | **Hypostatization and entrenchment** |
|---|---|---|---|
| **Creation** | nonce-formation: semantic and formal ambiguity and context-dependence | nonce-formation:<br>• individual occurrence by speaker/writer<br>• type-familiar to hearer/reader | • pseudo-concept<br>• no individual entry in the mental lexicon |
| **Consolidation** | stabilization of form and meaning | diffusion into the speech community | development of hypostatized concept with a tentative entry in the mental lexicon, loosely connected to other entries |
| **Establishment** | lexicalized lexeme (possible demotivation and idiomatization) | • institutionalized and conventionalized lexeme for the majority of the speech community<br>• item-familiar | hypostatized holistic concept with distinct entry in the mental lexicon, firmly connected to other entries |

It is important to note that these three perspectives, like the individual stages, are closely related to and influenced by each other. An example will illustrate this point. *Encore career,* defined as a second career after retirement in the context of more socially-oriented occupations, initially required a maximally specified context to elicit the intended meaning on the part of the hearer-reader. The informative context is required because of the compound's non-compositionality and high degree of lexicalization from the outset and not as an effect of its recurrence. Further lexicalization, as described in the table, context emancipation and semantic disambiguation and enrichment only emerge with continuing recurrence. This recurrence is however only possible if *encore career* exceeds its ad-hoc formation phase and gains currency, which can stay limited to certain types of source and fields of discourse. *Encore career* may thus not be or become completely institutionalized, whereas it does represent an advanced stage of lexicalization. From a cognitive perspective, the inherent semantic non-compositionality presupposes a certain degree of hypostatization prior to this initial spread and even when relatively new, it emerges in discourse as a tentatively hypostatized and entrenched concept. Moreover, new lexemes can be lexicalized, institutionalized /conventionalized and hypostatized/entrenched to different degrees. New words in instant messaging (SMS, chat, etc.), for instance, like *LOL*, 'laughing out loud/lots of love' or *OMG* 'oh my god' are firmly entrenched and lexicalized in the minds and language of only a restricted part of the speech community, i.e. those that frequently use these messaging services. Many of these medium-specific abbreviations, though widespread in subcommunities, are not fully institutionalized and conventionalized.

### 2.1.3. Two empirical studies on institutionalization

The first large-scale empirically-driven research on institutionalization from a longitudinal, dynamic perspective was published by Roswitha Fischer in 1998[41]. Using a corpus from newspaper articles from *The Guardian* between 1990 and 1996 and *The Miami Herald* from 1992, she investigated the motivation, productivity and institutionalization of "creative neologisms", i.e. products of word-formation processes other than derivation and compounding, of moderate frequency (cf. 1998: 2-3, 79). She introduces the concept of *topicality*, which describes the linguistic and extralinguistic phenomenon when "a word is used in connection with current affairs for a short period of time" (1998: 16). As a result, such lexemes are characterized by "short-lived frequency" (1998: 16) in contrast to the long-term, i.e. covering several years, attestations of lexemes in the course of the institutionalization process. The two concepts can become intertwined such that a repeated alternation between topical and non-topical stages is observed for both institutionalized and non-institutionalized lexemes (cf. 1998: 173, 175). Fischer concludes by claiming that topicality in society is the primary factor that promotes the institutionalization process (cf. 1998: 176).

41 As mentioned in 1.1, the study by Boulanger (1997) addresses the establishment of English neologisms from a static and synchronic approach.

The establishment of *sitcom,* for instance, is due to the high topicality of the word in the 1990s, when broadcast companies started to create such shows and the relatively new genre became established (cf. Fischer 1998: 94-98). Fischer assumes that not only an increase in frequency is evidence of advancing institutionalization, but also the occurrence of the lexeme in different semantic fields of discourse, orthographical stability, reduction of explanations, paraphrases or explicit contextual clues, its use as a modifier in noun phrases or base for further word-formation processes among others (cf. 1998: 69-70). With regard to *sitcom*, the establishment is evidenced by the dominance of the concatenated spelling (occasionally *sit-com* or *sit com* are still found), its appearance in noun phrases like *sitcom star* or *sitcom plot* as well as the creation of new coinages like *sitcom-funny*, *sitcom-type* (cf. 1998: 94-98). The absence of metalinguistic paraphrases and explanations that accompany the neologism during the initial stages of institutionalization is particularly conspicuous for the lexeme *techno* (in the sense of the music genre). Whereas such definitions were found in articles from the initial years of collection, by 1995 they have disappeared from the texts altogether (cf. 1998: 103-106).

On the basis of these linguistic and extralinguistic observations, Fischer divides the institutionalization process into three gradual stages. In the initial period, a neologism is introduced into the language and the speech community with the help of profuse explanations. However, when the lexeme is predominantly used in specialist discourse or slang, or is semantically and morphologically sufficiently transparent, its meaning will be known to the speakers and these explanations will not necessarily be present. When topicality is significant enough, the lexeme will advance into an intermediate stage, in which explanations or paradigmatic contextual clues like hyponyms or antonyms are reduced. Simultaneously the lexeme might start to occur in headlines or as the topic of articles. Once the topicality is saturated, as a peak in a frequency graph would show, the final stage begins. At that point, a decline in frequency is observed and the explicit contextual support disappears entirely (cf. 1998: 122-123, 174). The resulting S-curve, which will feature prominently in the presentation of the results in chapter 4, is remarkably consistent with the spread of phonological changes in the language and might indicate a general diffusion pattern of linguistic innovation (cf. Fischer 1998: 174; cf. Aitchison 1991: 84, see also section 2.3). In terms of frequency, the institutionalization process is assumed to be completed when the lexeme has occurred around 50 times in a 25,000 000-word corpus over a couple of years (cf. Fischer 1998: 172).

As mentioned above, Fischer claims that the most dominant positive effect on institutionalization is caused by extralinguistic topicality (cf. 2.1.3). If the word and its underlying concept appeal to speakers for non-linguistic reasons embedded in society and its current events, the lexeme stands a better chance of becoming institutionalized. However, language-internal factors too were found to have an impact. She notes, for instance, that the existence of lexical alternatives that are shorter, structurally less complex, easier to pronounce and with neutral or positive associations can inhibit the institutionalization of a near-synonymous neologism (cf. Fischer 1998: 178-179). Thus, the diffusion of *right-to-life* was arrested due to the existence of the phrase *pro-life* (cf. 1998: 178). Nevertheless, these linguistic aspects can again be overridden by two extralinguistic factors: the authority of the user and the general "fashion" (Aitchison 1990: 107, cf. Fischer 1998: 179). Despite the linguistic complexity of a given neologism, it might still become institutionalized if the societal pressure of prestige, authority and identity is sufficiently large.

In an attempt to resolve the limits of theoretical introspection and exposure experiments with speakers, Hohenhaus (2006) introduces a new method of tracking the institutionalization process of neologisms by monitoring their behavior on the Internet. He claims that this innovative method has several important advantages over traditional approaches. Not only can the first occurrence of a novel lexeme be unambiguously attested and the subsequent diffusion chronologically charted, but linguists also gain a detailed insight into the reception and interpretation of the new word by the speakers (cf. Hohenhaus 2006: 18). Although I do not entirely share his uninhibited enthusiasm regarding the unrestricted application of the Internet for such purposes (which will be discussed in the next chapter), Hohenhaus successfully presents a cutting-edge approach to institutionalization. He is one of the first linguists to make the institutionalization process of one particular word, *bouncebackability*, visible and tangible. According to Hohenhaus, the word was coined by the manager of the English football club Crystal Palace, Iain Dowie, in November 2004 to express what had just taken place during the match: after trailing by one goal against Arsenal[42], Dowie's team managed to equalize and obtain a draw. However, the OED lists earlier attestations from 1972 and 1991. From the start, some degree of lexicalization, consistent with the claims by Lipka discussed above, seems to be present, since *bouncebackability* is not simply 'the ability to bounce/come back', but gains the more specific meaning of 'the ability to equalize after having been one or more goals behind in a football match' (cf. Hohenhaus 2006: 19). *Bouncebackability* in this specific sense was swiftly adopted by sports

42 soccernet.espn.go.com/report?id=153242&cc=5739.

TV shows and sports commentators and became the subject of a true hype in which *bouncebackility* merchandise became available, a petition was launched to have it entered into "the dictionary", presumably the OED, and a preliminary entry in the *Collins* open user-generated dictionary was set up (cf. Hohenhaus 2006: 19-20). In all these instances, the word was used with reference to football (cf. Hohenhaus 2006: 19). Hohenhaus not only noticed an expansion into other sports, but also into other contexts, mainly business. He concludes that a "real" diffusion seemed to be happening with a concomitant semantic extension (Hohenhaus 2006: 19). By early 2006, however, the initial diffusion had been arrested as evidenced by the dwindling activity on the online petitions and decreasing amount of search engine hits. While the Google query had produced 50,700 returns in January 2006, the number decreased to 43,600 in May 2006 (cf. Hohenhaus 2006: 20-21). Although these figures cannot be interpreted in absolute terms due to the logarithms underlying Google's calculations, they do show a tendency that *bouncebackability* was on the decline in 2006. Hohenhaus concludes that despite the initial hyping and active propagation by speakers, the word did not make a lasting contribution to the common vocabulary and might only survive in slang or other subcultural varieties, because it illustrates a case of "artificial institutionalization" (2006: 21-22). Even after real-world events in which the phenomenon was highly salient (like other spectacular football matches where a team equalized after having been behind during the 2006 FIFA World Cup), the word did not occur in reports (cf. Hohenhaus 2006: 22-23). Additional evidence of this artificial institutionalization was found in the frequent accompaniment of the word by hedges and quotation marks and its use as an "attention seeking device" (Hohenhaus 2006: 22) in titles. Moreover, *bouncebackability* also seemed to evoke open rejections as in the case of *The Guardian,* which called it a "non-word" (Hohenhaus 2006: 22). In March 2012 it appeared above the radar again when the OED *Online* featured it as *Word of the Day*[43]. As I will show below, the presence of metalinguistic comments and attention seems to have a significant effect on the institutionalization/conventionalization of English neologisms.

So far the discussion of the establishment process of English neologisms has focused on traditional approaches largely neglecting the fact that new lexemes not only become established in the language of the speech community, but also

43 oed.com/view/Entry/266201, accessed 14 March 2012. The word is included in the third edition of the OED (March 2006) and since December 2011 in the online version.

in the mental lexicon of the individual speaker[44]. Since language use takes place both on the communal level and on the individual level, any comprehensive theory of establishment cannot afford to ignore important insights from the cognitive sciences. In fact, one could argue that the cognitive processes in the mental lexicon are the necessary conditions for any kind of socio-pragmatic establishment, especially from the perspective of the hearer-reader. In order for a novel item to diffuse, i.e. being used by an increasing number of speakers, the meaning of the item will need to be understood by each hearer-reader and the neologism will need to leave a mental trace for subsequent retrieval from the lexicon in language production. In the following section I therefore introduce the most important findings from psycholinguistic studies regarding the interpretation, mental processing and storage of neologisms.

## 2.2. Cognitive-linguistic aspects of neologisms

With regard to production, the coining process of novel lexemes seems clear[45]. At a given point in time, a speaker or writer relies on the morphological toolkit of a language to create a linguistic surface realization for an underlying conceptual or stylistic need. Since the speaker desires their (referential and/or emotive) meaning to be correctly understood, they will attempt to aid this interpretation in various ways, e.g. by assuring morphological transparency or embedding semantic clues in the context (cf. Dunbar 2005: 217, 218). However, despite these efforts, speakers or writers can never guarantee that listeners or readers recognize their intentions and follow an identical process of meaning retrieval to that followed in meaning creation on the part of the speaker-writer because these comprehension processes remain hidden in the mental lexicon. From a psycholinguistic perspective, therefore, it is more rewarding to study the hearer-based retrieval of meaning and the cognitive processing and potential subsequent storage of novel formations.

Nevertheless, it is necessary to briefly discuss one particular production issue, *nameworthiness*, which is considered as a factor of influence on the conventionalization process of English neologisms (see 1.2). A pioneering and much-quoted study on speaker-, hearer- and community-based conditions affecting noun-noun

44 A notable exception is Schmid (2003, 2005, 2008), who introduces the (socio-)cognitive terms *conventionalization* and *entrenchment* into the field and elaborates on the notion of *hypostatization*.

45 A discussion of cognitive models of language production can be found in Schmid (2008: 13-19).

compounding was published by Pamela Downing in 1977. In a series of experimental tasks, she attempted to formulate linguistic and extralinguistic constraints that take effect when language users produce and comprehend non-lexicalized compounds. In one of the production-focused tasks, the so-called "naming task" (1977: 817), subjects were presented with drawings of entities for which they were asked to create names. Downing argues that speakers first of all exploit the informational resources that are present in the speech situation. If the relationship between two concepts is predictable or characteristic, the use of a lengthier compound is not justified. However, subjects frequently provide explicit specification even if not required by the situation, for example, when specifying the kind of door (back/front/side door) they saw on a drawing even if there was only one (cf. Downing 1977: 833, 837). Moreover, Downing found evidence indicating that the category denoted must be relevant. By naming a new category, the speaker implies that this category is conventionalizable. Inconventionalizable categories may be named, but are "unlikely to survive beyond the context in which they were originally created" (Downing 1977: 838). Downing claims that these production-based constraints on the part of the speaker guarantee interpretability on the part of the hearer. Hearers can rely on habitual or generic characteristics or relationships between the concepts that are deducible from the context and background knowledge (cf. Downing 1977: 837). These assumptions with regard to the comprehension-facilitating function of context will be taken up in section 2.2.1.

In the following section I will present a brief overview of psycholinguistic studies that have investigated the interpretation and storage process of novel words. I will discuss three central questions that have been addressed so far:

- Which linguistic and extralinguistic resources does the hearer rely on? (2.2.1)
- Which factors influence the comprehension and storage processes? (2.2.2 and 2.2.3)
- Which storage and retrieval model seems to fit best to describe the underlying processes in the mental lexicon? (2.2.3)

In answering these questions, it should be borne in mind, however, that no such thing as a uniform comprehension process exists. Barz (cf. 1998: 11-14) argues that the comprehension of novel formations is determined by semantic-pragmatic expectations that the hearer has developed on the basis of linguistic and extralinguistic knowledge. It is therefore a highly individual process, which accounts for different hearer-dependent degrees of novelty (cf. also Clark and Clark 1979: 801, 803; Wilso 1985: 280). As a consequence, Barz introduces the notion of "novelty effect" (1998: 12) to better accommodate the various idiosyncratic concerns that influence reception and comprehension. Typically, the novelty effect will arise more strongly when these expectations are not confirmed by the form and the meaning of the new word. Whereas the novelty of a new lexical item as such, i.e. in the speech community, can be more or less objectively and reliably confirmed by means of identifying its first attestation, the novelty effect on the individual language user can only be measured with the help of informants. Since, as Barz claims, novel formations are not stored in speakers' long-term memory, they need to be processed consciously and are received as unusual, producing a novelty effect (cf. Barz 1998: 12-14). In spite of these insights concerning the individuality of processing, some general effects on linguistic and cognitive processing of novel lexemes have been observed, which will be discussed in the following sections.

### 2.2.1. The importance of co(n)text

A substantial body of evidence shows that from an adolescent age[46] on word meanings are learnt from the context[47] without additional paraphrases or glosses (cf. Chaffin et al. 2001: 225; cf. Aitchison and Lewis 1995; cf. Nagy et al. 1987; cf. Nagy et al. 1985; cf. Stahl 1991; cf. Sternberg 1987; cf. Landauer and Dumais 1997). As a consequence, without such a supportive context, new words pose substantial comprehension difficulties to informants (cf. Gleitman and Gleitman 1970; cf. Downing 1977). Claims of this kind were tested in two eye-tracking experiments by Chaffin et al. (2001) among others. They first presented 36 subjects with a two-sentence text that contained a highly familiar, a less familiar or a new target word in an informative context in the first sentence and a related word in the second sentence, e.g.[48]

S1 = Joe picked up the **guitar/zither/asdor** and *began to strum a tune.*
S2 = He played the *instrument* to relax.

Chaffin et al. measured the initial processing time[49] of each of these parts and the regressions made into and out of them to reflect rereading of particular elements (cf. Chaffin et al. 2001: 227-228). As expected, initial processing time was longer

46 See also Nagy and Gentner 1990: 169-170 for a similar statement on children's abilities.
47 It is important to note that *context* in the current section is used as an umbrella term for linguistic cotext and extralinguistic context.
48 Taken from Chaffin et al. 2001: 227. The words in bold represent the targets, highly familiar, less or low familiar and new respectively. The italicized phrase in S1 represents the informative context and the italicized word in S2 the related word.
49 Initial processing time is measured by means of the duration of the first fixation on the target, the duration of the gaze and "spill over", i.e. duration of the first fixation after the target (Chaffin, et al. 2001: 227-228).

for novel than for highly familiar targets and more time was spent on the context following such a new word. In addition, more regressions out of this context and into the novel target were observed as well as more frequent refixations of this new word, suggesting that readers strongly rely on the context for the interpretation of new words and construct its meaning online in the first sentence (cf. Chaffin et al. 2001: 227-229). The effect of context was investigated further in a second experiment, in which the less familiar words were removed and a neutral, non-informative context was introduced. Thus, readers did not always have the full support of the context as in S1 of the example above, but the contextual information was replaced with unrelated information, e.g. *Joe picked up the asdor and began to walk home* (cf. Chaffin et al. 2001: 229). Since this neutral context was insufficient to deduce the meaning of the new target, the total time spent in this region was shorter than in informative, supportive contexts. The participants moreover did not regress as often as in the informative context condition. Readers were thus aware that this information would not aid their meaning construction and did not pay closer attention. Chaffin et al. (cf. 2001: 234) conclude that readers (or hearers) are highly sensitive to the informativeness of context when they are confronted with novel formations, since they strongly rely on the contained clues to construct meaning online. Moreover, contextual information is important in both visual and auditory word recognition, despite processing differences in both modalities (cf. Holcomb and Neville 1990: 282, 303-304).

The importance of context arises from its disambiguation function. A given context restricts the amount of possible interpretations elicited by a particular wordform, because it highlights salient features of the concepts involved (cf. Dunbar 2005: 219-220; cf. Clark and Clark 1979). The interpretation is assumed to be based on the diagnostic properties, i.e. the identification of the constituents. Diagnostic properties are those properties that occur frequently in the concept, but not in others (cf. Costello and Keane[50] 2005: 211). From the speakers' perspective, this corresponds to their intention to select particular words because they are the most accurate for the novel concept, e.g. shooting is diagnostic for *gun* in the example of *rose gun,* 'a tool to dispense insect repellent' given by Costello and Keane (2005: 205). The gun-tool will dispense the repellent in such a way as to exterminate the insects, an act more harmlessly, but similar to actual shooting. Because shooting represents a diagnostic property of gun, the imagery evoked narrows down

50 In order to construct the meaning of a new noun-noun compound, the listener makes pragmatic assumptions about the speaker's intentions (cf. Barz's "expectations" mentioned above), which are realized as pragmatic constraints in the framework developed by Costello and Keane (cf. 2005: 210).

and restricts the possible interpretations. Secondly, the interpretation should be plausible or conceptualizable and similar to other previously encountered combinations of concepts, e.g. a *rose gun* is similar to other garden products such as fertilizer sprays that dispense liquid to improve growth and keep the vegetation healthy. Lastly, the listener also relies on new information not contained in either of the constituent words and thus inferred from background knowledge. The two constituents are deemed necessary but not sufficient (cf. Costello and Keane 2005: 210-212): a *rose gun* is a tool to dispense insect repellent, the latter aspect, however, is not formally present and only metonymically implied by *rose*.

Dunbar also argues that particularly novel noun-noun compounds need contextual information to enable an interpretation, because the constituents and their combination can conceptualize a variety of properties and relations and are therefore not sufficient to elicit a correct understanding (cf. 2005: 217-218). Thus, confronted with a novel formation in isolation, the hearer cannot rely on the disambiguation effect otherwise triggered by the context (cf. Dunbar 2005: 220). Upon encountering the novel compound *bedroom producer* (my example), an addressee will apply the general compound-specific schema of concept combination in addition to the *-er* agentive nominalization. Any of the following interpretations in a contextless environment become possible: (i) a manufacturer of bedroom furniture, (ii) a music producer who records music in his or her bedroom, (iii) a music producer who records music to be listened to in bed or (iv) a music producer who records music with the help of bedroom furniture. Resulting from the presence of the lexemes in bold, explanations (i), (iii) and (iv) are cancelled out in the example (1), explanations (ii) - (iv) in example (2), both of which were taken from the Internet.

(1) Progressing from a *bedroom producer* to the studio. Like most producers I started out **making beats** in my **dorm/bedroom**. I've spent the last couple of years trying to improve and develop a solid technique. Now I'm thinking about performing live[51]. (post on a discussion forum, August 5, 2011)

(2) The U.S. **Department of Commerce** has assigned a 7.24% antidumping duty rate for the 2009 shipments of Chinese *bedroom produce*r Zhangjiagang Zheng Yan **Decoration Company** Ltd., sharply lower than the 41.75% that was previously announced[52]. (*Furniture Today*, September 29, 2011)

51 futureproducers.com/forums/music-genres/rap-hip-hop-r-b/progressing-bedroom-producer-studio-367611/.

52 furnituretoday.com/article/543611-DOC_Corrects_Antidumping_Duty_for_Chinese_Bedroom_Producer.php.

In order to test the disambiguation effect of context, Dunbar extracted compounds with *Goldilocks* as a first element from the *Wall Street Journal* issues between January 1991 and July 1998 and the *Financial Times* issues between January 1992 and July 1998. He presented 17 informants with the *Goldilocks* term as well as other known and novel compounds and asked them to provide a meaning (cf. 2005: 223). Not surprisingly, participants were not able to give an accurate interpretation without a context (cf. 2005: 223).

If we assume that the context provides a vital comprehension aid for the hearer or reader, the precise role of the knowledge culled from the linguistic context merits some further attention. Research suggests that the disambiguation effect, informed by the contextual information, results from constraints on possible interpretations (cf. Nagy and Gentner 1990; cf. Dunbar 2005; cf. Clark and Clark 1979). In their study addressing this issue, Nagy and Gentner claim that "[n]atural contexts [i.e. cotext, dk] are often uninformative […], so that gaining an adequate representation of a word's meaning should require a large number of exposures to the word in a variety of meaningful contexts" (1990: 170; cf. Nagy et al. 1985). In particular, several conceptual and linguistic constraints seem to be active which narrow down the hypotheses hearers formulate when extracting meaning from the context (cf. Nagy and Gentner 1990: 173). A first type of constraint concerns the possible concepts that might be coded in words, which explains the bias against highly specific concepts researchers have observed (cf. Nagy and Gentner 1990: 174, 175, cf. Downing 1977: 824). This indicates that "a language-universal bias against impossible concepts" exists (Nagy and Gentner 1990: 173). A second factor relates to the perceptibility of the relationship between the referents of the constituents (cf. Downing 1977: 824). In Downing's study, subjects were unable to provide interpretations for words like *butler-maid, circle-square* and *loaf-pie*, because no perceivable relationship seemed to exist between the two elements. Similarly, when the relationship was logically and/or pragmatically impossible or even just unlikely, as in *night-Democrat* (naturally, one is not only a Democrat at night), the given interpretations were rated impossible (cf. Downing 1977: 824-825).

Among the possible linguistic constraints, Nagy and Gentner, building on evidence from language acquisition research, attribute the most powerful effect to the semantic constraint, i.e. the acceptability of a concept as word meaning (cf. 1990: 174). In an attempt to investigate the psychological innateness of these constraints or biases, they conducted several experiments (cf. 1990: 177, 180). In the first one, they tested the effect of semantic constraints. One group of subjects was asked to fill in the appropriate word, selected from a set of four possibilities that were either conceptually appropriate, lexically appropriate, both or neither, in a sentence. The other group was presented with the same sentence, in which the slot was filled by an unknown word, and asked to select a definition from the same set of possibilities. As hypothesized, both groups preferred the conceptually appropriate words, and, moreover, the group in the linguistic condition, i.e. the definitional task, favored the lexically appropriate options over the inappropriate ones. Thus, semantic constraints are active when people are required to formulate more explicit hypotheses about the meaning of a word (cf. Nagy and Gentner 1990: 178-187). In a follow-up experiment Nagy and Gentner tried to reduce the possible effect of explicit, direct judgements (which may involve knowledge not used in natural processing). Subjects were presented with a text in which a nonce word, a verb or a noun, occurred twice, first in an informative context, the second time in a vague one. Subjects were asked four questions afterwards: two about the word in the first context, two about the word in the second context. One question concerned the manner of the action, one the object of the action. The responses clearly showed that in the informative context condition, subjects were able to answer both questions correctly. When they did not have such an elaborate context to draw inferences from, the participants were only able to answer the manner question for verbs and the object question for nouns, because only the generic characteristics of word classes were activated (cf. Nagy and Gentner 1990: 187-192). This indicates that the context provides linguistic clues that provide the mental lexicon with valuable input to elicit more precise interpretations and increase comprehension. A detailed discussion of all the possible constraints on the meaning construction of novel lexical items such as the taxonomic constraint and language-specific preferences regarding semantic patterns of meaning encoding, is beyond the scope of this survey (cf. Nagy and Gentner 1990: 173-176).

A final aspect to be discussed here concerns the nature of the contextual linguistic material that serves as input into the comprehension process. The disambiguation effect of context is claimed to emerge in the form of explicit linguistic cues. Baayen and Neijt (1997) introduce the notion of "contextual anchoring" (1997: 569)[53] in their corpus study of high-frequency and low-frequency or hapax legomena derivations with the Dutch prefeix *-heid*, '-ness'. They distinguish between "morphological anchoring" (1997: 569), when the base is repeated in the context, e.g. *snelheid* and *snel* ('speed' and 'fast') and "semantic" or "thematic anchoring" (1997: 569, 571), when semantically related words occur in the vicinity of the word in question, as in

53 The notion of contextual anchoring is closely knitted to Clark and Clark's "contextuals" (1979: 782). However, they reserve this term for a specific class of noun-to-verb conversions, like *to houdini* or *to porch*, who are characterized by a "shifting sense and denotation" (1979: 782) and as a result, high context-dependence (cf. 1979: 782-783).

the example of *snelheid* and *een opzienbarende 2.07,51 uur* (*'speed'* and *'a remarkable 2.07,51 hours'*). Their empirical analysis shows that both the amount and the type of anchoring differs for the two classes of derivations. Overall, 22% of semantic anchoring was found (cf. 1997: 571), mainly for the low-frequency words. The high-frequency words, which were predominantly used with a referential rather than syntactic function, are characterized by a low degree of contextual anchoring, which was mainly of the morphological type (cf. Baayen and Neijt 1997: 568, 570). Baayen and Neijt claim that the morphological anchoring results from the higher probability of high-frequency derivations co-occurring rather than from the need for a supportive context (cf. 1997: 570). Such high-frequency complex lexemes are formally entirely regular, but nevertheless need to be retrieved holistically from memory because of their irregular semantics, i.e. non-compositionality (cf. 1997: 568). Low-frequency *-heid* derivations, including hapax legomena, on the other hand are more firmly embedded in the context by means of semantic associates. Their function is predominantly anaphoric or syntactic; they are semantically and morphologically regular derivations, used to meet the requirements of grammar and text cohesion and are assembled by rule during comprehension (cf. 1997: 568).

The importance of context, however, is partially contested by Renouf and Bauer (2000), who investigated approximately 5000 novel compounds and derivations, automatically extracted from a corpus comprising ten years of *Independent* issues (cf. 2000: 231, 234-235). For each of these new words, they assessed the potential overt, i.e. quotation marks, glosses and explanatory phrases like *so-called* and *what X call(s),* and covert contextual clues such as root or base repetitions, e.g. *OJ outsoaped the soap* (2000: 242), whole-word repetitions or collocations and other lexically or semantically related lexemes (cf. 2000: 236-252) and concluded that a mere 2,5% of the texts provided overt clues (cf. 2000: 254). Quantitative results for instances of the covert clues were not given. In view of the frequent absence of linguistic clues provided by the writer, Renouf and Bauer question the extent to which the cotext can facilitate comprehension on the part of the reader. They admit that the apparent lack of such clues might be explained by the newspaper character of the texts, in which journalists appeal to the shared knowledge of their regular audience and consequently provide textual support only sparsely. However, Renouf and Bauer argue that the morphological make-up is in most cases, notable exceptions being figurative language use and polysemy, sufficient to elicit a correct interpretation of a novel word (cf. 2000: 254). It should be borne in mind that the degree of contextual reliance is also influenced by the degree of morpho-semantic transparency of the novel lexeme, an aspect which will be discussed in section 2.2.3. Given the size of the Bauer and Renouf sample though, it is unlikely that the lack of contextual support is explained by the transparency of each of the lexemes under investigation.

Once the interpretation of a novel formation has been felicitously inferred, several possible storage processes might become activated to potentially file the word in the mental lexicon and facilitate future retrieval. A first theoretical school advocates holistic processing, also known as *direct-access models*: complex lexemes are stored as and retrieved from memory like simplexes, i.e. without morphological parsing (cf. Schmid 2008: 22). A second type of model, the so-called *(de)compositional model*, argues that complex lexemes are parsed and decomposed so that no distinct entry is needed and the complex word assembled from its stored parts (cf. Schmid 2008: 22). A third type, the *dual-route* or *race-horse model* (cf. e.g. Baayen and Neijt 1997), seeks to unite these two approaches. The dual-route model predicts that holistic and decompositional retrieval are simultaneously active[54]. Prior to assessing the viability of each of these models in 2.2.3, it is necessary to discuss two further aspects that have been argued to influence cognitive processing, storage and retrieval.

Robust frequency effects that facilitate routinization have been attested in a multitude of studies which will be discussed in 2.2.2. However, evidence seems to suggest that not the raw frequency of a lexeme speeds up recall from lexical memory, but the diversity of the contexts in which it appears (cf. Adelman et al. 2006; Verkoeijen et al. 2004). In a series of lexical decision and naming tasks for words in contexts extracted from several corpora, they observed faster response times for words with high "contextual diversity" (2006: 814 ff.), whereas no such facilitatory effect was present for words with high frequency (cf. 2006: 815). On the contrary, Adelman et al. state that frequency was rather an inhibitor (cf. 2006: 815). The same result appeared if variables like the semantic properties of the word or the potential correlation between frequency and contextual diversity were eliminated. They conclude that the effect of contextual diversity is caused by demand. A word is likely to be needed again if it has occurred in a multitude of contexts before. Mere frequency thus cannot accurately predict such a future need (cf. Adelman et al. 2006: 822). Since the words used in the study were all more or less familiar words, further research is necessary to determine the extent of the effect of contextual diversity on the processing of novel

54 Consequently, the model has been criticized for its inefficiency: the parallel operation of two separate processes in a first-past-the-post fashion would contradict the assumption that lexical memory is organized in terms of economy of processing and storage (cf. Schmid 2008: 22-23). Building on experimental research, Libben therefore proposes an improved version of the model (2006).

words. It furthermore remains unclear how these results are compatible with those that will be presented in the next section and focus on mere frequency[55] without taking into account the contextual diversity.

### 2.2.2. The importance of exposure

In their discussion of previous research on children's ability to learn new words[56], Nagy and Gentner (cf. 1990: 169-170) write that even a single exposure in context is sufficient to observe a learning effect[57]. Bloom (2000: ch. 2) has labeled this "fast mapping". If children are indeed able to develop an approximate meaning for unknown words after only one encounter, the fast mapping principle might be generally responsible for initiating tentative anchors for holistic processing of complex words in the mental lexicon (cf. de Vaan et al. 2007: 2)[58].

In two priming experiments de Vaan et al. (2007) investigated the claim that even morphologically regular but complex lexemes, like the Dutch *-heid* derivations, leave traces in the mental lexicon. Both experiments contained a base-primed condition, in which the neologism followed the base after 39 words, e.g. *gammel* preceding *gammelheid* ('wobbly' - 'wobbliness') and a neologism-primed condition, in which the neologism was repeated after the same interval of 39 words, e.g. *gammelheid - gammelheid.* They assumed that no difference in the two conditions would be attested if complex but regular lexemes were not tentatively stored after the first exposure (cf. de Vaan et al. 2007: 3); the results in the two experiments should be similar for the two groups. The first experiment consisted of a lexical decision task in which subjects were asked to indicate whether the encountered words in isolation were true Dutch words or non-words. De Vaan et al. observed that a priming effect, as reflected in shorter response times for the target, exists for both groups. However, they did discover that the priming effect was more significant after higher-frequency

55 See also Plaut et al. (1996), Seidenberg and McClelland (1989), Zorzi, et al. (1998), Coltheart et al. (2001), Murray and Foster (2004), Sandra (1994).

56 See also Bybee and Slobin (cf. 2007: 106-107) for similar findings regarding children's acquisition of irregular past tense forms.

57 Philip Johnson-Laird remarks that children do not only learn the new words from the context, but are able to remember them "for at least a week" (1983: 224). Unfortunately, Johnson-Laird does not expand on this claim nor substantiates it with empirical evidence.

58 The speedy acquisition of new words by children has also been claimed to be an effect of their learning being a constant activity during those initial years (cf. Tomasello 2003: 50-51).

bases. Subjects responded faster in the neologism-primed condition than in the base-primed condition. Moreover, if the neologism prime had been rejected as a word, subjects needed longer to judge the acceptability of the neologism at second exposure. Since they did not detect any effect of family size for neologisms compared to established words, de Vaan et al. assume that the facilitatory effect appears after one single encounter and continuously increases with each further exposure (cf. 2007: 6-13).

In the second experiment, a self-paced reading task, de Vaan et al. observed tentative traces in memory for morphologically complex neologisms when they had been primed by the neologisms instead of their bases. When the readers had already encountered the entire neologism before, they moved on to the next word faster than when they had only encountered the base. They conclude that speakers recognize a neologism after a single exposure, which implies that some sort of trace is present in lexical memory (cf. de Vaan et al. 2007: 13-18). The nature of these traces, i.e. as results of holistic or rule-assembled activity, however, deserves further research (cf. de Vaan et al. 2007: 19)[59].

Moreover, Dumay et al. (cf. 2004: 339) observed that after a mere 24 hours, more importantly one night's sleep, the activation of familiar words like *cathedral* was slowed when subjects had been repeatedly presented with the pseudoword *cathedruke* (cf. Davis et al. 2009: 814 for evidence from fMRI research). This indicates that a distinct entry for *cathedruke* had been set up, competing with *cathedral* during subsequent retrieval.

In addition to frequency of exposure and context, morpho-semantic transparency has been argued to be of importance for the processing and storage of novel formations. In the following section I will discuss this issue in detail and conclude with the discussion of the viability of the two competing processing models that are assumed to reflect the mechanisms of lexical storage, access and retrieval, which were introduced in 2.2.1.

### 2.2.3. The importance of transparency

The notion of *transparency* has two poles: the morphological one and the semantic one (cf. Schmid 2008: 11-13). The former refers to the formal structure of the word. Transparent coinages are those that can be segmented into morphemes without difficulties and thus provide indicators for their morphological

59 According to Pinker and Ullman (2002), storage in memory for such perfectly regular words is redundant, since they can be assembled by rule and only high-frequency words of this type will merit an independent, distinct entry in the mental lexicon.

make-up, e.g. *ghost surgery, Eurofascists, intexticated*. Although their structure is straightforward, the hearer's rule knowledge of regular word-formation patterns might not be sufficient to recognize and arrive at a correct interpretation, which means that morphological transparency does not guarantee semantic transparency. Even if *ghost surgery* is successfully parsed as a compound, which the hearer recognizes as a combination of concepts, they might not fully grasp exactly how these concepts are combined, i.e what the semantic relationship between *ghost* and *surgery* is. Thus, the second pole, semantic transparency, conveys complementary and necessary information during lexical processing.

Semantic transparency is a function of several more specific factors. A first factor that increases the semantic transparency of a novel formation is the familiarity with its morphemes, represented by their frequency in the language (cf. Schmid 2008: 12)[60]. Although *elephant food* might not be in the dictionary and might occur infrequently in the English language (in western parts of the world), it will present less recognition and processing difficulties than *baiji food*, because bajis[61] do not occur in English-speaking countries in the western hemisphere, while elephants do form a part of these cultures, even if not indigenously. Specifically in compounds in which the two free lexemes represent different degrees of frequency and familiarity it is debated which of the constituents contributes the most information. Schmid, for instance, argues that it is the first constituent that has been shown to be of more importance in lexical processing, probably due to its more salient initial position (cf. 2008: 12). Barz, however, contests this view and places more prominence on the second constituent. In her experiments she observed that the novelty effect (cf. above) was much stronger for *Igelflut* ('hedgehog flood') than for *Igelfutter* ('hedgehog food') (cf. 1998: 18-26). I do feel that a further factor, which is not mentioned by Barz, explains the distinction between *Igelfutter* and *Igelflut*, namely the feasibility of the concept. *Igelfutter* follows the well established, transparent pattern *animal + food* (*dog food, animal food, elephant food*). *Igelflut* on the other hand does not represent a concept that can be readily called up mentally. In addition to the opacity of the semantic relation between the two constituents, the entire compound is simply nonsensical in ordinary reality. It might very well be that it is the general salience of the entire compound,

60 For an overview of experimental studies regarding the effect of frequency see Schmid (2008: 12).

61 A baiji is also known as a Yangtze river dolphin and is an almost extinct species of dolphin indigenous to China's Yangtze river. (cf. *Encyclopaedia Britannica Online*, February 13, 2011, britannica.com/EBchecked/topic/708626/baiji).

or better lack of it, rather than the salience of the second element that explains her findings.

Secondly, semantic transparency also depends on the family size of the constituents. Novel formations coined according to a pattern that has a substantial size of analogous formations are processed faster than words whose constituents do not follow such patterns (cf. Schmid 2008: 12). In an experiment with high- and low-frequency words, Schreuder and Baayen (cf. 1997: 121-124) noticed that response times to words with the same base frequency were significantly faster when the word belonged to a large morphological family. Therefore, prefixations such as *e-friend* or *e-novel* will be understood and processed faster than blends like *globesity* or *burquini*, because the *e-* prefix has become highly productive in recent years and constitutes an expanding family. The blend *globesity* on the other hand cannot benefit from the recognition advantage that established or productive family members offer, because it represents a unique fusion of two words (*global obesity*).

A third component that increases the semantic transparency of a novel formation, more specifically a novel compound, concerns the semantic relationship between the constituents (cf. Schmid 2008: 12; Downing 1977; Gagné 2002; Gagné and Spalding 2006). Given the huge diversity of semantic relations that can hold between the two elements of a compound, the interpretation will require less cognitive effort in cases in which this relationship is prototypical. Novel compounds with *jacket* as a second element coined according to the pattern 'first element specifies the function/occasion of the second element', e.g. *cleaning/hockey/couch jacket* will be easier to process than new compounds in which the first element conceptualizes other aspects that might require a context, e.g. *London jacket* ('jacket bought/lost/stolen in London'). Thus, it seems that hearers' knowledge of word-formation schema and the prototypical or salient semantics conveyed by them are additional supportive means to recognize and understand novel formations. Wilso, for instance, assumes that a more extensive knowledge leads to less processing problems (cf. 1985: 282).

To sum up, four decisive factors determine the ease of lexical retrieval:

- the context (cf. 2.2.1)
- the frequency of prior and subsequent exposure (cf. 2.2.2)
- the semantic and morphological transparency of the lexeme and its constituents (2.2.3)
- the conceptualizability of the denotatum (cf. 2.2, 2.2.1 and previous paragraph)

The question that still needs to be addressed here concerns the nature of lexical retrieval. As mentioned above, the direct-access model advocates holistic processing. However, such an approach would imply that new lexemes, which by definition do not have any entries in the mental lexicon, are incomprehensible to hearers. A multitude of research studies have convincingly shown that despite processing difficulties, hearers are able to interpret novel formations accurately. The *(de)compositional model*, on the other hand, cannot account for highly lexicalized items or high-frequency words. Both types would unnecessarily slow down retrieval and understanding (cf. Schmid 2008: 22). The *dual-route* or *race-horse model* has been suggested as a compromise. On the basis of experimental evidence from response times for compounds, the decompositional route is assumed for semantically transparent compounds while opaque compounds are accessed holistically (cf. Sandra 1990; Zwitserlood 1994; Libben et al. 2003). However, if a further important factor, the frequency of occurrence, is considered, the conclusions are slightly altered in favor of one-route models. Both high-frequency opaque and transparent lexemes are characterized by a holistic entry, whereas low-frequency transparent lexemes are processed via their constituents. A special case is represented by the low-frequency opaque lexemes, where the parallel activation of both routes seems the most likely process (cf. Baayen and Neijt 1997: 568; Baayen 1993: 181; Bauer 2001: 122; Schmid 2008: 24-25).

Given its focus on the cognitive processing of linguistic structures, the degree to which these structures are activated automatically has been of great concern since the advent of cognitive linguistics. Ronald Langacker introduced the term "entrenchment" for this idea of routinized activation (1987: 59, 100). For a long time, the notion has been and is being used both on the level of the individual speaker and the speech community at large (cf. Langacker 2008: 17; Geeraerts 2010). Schmid[62] (cf. 2010: 117), however, convincingly argues that in view of the differences between the two on both levels, a distinction should be made: *Entrenchment*[63] is concerned with the degree to which lexemes are holistically established on the microlevel of the mental systems of individuals, whereas *conventionalization* refers to the degree to which lexemes are established on the macrolevel of the speech community, which is discussed in 2.3 (cf. Verhagen 2011; 2012: 2, 10).

In his much-quoted statement, Langacker (1987: 59) describes the routinization of lexical retrieval as

62 Note that his earlier publications do not make such a distinction yet (cf. Schmid 2000: 39, 2007: 119).

63 Since entrenchment is a highly individual notion that requires experimental testing, it is beyond the scope of the present study and will only be discussed briefly.

> […] a continuous scale of entrenchment in cognitive organization. Every use of a structure has a positive impact on its degree of entrenchment, whereas extended periods of disuse have a negative impact. With repeated use, a novel structure becomes progressively entrenched, to the point of becoming a unit; moreover, units are variably entrenched depending on the frequency of their occurrence […].

Thus, a lexeme like *dog food* will be more firmly entrenched and its retrieval automatized to a higher degree than the novel lexeme *ghost surgery*. However, if the latter becomes used, actively or passively, with increasing frequency, the activated call up leaves "a slight trace in the lexicon [and] increases in lexical strength" (Bybee 1985: 117). After repeated exposure, these traces will be embedded deeper and activation will accordingly proceed faster and more automatic (cf. Bybee 1985: 117).

Entrenchment is hence said to correlate with frequency in two ways. Firstly, on the methodological level of linguistic analysis, high frequency in the data reflects a higher degree of entrenchment in the mental lexicon. Secondly, on the level of cognitive processing, high frequency not only reflects a higher degree of entrenchment, but increasing frequency also instantiates a higher degree of entrenchment (cf. Langacker 1987, 1991: 48; Schmid 2010: 102). Secondly, entrenchment tangibly surfaces as observed frequency of linguistic structures in language corpora (cf. Schmid 2010: 102 for a detailed survey of applications). The latter statement should be treated with care. A first issue of concern is the type of frequency counts. Is the degree of entrenchment reflected by the absolute or the relative frequency of linguistic units in a corpus (cf. Schmid 2010: 117-119)[64]? Moreover, research has shown that lexical retrieval is also speeded up by the presence of homonymic forms (cf. Schmid 2010: 119 for an overview). As a corollary, not only will the frequency of contextually-specified instances foster entrenchment, but also their cotext-free, overall occurrences (cf. Schmid 2010: 119-120). Since cognitive corpus linguistics has grown very attached to mathematical and statistical models to objectively (but perhaps mistakenly) capture the cognitive underpinnings of language by means of corpus usage counts, these models might not always accurately reflect or clarify the nature of the mental lexicon if the frequencies entered lack proper justification (cf. Schmid 2010).

Rather than trying to resolve these issues, one last point to be made here concerns the (non-)entrenchment of neologisms. Since entrenchment arises by virtue of frequency, nonce-formations are by definition not entrenched insofar

64 Schmid furthermore notes that not only the frequency of the linguistic unit matters, but also that of its constituents (cf. 2008: 21).

as they do not have a distinct gestalt-like entry in the mental lexicon and are processed computationally with a greater effort. If a speaker, however, repeatedly encounters the nonce-formation, which, strictly speaking, has then become a neologism, feeble traces in the form of faster response latencies are detectable and tentative entries set up (cf. 2.1.2). On the basis of response latencies in naming tasks Forster (cf. 2007: 42) has demonstrated that frequency of exposure has a much more substantial impact during the initial repetitions than at a later stage; the degree of entrenchment is therefore non-linear (cf. Schmid 2008: 21). Moreover, Schmid surmises that the degree of transparency also takes effect[65]: Opaque neologisms require less repetitions to become (partially) entrenched than transparent ones, because their more laborious processing instantiates deeper and more robust traces (cf. 2008: 25). He remarks that most notably peculiar or eye-catching neologisms, as abundant in advertising and the media, stand a better chance of achieving "almost immediate entrenchment" (2008: 25). In the light of these highly individual aspects, i.e. frequency of exposure and transparency, it becomes clear that entrenchment affects establishment or storage at the micro-level of single speakers. Since the mental lexicon of the individual speaker remains largely inaccessible for a longitudinal study of the establishment process of new words, the present study investigates the establishment of novel lexical items on the macro-level of the speech community, i.e. the conventionalization process. The next section will discuss the core issues of establishment in the speech community and introduce Schmid's *entrenchment-and-conventionalization model* (2014), which provides the theoretical framework for the present study.

## 2.3. Establishment revisited: Conventionalization[66]

As mentioned in the introduction, the conventionality of linguistic structures constitutes an important prerequisite for successful human communication. In order to describe the processes by means of which conventionality of forms and meanings in the speech community emerges, attempts have been made to incorporate findings from theoretical-philosophically-oriented work on

65 Although the entrenchment level of related linguistic structures has also been assumed to influence the entrenchment process, the precise direction is not entirely clear. Both a facilitatory and an inhibiting effect have been observed (cf. Langacker 1991: 161; Schmid 2007: 121).

66 This section is based on a version of the EC-model as described by Schmid (2014), supplemented with more detail by the author when relevant for the present study.

conventionalization (cf. de Saussure 1916; Keller 1998) and research on socio-linguistic mechanisms of language change (cf. Labov 1972, 1980, 1994, 2001; Clark 1996; Eckert 2000; Brinton and Traugott 2005; Trudgill 2008), most notably in Croft's book on language change (2000; see also Hruschka et al. 2009 for a detailed bibliography)[67]. Although many valuable insights have been obtained from research on language change, the socio-cognitive or socio-pragmatic process by means of which a lexical innovation becomes accepted by the members of the speech community as a new convention has been neglected in favor of a description of more easily observable or more conspicuous concrete instances of phonological innovation. Blythe and Croft (cf. 2009: 47-48; Hruschka et al. 2009: 464) convincingly argue that language is subject to social and cognitive influences. In addition to the role of context, conversation and discourse partners, long since recognized in (socio)linguistics, they also maintain that cognitive processes like memory, production and conceptualization influence the structure of language and subsequent change. A recent approach that has tried to integrate these various strands of research into one framework and develop a fine-grained process model is the *entrenchment-and-conventionalization model* (EC) (cf. Schmid 2014), which will be presented in detail in the following. The EC-model provides an implicit integration of cognitive factors, which were not taken into account in the traditional institutionalization framework.

In a slimmed-down version of Lewis' (1969) definition of a convention (cf. Croft 2000: 97-99 for a detailed explanation), Clark states that a convention is (1996: 71):

1) a regularity in behaviour
2) partly arbitrary
3) that is common ground in a given community
4) as a coordination device
5) for a recurrent coordination problem

Thus, in order to solve the recurrent naming problem for an object with dark-colored bark that carries leaves or flowers from spring to autumn (part 5), speakers have agreed on the orthographical and phonological form *tree* (part 3 and 4). There is no form-internal reason why this particular sound sequence for the particular object has been chosen (part 2), an alternative would have been fathomable, if at least the majority of speakers had conformed to it (cf. Croft 2000: 97).

67 See p. 53-73 as well as chapters 4 and 7.

This form *tree* represents the convention, i.e. the standard, regular and systematic way of referring to the denoted object with bark and leaves (part 1).

Linguistic innovations are by definition nonconventionalized, even if they make use of conventionalized material (cf. Croft 2000: 98; Keller 1998: 157). If speakers do not have an adequate lexeme or phrase for their intended meaning, which is of primary concern in everyday communication, they will resort to established lexemes and word-formation patterns instead of creating words ex nihilo to guarantee comprehension[68]. Innovations constitute the first step of the conventionalization process. They represent individual-based constructions of novel expressions (or pronunciation instances) and mental representations (cf. Milroy 1992: 164). As Milroy remarks, "[i]t is speakers, and not languages that innovate", because "speaker innovation [is] an act of the speaker which is capable of influencing linguistic structure" (1992: 169). The speaker who initiates the innovation is often labeled "innovator" (Milroy 1992: 175) or "introducer "(Croft 2000: 179). Their conceptions of an innovator differ from Labov's (1980), who characterizes them on the basis of social features like high status and prestige within and outside of the community. Milroy (cf. 1992: 175-185, Milroy and Milroy 1985, 1989) contest this view, which will be discussed below. The influence of the innovator moreover is not always permanent nor successful. Even speakers that belong to the same community might not adopt the innovation at all, or only temporarily (cf. Milroy 1992: 165-168, 169). This temporary adoption is indeed a very frequent phenomenon, especially for vogue words, as I will show in section 4.1 when discussing various degrees of conventionalization.

In order for a novel formation to be adopted by other speakers, i.e. develop from a nonce-formation into a true neologism, *accommodation* needs to take place. The notion derives from Giles' Speech Accommodation Theory (1973; Giles, Coupland and Coupland 1991: 5), which explains a speaker's shifting speech styles in different speech situations in terms of speech behavior modifications as a response to the language use of the other conversation participants (cf. Auer and Hinsken 2005: 335-336, 343; Kristiansen 2008). Giles et al. (cf. 1991: 5), for instance, claim that the accent shift of an interviewee to that of the interviewer might not result so much from the formality of the context, but from the conscious or unconscious alignment on the part of the interviewee, who will (want to) sound similar to the interviewer. Accommodation does not always entail convergence, i.e. adoption of linguistic, prosodic or gestural

68 For an overview of established linguistic processes to create new words, see, for instance, Schmid (2011: 69-71) or similar handbooks on word-formation.

features of the other speakers. Convergence will typically only arise when the relationship between speakers is characterized by socio-emotional proximity, peer group membership or behavioral mirroring (cf. Giles et al. 1991: 7, 18; Auer and Hinskens' weaker version of "identity projection" 2005: 336). However, when speakers are socio-emotionally distanced or reject each other outright, they will avoid accommodating to the other's speech styles and emphasize linguistic, prosodic and non-verbal differences so that divergence arises (cf. Giles et al. 1991: 8). Instances of accommodation are gradual phenomena. They may be unimodal or multimodal, depending on the amount of modification of linguistic structures taking place and can be symmetrical or asymmetrical, i.e. not every speaker in a conversation will adopt features from the other participants (cf. Giles et al. 1991: 11-15). Moreover, Croft (cf. 2000: 182) distinguishes between the speakers' motives. Whereas convergence and divergence are characteristic for interactions of speakers from the same community that might accommodate to reflect their (rejection of) social identification, speakers from different communities will typically accommodate to facilitate communication. Speakers from different sociohistorical or regional backgrounds possess different codes, i.e. linguistic, prosodic, non-verbal features or mental conceptualizations, which might complicate communication. In order to restrict or avoid miscommunication, such speakers might smoothen or weaken the most deviant aspects of their language and assure mutual intelligibility. With regard to conventionalization, instances of divergence, both on an inter- and intracommunity level, will interrupt the conventionalization process, since the required adoption of novel structures does not take place. As Auer and Hinskens remark, only "long-term accommodation" (2003: 335), i.e. accommodation that exceeds a temporally-restricted speech situation ("short-term accommodation", 2003: 335) and becomes an integral part of a speaker's verbal repertoire, will lead to language change and the conventionalization of innovative linguistic features. The exact nature of the accommodation mechanisms are fiercely debated. On the one hand, advocates of the deterministic view emphasize the automaticity with which accommodation processes happen unconsciously, only influenced by the frequency of exposure to the language (cf. Trudgill 2004, 2008). On the other hand, proponents of evolutionary selection, adapted from evolutionary biology, maintain that in addition to frequency, social values as associated with the language and its users also feed into the process (cf. Baxter et al. 2008, 2009 among others).

If a new lexeme, created by the innovator thus becomes adopted by a larger group of speakers in different speech situations, a process of *diffusion* or "propagation" (Croft 2000: 4, 98) is initiated. Diffusion affects different groups of speakers and types and fields of discourse (or text types and semantic domains) to different degrees, depending on the degree of accommodation or individual threshold level (cf. Granovetter 1978). In addition to the communicative need (cf. Große and Neubert 1982: 7), i.e. the linguistic expression for new objects or concepts, Hamblin et al. (cf. 1979: 809) also observe that imitation provides an important trigger for diffusion. They state (1979: 809):

> Diffusion models portray society as a huge learning system where individuals are continually behaving and making decisions through time but not independently of one another. They watch one another and talk with one another about one another's behaviour and the experienced consequences. [...]. Thus, the collective process involves some direct learning but mostly observational and symbolic learning.

The contact and the social relationship between speakers is of utmost importance in the diffusion process. Unlike Labov's (1980) model of the innovator as a prestigious community member with many social ties within and outside the community, Milroy claims that the fringe members are responsible for innovations and their initial spread to other speakers (cf. 1992: 175-185, Milroy and Milroy 1985, 1989). Such fringe members are less pressured to adhere to the community norm because their ties to the other members, and thus their degree of group identification, is much weaker. Simultaneously, they are more sensitive to community-external pressure and maintain more contact to other groups and networks, increasing the range of influence (cf. "weak ties" in Granovetter 1973). Because they are more numerous than the prestigious, privileged inner circle they will typically reach a bigger audience and thus a higher probability that the innovation might be adopted by other weak-tie speakers. Milroy does not refute the importance of the more prestigious members; he merely attributes them a different role, that of "early adopters" (1992: 183; Raumolin-Brunberg 2006). The early adopters are central, norm-conforming members who will spread the innovation fast and to the entire group (cf. 1992: 175-185; "opinion leaders" in Valente 1995: 33-38). Valente states that "[g]enerally, individuals wait until the most influential members of the group adopt an innovation" (1995: 34). Evidence supporting these claims is found in diffusion studies by Rogers and colleagues[69] (cf. for instance, Rogers and Shoemaker 1971) and reflected in the typical S-curve pattern innovations follow (cf. Rogers 1962; Aitchison 1991: 83-84; Kroch 1989: 203; Chambers 1992: 693-695; Reali and Griffiths 2009).

69 More studies are discussed in Valente (1995).

*Fig. 1: Integration of Milroy's and Rogers' model of diffusion stages into an S-curve*

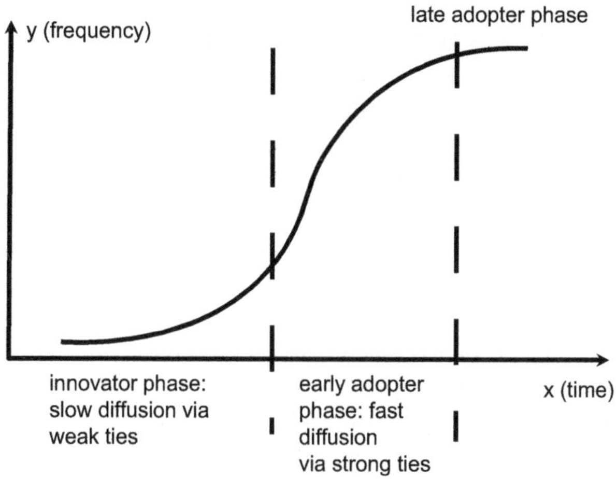


It should be pointed out that this kind of S-curve is predominantly based on sound changes; as I will show in 4.1, other patterns arise when lexical innovation is involved. Indeed, diffusion has been studied mainly with respect to social changes (e.g. the work by Rogers) and phonological innovations. This is apparent from the claim by Croft (2000: 176), who explains his "First Law of Propagation" as follows: "there seems to be a natural human tendency to increase the conventionality of one *variant of a lingueme* in a community at the expense of another, albeit over a long period of time in many cases" (my emphasis) and "[t]he propagation of a linguistic variant is a selection process" (2000: 178). He illustrates his claim with an example of newly coined technical terms that initially co-exist until the set is slimmed down to one option that becomes conventionalized. However, in everyday language, such initial co-existence or synonymy will tend to have a stylistic function and/or express connotational nuances so that the co-existence might persist. As a corollary, the question why some changes diffuse and others do not has prevailingly dealt with sound changes, whose diffusion mechanisms might tally well with, but do not necessarily need to correspond to those of neologisms.

Two such mechanisms have gained firm ground: Keller's invisible hand theory (1990, 1994) and the sociohistorical, evolutionary selection theory (cf. Labov 1980; Milroy 1985, 1989, 1992; Baxter et al. 2006; Blythe and Croft 2009). Keller argues that language change unintentionally arises from an intended action on the part of the speaker (cf. 1990; 1994: 57). Since the members of a speech community behave similarly with regard to their intentions, language change is merely the collective consequence of such intentions; it is a "neutral evolution" (Blythe and Croft 2009: 49)[70]. In contrast, selection theory claims that language change results from a socially-fueled selection of one variant over another (cf. Croft 2000: 60; see also Milroy's network model mentioned above). Recently, attempts have been made to model the selection process mathematically (cf. Baxter et al. 2006, 2009; Baxter et al. 2009; Blythe and Croft 2009, 2012). These approaches assume that speakers produce variation when "replicating" (Blythe and Croft 2009: 48; see also Johanson 2008 for *code-copying*) linguistic structures. Based on past and present interactions, one or more of these variants might be selected by the speaker for future use (cf. Blythe and Croft 2009: 47-48). Hence, the adaptability of language and its speakers is caused by cognitive events of memory and perception. In their application of the USM model, presented in detail in Baxter et al. (2006), Blythe and Croft (2009) tested the various selection procedures that might account for this kind of adaptability. They used three different models: the "replicator selection" or "fitness" model (2009: 49), which considers social factors like prestige, the "neutral interactor selection" model (2009: 50), which is determined by frequency, and the "weighted interactor selection" model (2009: 50), which incorporates both frequency and social factors. They conclude that the weighted interactor model looks the most promising, but requires more work (cf. 2009: 57-60). Indeed, in their more recent work, they assume that the weighted interactor selection model sparks the change, but continues by means of replicator selection after the weight of the interactor has been passed onto this replicator by the speakers (cf. Blythe and Croft 2012: 296). Despite the introduction of mathematical modeling, they do not consider (or at least not openly) the various social factors that might underpin the selection procedure in detail.

If a certain degree of diffusion has been achieved, a next step in the conventionalization process may take place, *normation*, which in turn will foster the diffusion further (cf. Lewis 1969: 99; Itkonen 2008: 389; Harder 2010: 217ff.). Normation may be implicit in the form of tacit agreement among the members of a speech community on the meaning or use of a given linguistic structure (cf. Blank 2001: 1596). On the other hand, such guidelines or instructions may also be explicitly laid down in dictionaries, text and grammar books (cf. Holmes 2008: 110ff.). Whereas implicit normation assumes a similar degree of entrenchment of a linguistic structure for most, if not all, speakers, the explicit normation

---

70 For a critique of the invisible hand process see Croft (2000: 60-62).

provides speakers with an external authority that actively steers entrenchment. Hence, conventionalization and entrenchment are intricately intertwined and mutually constitutive. Conventionalization is not merely entrenchment at large, but also influences the automatization of lexical access and vice versa. In other words, a novel lexeme of general use can only become conventionalized if it has had some kind of impact on the sociocognitive system of the speaker and the impact will be increased or reduced in accordance with its conventionalization process.

One last point to be made here concerns the practical operationalization of conventionalization. Like entrenchment, the frequency of a linguistic structure in large-scale corpora is assumed to correspond to its degree of establishment in the speech community. A recent case study by Schmid (2011b), for instance, uses this approach. Schmid traced the *not that* construction from its alleged innovation to its current widespread occurrence in a collection of historical and contemporary corpora. The earliest attestation of the construction is found in the Wycliffite Bible translation of 1380. In the following 200 years, the construction is almost exclusively used in translations from Latin and French theological texts such as treatises, sermons, homilies and instructions. Not until the end of the 16th century does the construction tentatively appear in other domains. Between the 17th and the 19th century, Schmid discovers a variable pattern. Sometimes the frequencies slightly increase, sometimes they slightly drop. In present-day English, however, the constructions seems to have become established, BNC frequencies from the fiction component reveal a frequency of 50 occurrences per million words (cf. Schmid 2011b: 302-312). Hence, one could simply state that a higher frequency reflects a higher degree of conventionalization and vice versa. However, two objections should be raised. As Schmid notes, the use of the *not that* constructions seems to depend on the author, with more occurrences in Aphra Behn's or Laurence Stern's work compared to Samuel Johnson's (cf. 2011b: 311). This speaker-dependent pattern is not an exception. Social background like age, profession and environment creates a group-specific vocabulary that might not be representative of the majority of the speech community. If for some reason or another, such texts appear in a corpus with a disproportional frequency, the researcher relying on frequency counts might be misguided with regard to the degree of conventionalization. The danger is particularly present for Internet material, which forms the basis for my investigation, because it is query-driven rather than consisting of a carefully balanced language sample. Moreover, which threshold should be taken? Do we assume a frequency of 10, 50 or 250 per million words to be sufficient to count as conventionalized? What happens if we do not know the sample size of the corpus, as in the present study?

Given the Zipfian distribution of words in a corpus and the fact that many words are well-established despite their low or context-constrained frequency in discourse, such decisions would be entirely arbitrary. *Christmas pudding* or *nursery rhyme* (my examples), for instance, occur 0.2 times per million words in the OEC, but it can hardly be claimed that these lexemes are not an established part of the English lexicon (cf. Bybee 2007: 16-17 for other examples). Unlike Fischer (cf. 1998: 172), who puts the threshold at 40 or 50 occurrences per 25 million words in a corpus covering "at least a few years" (1998: 172), I do not apply a fixed frequency threshold, but consider two further factors.

Therefore, a second measure is necessary. In addition to frequency, the degree of conventionalization should consider the *type of source* and the *field of discourse* (see 3.3.2). The size of the speech community affected by the innovation is also reflected in the socio-pragmatic types of discourse the neologism occurs in. If a word is exclusively found in scientific texts, the degree of conventionalization will be lower compared to a word that occurs in blogs, on Twitter and in established newspapers with the same (high) frequency. A similar assumption holds true for the diffusion of words into other fields of discourse, i.e. semantic domains. Obvious conventionalization cases of this kind are found in instances when a technical, jargon-based word gains general currency, e.g. *URL*. The inclusion of a socio-pragmatic or socio-semantic level into the quantification of conventionalization not only reduces the potential bias of frequency data, but also incorporates the social dimension of language change (cf. Milroy 1992; Croft 2000; Blythe and Croft 2009).

In sum, *conventionalization* refers to the sociohistorical and sociocognitive process by which innovative structures diffuse into the speech community, on the basis of accommodation strategies on the part of the speakers and possibly accompanied by some sort of normation, until they are actively and/or passively known by the majority of its speakers. In linguistic (and statistical) investigations of empirical data, the degree of conventionalization of a novel item can be operationalized in terms of its frequency in the entire sample and the type(s) of source and field(s) of discourse it occurs in. As a result, conventionalization[71] is not an all-or-nothing phenomenon, but is best described in terms of a continuum (see 4.1.) "of degrees of recurrence in the speech community" (Johanson 2008: 65).

71 Of course, if a word falls into disuse, before or after it has become fully established, a process of deconventionalization takes place (cf. Johanson 2008: 66).

# 3. Investigating English neologisms on the Internet

As mentioned above, most empirically-driven studies of nonce-formations and neologisms have focused on a particular genre or text type for which large corpora were available (Baayen and Renouf 1996; Fischer 1998) or being compiled by the researcher (Hohenhaus 1996, 2007). One notable exception which explores the potential of the Internet for monitoring the behavior of neologisms is Hohenhaus' case study of *bouncebackability* (2006) discussed in 2.1.3.

Hohenhaus, however, only investigated an isolated case. In contrast, the present study aims to investigate the behavior of neologisms systematically, which requires a more complex and advanced methodology. The following chapter[72] will discuss previous approaches to the use of the Web as a linguistic corpus (section 3.1), introduce a new tool for discovering and monitoring English neologisms online (section 3.2) and describe in detail how the present set of neologisms was collected and processed (section 3.3).

## 3.1. The Web as a corpus? Static and dynamic applications

### 3.1.1. General problems

The past decades in linguistics have yielded irrefutable evidence of the benefits and merits of corpus-based and corpus-driven approaches to language. As a result, both the number of corpora and the amount of words they contain has increased significantly, which has in turn triggered a new kind of empiricism in linguistics. Corpora provide linguists with a carefully compiled and representative cross-section of a given language during a given period. Despite their balanced range of different text types and stylistic, regional and social varieties, they are not devised or equipped to offer a dynamic portrait of linguistic structures, but remain temporally rigid. Precisely this snap-shot character of corpora is problematic in neologism studies. Whereas the majority of linguistic constructions only change slowly and need decades or centuries rather than months, innovation in the lexicon is a more rapid process. Researchers relying on corpora

72 The first two parts of this chapter are an updated and revised version of Kerremans et al. 2012.

for the close observation of neologisms would simply lose track of them, either because they have become obsolete or because they have already become firmly established in the language. Not only the temporal rigidity poses a problem, but also the time lag between data collection and public availability of a given corpus. Some monitor corpora (cf. Sinclair 1996: 11) like ukWaC[73], the OEC[74] or the Bank of English (cf. McEnery, Xiao and Tono 2006: 67-69) are being updated regularly, but even they do not allow monitoring on a weekly basis. Theoretically, it would be possible for lexicologists to string together different synchronic snapshots into one diachronic corpus (cf. Mair 2006; Leech et al. 2009), but this would be a time-consuming and costly enterprise. Therefore, I use the Internet, which is precisely such a progressively expanding collection of data needed to retrieve and track the development of (potential) neologisms.

The use of the Web as a corpus is neither new nor unproblematic. In principle, researchers wishing to dig into the linguistic goldmine of the Internet have three options. They can compile a corpus from web data, adhering to standard principles of corpus design, manually (cf. Hoffmann 2007) or automatically like the *WaCky* projects (cf. Baroni and Bernardini 2004, 2006) or simply scour the Web for useful data with commercial engines (cf. Lüdeling et al. 2007: 8). Since the first two options merely differ from standard corpora in the source of the material, i.e. online vs. machine-readable texts, and carefully select the material that will be included, the third option in particular is susceptible to criticism. As some researchers have pointed out, commercial search engines like Google, Bing or Yahoo are unreliable in qualitative and quantitative linguistics because of their volatility (cf. Kilgarriff 2003; Renouf 1998, Renouf et al. 2005; Lüdeling et al. 2007). Firstly, such search engines do not index, i.e. find and render, all the pages on the Web but restrict themselves to the Surface Web (cf. Lawrence and Giles 1999). Ideally, researchers should be allowed and able to access the entire index, including the Deep Web material, which remains hidden to commercial search engines and standard webcrawlers, unrestrictedly. To my current knowledge only Buchstaller et al. (2010), who were granted access to the entire Google newsgroups archives to investigate the decline and narrowing of use of quotative *all* in favor of quotative

73 *ukWaC* is the British English component of the *WaCky* family, which assembles corpora from the Web by crawling the national domains, i.e..uk for British English, with seeds (search terms) from newspapers or older corpora like the *BNC* in the case of British English (cf., Baroni and Bernardini 2004, 2006; Ferraresi 2007, Ferraresi et al. 2008; Baroni et al. 2009). Many of the *WaCky* corpora are available for free from wacky.sslmit.unibo.it/doku.php?id=start

74 The OEC is available under the SketchEngine license, see sketchengine.co.uk/.

*like*, succeeded in including such hidden, more comprehensive data. Moreover, the number of indexed pages and the speed with which the index is updated fluctuates over time and among the individual search engines, Google generally scoring best for both parameters (cf. Lewandowski 2008a: 320, 2008b). Research has shown that the majority of pages change only marginally, but since 20% of all pages disappear within a year and approximately 8% of the web consists of new pages that go online every week (cf. Ntoulas, Cho and Olson 2004: 3), the size and freshness of the index is of prime importance. However, despite its leading position in index size and freshness, Google does not display all the pages for a specific query but returns only the first 2000 hits (cf. Kilgarriff 2003: 1). More importantly, the ranking of the results is driven by commercial factors (cf. Renouf 1998; Renouf et al. 2005: 1), which implies that the most linguistically relevant results will not necessarily be displayed first. Thus, the frequency counts Google displays on top of the page, which are mere statistical guesstimates, cannot and should not be trusted, as they do not accurately reflect the actual frequency of a given lexeme or construction. It is true that the biased frequency issue is a serious problem that needs to be tackled before valid assumptions can be corroborated by it, but since neologisms are by definition low frequency words, at least in the initial stage when the monitoring process starts, neither the limitation of displayed results nor their commercially-motivated ranking speak against such an approach.

A second frequency-related problem concerns the orthographical or morphosyntactic insensitivity with which commercial search engines return queries (cf. Lüdeling et al. 2007: 14). Google, for instance, does not distinguish between capitalized and non-capitalized search terms, yielding an estimated 119,000 pages for both *Globesity* and *globesity* (on October 24, 2011) nor between spelling variants: the search for *detweet* will also produce *de-tweet* and *de tweet*. Since the latter form is not a legitimate orthographical form in English, but, among others, a standard noun phrase consisting of a definite article and a noun in Dutch ('the tweet'), advanced search options are necessary to avoid incorporating languages other than English in the sample. Rather than an obstacle, this formal insensitivity is an asset in neologism studies, because neologisms are characterized by precisely such orthographical flexibility.

A graver problem with commercial search engines Lüdeling et al. address is the fact that results cannot be validated and replicated by other researchers, because the data set cannot be reproduced (cf. 2007: 10-12). As mentioned above, indexing is unpredictable and unstable. Even if researchers want to repeat their original search and apply the same settings, the sample will never be an exact replica of the first one, like in corpus queries, because some pages will have been deleted or updated, some will have remained unchanged but included twice and others will be new. Two conciliatory remarks are in order here. Again, it is precisely the continuous update and inclusion of novel instances of language that makes the Web attractive to lexicographers and lexicologists, because it allows them to closely track lexical change and innovation. In addition, the less strict copyrights on much of the web material mean it is possible to download all the pages in the first sample and store them. As a result, a stable and fixed 'corpus' is available, which can be quantified (and thus form the basis for accurate frequency counts and subsequent statistical methods) and consulted by other linguists. These strategies imply that some kind of pre- and post-processing of the data yielded by search engines is necessary in order to provide linguistically and scientifically adequate and appropriate material. Post-processing features will, for instance, filter out undesired languages and duplicates (in order not to mess up frequency counts) and provide meta-data and classification options.

Precisely these custom-tailored, automatic queries via commercial search engines, the crawling approach, have been the center of attention in Internet-based empirical linguistics during the past years despite being forced to depend on their whims. The following sections will give a brief overview of two types of such webcrawlers and discuss some of their inadequacies, which have fueled the development of a specialized neologism-monitoring tool, the NeoCrawler. Despite its reliance on Google, the NeoCrawler provides solutions for some of the problems addressed above and allows the compilation of an "opportunistic corpus" (Teubert 1998: 157-158, 168) suited to answer the specific research questions addressed in the present study.

### 3.1.2. Downloadable crawlers

Unlike the crawlers presented in 3.1.3, KWiCFinder[75] (Fletcher 2001, 2007) and GlossaNet 2[76] (Fairon et al. 2008) need to be downloaded from the Web and installed on the user's computer. Since the storage space and crawling speed depend on the performance of the user's personal computer and its connection to the Internet, processing larger data sets can become slow and unreliable.

KWiCFinder accesses the Web via AltaVista and returns the submitted queries as HTML or TXT downloads. Alternatively, users can opt for a more user-friendly access via WebKWiC, a Java application, which collects cached website copies from Google (cf. Fletcher 2007: 36). A summary of the results is listed in a KWiC display. KWiCFinder offers a useful range of advanced search features

75 kwicfinder.com
76 glossa.fltr.ucl.ac.be/

such as wild- and tamecard options that extract orthographic and syntactic variants of the search term (cf. Fletcher 2001: 34). Furthermore, the user can include or exclude particular words, pages, hosts and dates in the search string and accordingly narrow down or extend the queries (cf. Fletcher 2001: 34). Although the author does not expatiate on available post-processing features, he mentions annotation and classification options and conversion of the pages into XML.

Whereas KWiCFinder accesses the Internet via commercial search engines, GlossaNet 2 uses RSS and Atom feeds[77] to retrieve and download web pages. Both in the first version of 1998, which was restricted to newspapers, and in the expanded later version, the user compiles a corpus from the websites to which the feeds belong. These feeds are either selected from a predefined set or individually added by the user. Once the corpus is assembled, queries are submitted and the relevant pages extracted and added to the corpus in regular intervals. The "Manager" (Fairon et al. 2008: 3) thus first follows the feeds to the web pages, retrieves their content and passes them on to another server that will strip the pages of programming code and remove duplicates. This second server subsequently compiles the corpus, performs tokenization, lemmatization and tagging and returns the pages to the Manager. Finally, the Manager adds any new pages to or updates existing ones in the corpus and informs the user that their corpus has been created and/or updated. Post-processing features like concordancing or socio-pragmatic classification are not mentioned.

Although GlossaNet 2 periodically generates a potentially suitable corpus for linguistic research, the selection of RSS and Atom feeds on which this corpus relies -even if the amount is unrestricted- captures too limited a range of genres and semantic domains to observe the diffusion of neologisms. Thus, the possible storage and crawling speed problems when processing a larger sample of neologisms and the lack of post-processing features in both applications are major drawbacks that necessitate an alternative method of fishing the Internet for linguistic data. Two very promising alternatives are presented in the next section.

### 3.1.3. On-demand crawlers

The on-demand crawlers presented here, like the NeoCrawler, are available online, where they can be consulted whenever necessary. Both the Linguistic

77 RSS and Atom feeds are web data tools that facilitate the update, publication and exchange of web content. Readers who have subscribed to such feeds for particular pages are automatically notified when the page content has changed. They contain information about the title and description of the page, its publication and the link in XML format.

Search Engine (Kilgarriff 2003) and Webcorp[78] (©RDUES 1999) reject the use of commercial search engines to extract empirical data from the Internet and advocate an independent linguistic search engine[79], tailored to the needs of linguistic research. However, at the time of writing the publicly accessible version of Webcorp still enters the Web via Bing and Google (see webcorp.org.uk).

Kilgarriff's Linguistic Search Engine (LSE)[80], whose precise configuration and difference from commercial search engines is not discussed in the available sources, daily crawls the Web and adds these data together with the source URL into a database. The LSE database is updated once or twice a year. Although Kilgarriff maintains that such an annual or bi-annual update is sufficient to observe language change (cf. 2003: 3), I will show in the next chapter that these intervals are too long to adequately monitor lexical innovation. In a second step, the data is filtered, converted into standard XML and classified. The LSE filters out all the material that is not written "in sentences" (2003: 3), like sound files, images, lists of prices, products and people. However, duplicates, i.e. webpages that are listed several times under various URLs, do not seem to be removed automatically. Kilgarriff suggests automatic classification of text type and semantic domains with the TypTex and TypWeb toolset (Folch et al. 2000), but remains vague about the feasability and accuracy in practice. Moreover, he assumes that several 100 text types will be found on the Web, a number which would be impractical to work with in larger samples. The sociopragmatic classification of web pages is not entirely unproblematic, as will be discussed in section 3.3.2. As I will show below, the NeoCrawler's set of nine text types (or "types of source" as they will be called, see 3.2.2 and 3.3.2) is able to capture the diversity of the online English language, albeit on a broad rather than fine-grained level. Further post-processing features include tagging, parsing and lemmatization in addition to statistical summaries of the search term's behavior with Word Sketch[81]. Unfortunately, tokenization does not seem to be included during post-processing. It is however indispensable to obtain valuable quantitative profiles of the linguistic data, especially in the light of concordancing and collocation research.

78 webcorp.org.uk

79 One specialized search engine for linguistics, Elkiss and Resnik's *The Linguist's Search Engine*, which went online in early 2004, is no longer active (see Resnik and Elkiss 2005 and their homepage on lse.umiacs.umd.edu/).

80 To my current knowledge, the project has not been realized in the proposed form.

81 wasps.itri.bton.ac.uk/

As shown in Figure 2 the NeoCrawler's underlying relational database consists of a number of connected tables that contain information fields on a given neologism on various levels, as expressed in the table headline:

- The *process_info* table summarizes the (non-linguistic) details of each search process and its outcome under a unique ID. This table saves information on the date, the time restriction and the precise search string(s) that was/were submitted as well as the amount of returned pages and the number of tokens of the query on these pages.
- The *lemma* table, linked to the process_info table as illustrated by the '#', contains a manually compiled linguistic fact sheet that lists the word-formation process(es), possible types of semantic transfer such as metaphor and metonymy, and any morpho-semantically related lexemes that might exist (e.g. *diabesity* and *globesity* both blended with *obesity*). The meaning or meanings are also recorded here.
- Because the lemma table contains type-level information, which gives a basic linguistic summary less prone to change (except for the meaning), the *token* table contains additional information about the specific behavior of the neologism. This field describes the token from a socio-pragmatic perspective, such as its position in the text and presence or absence of novelty markers like quotation marks. It furthermore shows the extended cotext and provides links to information on the source, the version and the author.
- The *source* table is, like the token table, the most interesting from a linguistic point-of-view, because it also contains socio-pragmatic details. Listed here, for instance, are the type of source, the field of discourse, as well as the URL to the original page, which is necessary to create a stable data sample, as mentioned above.
- Like the process_info table, the *version* table is a non-linguistic summary of details pertaining to the page, i.e. the date of creation, title, size etc.
- Unfortunately, the *author* table often remains empty, since the socio-economic background of the author is frequently not available.
- A useful option we have incorporated in the NeoCrawler is reflected in the *blacklist* table. Occasionally, pages will be returned that are irrelevant. The blacklisting feature allows us to exclude such pages or search strings from further crawling sessions.

Since the tables are all linked together in multiple ways of increasing specificity, information does not have to be entered repeatedly as it does in XML, but is speedily available for each single token, which inherits all the information from the connected tables.

This database serves as the foundation for the two modules of the NeoCrawler that perform the actual crawling. The Discoverer, in charge of detecting potential neologisms on the Web, yields a selection of candidates, which are added to the database after a manual review by the researcher(s). The second module, the Observer is responsible for regular web crawls. It retrieves the queries from the stored neologisms in the database, sends them to Google and feeds the results into it after completion. The next sections will discuss the mechanisms and procedures of both modules in detail.

### 3.2.1. The Discoverer

In order to be able to closely observe the linguistic and extralinguistic behavior of neologisms, a timely discovery, ideally on the day of coinage is of utmost importance. On the one hand, retrospective collection of data, which might be unreliable given the flux of search engine indexes, is reduced to a minimum and on the other hand, researchers stand a better chance of monitoring the diffusion on the Web before the neologism becomes too frequent to keep track of it. In contrast to other approaches using specific sources like newspaper corpora (Fischer 1998) or novels (Hohenhaus 1996) to extract potential neologisms, we have attempted to implement an Internet-based method[84]. The Web not only offers an unlimited amount of data, estimated at close to one billion pages as of June 2014 (cf. Netcraft's June 2014 Web Server Survey[85]), but more importantly, a wide array of stylistic and sociolinguistic varieties that enable us to overcome genre or topic restrictions and thus search the language at large.

At present, the Discoverer sweeps the Web for potential neologisms in two ways. The first method consists of standard web crawling with metalinguistic markers as search strings. The underlying assumption is that people who have encountered or coined a new word will comment on it. Thus, target constructions include:

- *coined/came up with/made up a/the (new) word/term*
- *invented a/the (new) word/term*
- *heard/read/encountered/stumbled upon a/the (new) word/term*

---

84 For a similar approach restricted to the Wikipedia domain called *Zeitgeist* see Veale and Butnariu (2010). For a related approach see AVIATOR and APRIL at RDUES, rdues.bcu.ac.uk (cf. Renouf et al. 2005).

85 Published on June 6, 2014, news.netcraft.com/archives/category/web-server-survey/. Other sources claim figures close to two billion pages (cf. de Kunder on worldwidewebsize.com).

These metalinguistically-oriented searches were conducted prior to the development of the actual Discover and did not elicit the required results. First of all, the manual assessment of these candidates was a time-consuming process, because only the search terms were highlighted in the cotext and we had to gather both the candidate and evidence for its status as neologism from the entire cotext. Frequently, these candidates were nonce-formations, often resulting from typing mistakes: save for the coiner's comment, no further occurrences were found. More problematic, however, was the fact that even with time restrictions, older words that had already become established or obsolete ended up in the list. When people start talking about a given word, its novelty has already been slightly eroded, either because these people did not encounter the word in its coinage phase but only much later, or because individual speakers have individual perceptions of what is new. As a result, the need for a more timely discovery arose. Table 2 illustrates the results of such a metalinguistically-driven search process and its drawbacks.

*Table 2: Examples of results of metalinguistically-driven searches for neologisms*

| Query phrase | Candidate | Date of retrieval | Date of posting | Problem |
|---|---|---|---|---|
| ***came across a new word*** | *carental* | October 24, 2011 | October 20, 2011 | writer misread *car rental* |
| ***heard a new word*** | – | – | – | – |
| ***coined a new word*** | *omnicontra* | October 24, 2011 | October 23, 2011 | nonce-formation |
| | *doucheboob* | October 24, 2011 | October 24, 2011 | |
| | *detalization* | October 24, 2011 | October 23, 2011 | • typo mistake of *detailization*<br>• nonce-formation |
| ***invented a new word*** | *Gourgeois* | October 24, 2011 | October 23, 2011 | nonce-formation |
| | *favred* | October 24, 2011 | December 9, 2010 | • nonce-formation<br>• older posting |
| | *ciderific* | October 24, 2011 | October 11, 2011 | • nonce-formation<br>• older posting |
| | *rolling average index* | October 24, 2011 | October 24, 2011 | |

| Query phrase | Candidate | Date of retrieval | Date of posting | Problem |
|---|---|---|---|---|
| | *adorlable* | October 24, 2011 | October 18, 2011 | • typing mistake of *adorable*<br>• nonce-formation<br>• older posting |
| | *trousers* | October 24, 2011 | October 21, 2011 | ironic comment |
| ***made up a new word*** | *trollex* | October 24, 2011 | October 24, 2011 | nonce-formation |
| | *ingredientzes* | October 24, 2011 | October 24, 2011 | nonce-formation |
| | *fluke* | October 24, 2011 | October 23, 2011 | word already exists (e.g. in Urban Dictionary) |
| | *volumptuous* | October 24, 2011 | unknown | • word already exists (e.g. in Urban Dictionary)<br>• unknown date of coinage |
| | *waderish* | October 24, 2011 | October 19, 2011 | • nonce-formation<br>• older posting |
| | *whoopoo* | October 24, 2011 | May 20, 2010 | • typing mistake of *whoopee*<br>• older posting |
| ***stumbled upon a new word*** | – | – | – | – |
| ***came up with a new word*** | – | – | – | – |

The Discoverer[86] proceeds in a radically different manner. Instead of relying on people's judgements as evidenced by their metalinguistic usage, it automatically analyzes web content[87] for unknown grapheme sequences, presently limited to Google Blogs[88], a selection of URLs and local files. It then extracts those grapheme

86 I am greatly indebted to René Mattern, who programmed the Discoverer as part of his M.A. thesis in computational linguistics. A detailed documentation of the Discoverer is found in Mattern (2010).

87 Other, similar automatic detection procedures of neologisms are found in Renouf et al. (2005) and Cabré et al. (2003) for Spanish and Catalan novel monolexemes in newspapers. For a detailed description of Larousse's manual detection procedure, see Sommant (2003).

88 Since the Discoverer was developed recently, it is still very much in its infancy. In the near future, we aim to expand the search and incorporate other blog providers.

sequences that are not contained in the Discoverer's dictionary, which will be discussed below, as neologism candidates. As illustrated in the left-hand column of Figure 4 on page 85, the NeoCrawler thus first accesses an individually specified number of Google blogs, URLs or files from the private hard disk (steps a and b) and downloads the contents (step c). These downloaded HTML pages are then stripped of all programming code and HTML tags until only the linguistically relevant body remains. Next, the plain text of the body is split into words; spaces, capital letters and punctuation marks serve as delimiters between single words[89]. These words are then sorted into a frequency list, which provides the basis for the detection of potential neologisms, because in this list the unknown grapheme strings are identified. In order to assess the neologism potential, several filters are applied to this word list to exclude the least likely candidates. Such words include:

- stop words, i.e. highly common words which are by definition filtered out in natural language processing, because they cause various problems (cf. Luhn 1958)
- words with fewer than three letters
- words that contain more than two digits
- proper names[90]

In the next step, (d) in the figure, the remaining words are tested for 'knownness' through comparison to a reference dictionary, compiled from the English version of Wikipedia, and a catalogue of N-grams representing known words. These N-grams were extracted from Google's 2006 N-gram corpus[91], which consists of roughly a trillion running words from websites, and is divided into unigrams, i.e. single words, bigrams, trigrams and so on up to five-grams. For the present purpose, only the 14 million unigrams were considered and filtered for non-words according to the same criteria used by the Discoverer for new candidates. The resulting sample consists of approximately 7.8 million tokens and ensures that only those grapheme strings that did not occur before 2006 are detected as potential neologisms by the Discoverer. Unfortunately, in the present detection procedure on the basis of known unigrams, non-concatenated compounds cannot be recognized as potential neologisms.

---

89 An obvious drawback of this method is the incapability of finding non-concatenated compounds, because they will be rendered as two single words in our splitting analysis.

90 A list of proper names was provided by Michaela Geierhos from the Centrum für Informations- und Sprachverarbeitung at the LMU München.

91 The Google N-grams are available free of charge from catalog.ldc.upenn.edu/LDC2006T13.

Since the Discoverer recognizes unknown grapheme strings, a further selection procedure is required to exclude non-words, i.e. sequences of letters that resemble words but in fact are not. These word-like elements often result from typing errors or misspellings. In order to assess the likeliness that a grapheme combination will be a valid English word the Discoverer performs a frequency-of-occurrence analysis of these grapheme strings. In this trigram, i.e. a combination of three letters, analysis, the Discoverer matches the grapheme sequence under investigation with a database of trigrams and their frequencies in English. It is assumed that these three-letter strings, collected from Google's N-grams, are typical combinations of English graphemes and thus represent real words. During this matching process, the Discoverer compares the three-letter strings in the candidate word[92] with the frequency with which this sequence occurs in the trigram database and calculates the probability that the candidate is an English word. The word *baby-trafficking*[93], for instance, receives a higher average trigram frequency of 9.72% in comparison to *2min*, extracted in the same identification run, scoring merely 0.90%. These scores indicate that *baby-trafficking* is more likely to be a valid English when compared to *2min*. The candidate strings with the lowest values are removed and will not be displayed. Despite this kind of rigorous filtering and matching drastically reducing the number of potential neologisms, a further rating system was implemented to increase the Discoverer's efficiency and decrease the researcher's expenditure in time when manually reviewing the candidate list.

Each candidate is awarded a 'type quality' figure between 0 and 10 that further estimates the likeliness it is a neologism. Points are detracted when the grapheme string:

- contains numbers: (-1)
- contains numbers other than 1, 2, 4, 8: (-1)
- contains consecutive numbers: (-3)
- contains non-Latin or non-letter characters other than hyphens or single quotes: (-5)
- contains capitals following lowercase letters: (-1)

As a result, a word like *$70-million* receives a type quality score of 0 because it violates many of the listed specifications, even though it has a trigram frequency

92 This implies that strings consisting of less than three graphemes are discounted as being potential neologisms.

93 *Baby-trafficking* and *2min* were retrieved by the Discoverer from the *Guardian* on June 28, 2014 as unknown grapheme strings.

of 2.42% and would not have been removed on the basis of this frequency alone. Before every Discoverer run, the researcher can decide whether all type qualities should be shown or only those with a particular score.

The Discoverer lists all potential neologisms in their cotext, together with their type quality score and trigram frequency (step e in the figure). At this point, the manual review starts (steps f and g). If a word is shown which, despite the extensive filtering and selection, is to be discounted, like *$70-million*, the researcher selects it as 'garbage' and indicates the reason as illustrated in Figure 3 below with a search of *The Daily Mirror* on November 2, 2011. The word might be a garbled string, i.e. a combination of typographical characters that is a non-word, a proper name such as *Mulheirn* in Figure 3, an orthographical error, a known compound, a foreign language word or a word that is simply missing from the dictionary like *Q&As* in Figure 3. The words that belong to the latter four categories are added to the user-generated dictionary discussed above and will not be listed in future searches. If a researcher decides that the word is a candidate, based on intuition, the type quality scores, trigram frequencies, context and cotext, the candidate is preliminarily classified according to its word-formation pattern. Ambiguous cases are initially marked as 'ignore' and discussed with the team before final decisions are made.

*Fig. 3: An overview of potential neologisms and their processing options*

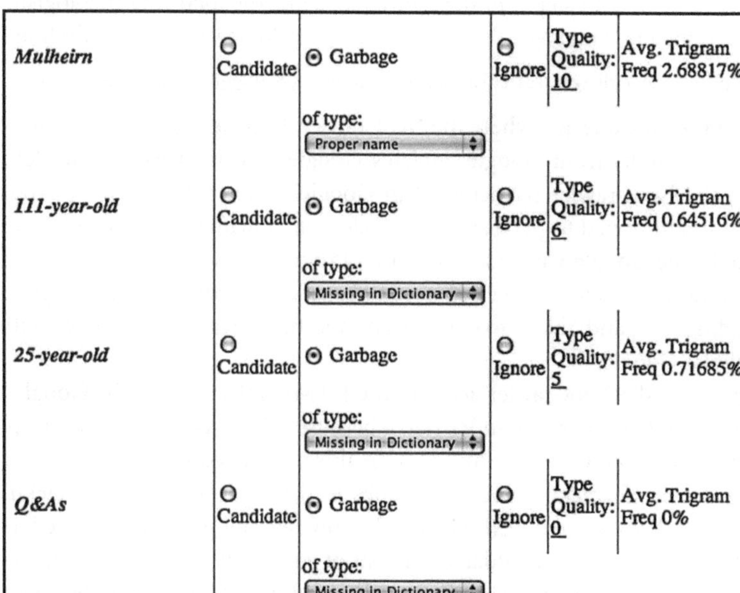

Once a potential neologism is marked as such by adding it to the database (step g in Figure 4 below), a first search with unlimited time restriction is conducted and included in all future crawls by the Observer to monitor its diffusion, as illustrated by step 1a in Figure 4 on page 85. The next section will discuss the mechanisms and features of the Observer in detail.

### 3.2.2. The Observer

The Observer module not only contains the actual web crawler, but also the core of linguistic tools that are necessary to describe a neologism's socio-pragmatic behavior in the speech community, i.e. the classification system. Since the NeoCrawler's classification scheme is rather idiosyncratic, it will be discussed in detail in section 3.3.2 and merely a brief overview will be presented here. Each Observer crawling round starts similar to a manual Google search that users conduct. However, the NeoCrawler does not require such manual input by its users, but assembles a URL code automatically prior to feeding it into Google. This URL code is a condensed version of manually selected advanced search options in the Google interface. It contains the query word and specific parameters such as date, in our case limited to the past week to ensure seamless coverage of data, and language.

Thus, a slightly simplified URL code the Observer builds for 100 results for the word *detweet* in step 2 in the figure looks like the following (neologism "q" and parameters "language", "number", "date" and "start value" are underlined):

http://www.google.com/search?q=detweet&num=100&hl=en&tbs=qdr:w&start=100

Such automatic queries, where the NeoCrawler disguises itself as a web browser to retrieve links from Google, violates Google's terms of use. Until October 2011, the NeoCrawler participated in Google's University Research Program and was authorized to perform large-scale web crawling automatically. Unfortunately, the Google University Research Program was discontinued until further notice. The NeoCrawler will need to broaden its scope of search engines by including Bing and Yahoo to compensate and find alternative ways of continuing to use Google.

In step 3, the NeoCrawler accesses the HTML links returned by Google and parses them (summarized under step 6 because this process does not take place online, but in the Observer module). In this automated process all web links, Google-internal tracking and cache links in these pages as well as blacklisted sites (see below) are removed. Thus, only truly relevant pages are retained. False positives, duplicates and outdated versions of pages that are already contained in the database are removed. This ensures the validity and integrity of the collected

inadequate for the present purpose. The various shortcomings of those systems and the subsequent development of a distinct classification system, based on Herring's "faceted classification scheme" (2007) are discussed in detail in section 3.3.2. For now, I will restrict myself to a rudimentary outline of the three-level multidimensional[96] classification procedure.

The first two levels are concerned with the page classification, where homogeneity regarding certain social and linguistic characteristics like audience, author, topic is assumed to be high. The first level distinguishes between the linguistic *modes of usage*, i.e. meta- versus objectlinguistic uses. Since it is my aim to investigate the possibility of these metalinguistic uses inhibiting conventionalization, they are identified first. Admittedly, the mode of use of a lexeme can only be assessed for each of its individual tokens. However, given the size of the sample, token-level description of mode of use proved to be infeasible, bearing in mind that the classification is still a manual process. Moreover, obvious instances of metalinguistic use, as in dictionary or encyclopedia entries, would apply to the page and token level simultaneously and thus do not bias the overall result. These instances are stored in the distinct category DICTIONARY/THESAURUS, as listed in Table 3 on page 90. Metalinguistic use is found not only in reference works, but also in various instances in which the writer does not use the word to refer to an object or event in reality, but comments on its existence, use, meaning and form or refers to the coiner and/or the coinage event without applying the neologism to new classes of referents. Examples are given in 4.1.2 and 4.1.3. Pages that contained multiple tokens were assigned the relevant mode of use on the basis of dominant frequency. Thus, if a neologism occurred five times on a given page, four times metalinguistically and only once objectlinguistically, the page was classified as metalinguistic and vice versa.

The second level, still concerned with page classification, involves the dimensions *field of discourse*, i.e. the topic, *type of source* and *authorship* as illustrated in Table 3 on the next page. The term *type of source* was explicitly chosen to avoid the quagmire of ambiguity surrounding *genre*, *style*, *text type* and *register*, and indicates the deviation from classical sociolinguistic approaches to discourse types to incorporate features of Internet language. A *type of source* in the present approach is a set of textual units with shared graphical, structural and linguistic properties. In a selection of types of source, most notably in blogs, authorship

---

96 *Dimension* is not used here in the sense intended by Biber and Kurjian (2007) as a synonym for different kinds of texts. The dimensions represent language-internal and -external perspectives on classification.

also needs to be assessed, because blogs do not contain an inherent authorship. People who write for newspapers tend to be professional journalists; people who publish in scientific journals are almost exclusively scholars. However, in blogs this one-to-one relationship does not exist, since they are used for a variety of purposes, ranging from personal diaries to professional marketing. Examples of the various types of source and instances of authorship will be discussed in section 3.3.2.

*Table 3: Page-level classification scheme*

| **Mode of use** | | |
|---|---|---|
| | Metalinguistic | |
| | Objectlinguistic | |
| **Semantic features*** | **Field of discourse** | **Sub-field of discourse** |
| | general | |
| | politics | |
| | law | |
| | business | |
| | sports | |
| | science | |
| | advertising | |
| | lifestyle | celebrities, food and drink, fashion, health |
| | entertainment | radio and TV, movies, music |
| | computing/Internet | gaming, technology |
| | other | |
| **Socio-pragmatic features** | **Type of source** | **Sub-type of source** |
| | blog | |
| | news | |
| | discussion forum | |
| | portal | community, directory, job, Hollers, Gather, Bebo, Blippy, other |
| | social network | Facebook (public), MySpace, Meetup, other |
| | filesharing | documents, music, video, photo, blog |
| | microblogging | Twitter, Tumblr, other |
| | academic | |

| | | | |
|---|---|---|---|
| | dictionary/ thesaurus** | | |
| | **Authorship** | | |
| | private | | |
| | professional | | |

* not applicable to metalinguistic uses
* * only applicable to metalinguistic uses

A further dimension on the top level classifies pages semantically according to their field of discourse[97]. These fields of discourse largely correspond to the thematic sections found in corpora or newspapers. Fields of discourse are only assigned to objectlinguistically used instances of neologisms. Sub-field classification is optional and used whenever finer topical distinctions are necessary and noteworthy.

The third level captures the linguistic dimensions of the individual token. An overview is presented in Table 4. In addition to simple part of speech assignment, to be extracted automatically in the future, and the description of the position in the text, this level offers the possibility of adding precise information on the kind of metalinguistic use that was observed, i.e. whether a definition or paraphrase was present, on the style of the text and the referent of the neologism.

*Table 4: Token-level classification scheme*

| Linguistic dimension | Class label | Class realization label |
|---|---|---|
| Syntax feature | part of speech | verb, noun, adjective, adverb, interjection, phrase |
| Text feature | position | title, headline, body, caption, category, tag |
| Metalinguistic feature | explanation | definition, paraphrase, none |
| Sociolinguistic feature | style of use | neutral, informal, formal, vulgar, e-speak |
| Cognitive feature | new class of referent | yes/no |

The NeoCrawler thus presents a new and advanced tool for the identification, retrieval and analysis of novel linguistic material on the Internet. Since these

97 In order to avoid confusion, the term *field of discourse* was preferred to *semantic domain*, since *domain* is frequently used in an online context to refer to the location and address of a page or collection of pages.

three components are seamlessly integrated into one program, it is a convenient, reliable and fast application for investigating the development of English neologisms on the web. Its rigorous filtering, useful options like blacklisting and not least, its storage of the original pages are all features that successfully overcome some of the objections raised by linguists. Moreover, the inclusion of a distinct classification system, tailored to the current needs of socio-pragmatic and linguistic analysis, proved to be a novelty not yet found in the existing crawlers. The next section will discuss in detail how the neologisms in the present study were selected (3.3.1), illustrate the classification process by means of concrete examples (3.3.2) and describe how the nameworthiness factor was investigated (3.3.3).

## 3.3. Data selection and investigation procedure

At the time the neologisms were selected for the present investigation, the NeoCrawler contained approximately 270 entries. This number exceeded the capacity of manually analyzable neologisms. An overview of the various sources and criteria that were applied to this substantial set so as to compile a manageable sample is presented in 3.3.1. Subsequently, I will describe the classification procedure, its origin and precise application in 3.3.2 as well as discuss some minor adjustments required for the statistical modeling. The last section of this chapter, 3.3.3, is concerned with the investigation and operationalization of nameworthiness.

### 3.3.1. Data selection

The collection of neologisms began before the NeoCrawler became operational and thus tapped into a variety of sources to obtain the required sample. Collecting neologisms proved to be a difficult task for various reasons. A first method that was explored involved participant observation, i.e. appealing to native speakers' eagle-eyeing potential new lexemes. However, since these observations are mere individual perceptions of what is new, they elicited suboptimal results. Many of the words added on the basis of informants' hints turned out to be comparably older than assumed, a phenomenon that has been aptly labeled *recency illusion*, a neologism in itself, by Arnold Zwicky in a post on Language Log (August 2005[98]). According to Zwicky, people often assume certain words, expressions or societal changes are recent innovations, because they seem new to them (cf. also Barz's *novelty effect* discussed above). As a second corollary, some

98 itre.cis.upenn.edu/~myl/languagelog/archives/002386.html.

of these 'new' lexemes were already too frequent to monitor manually and well on their way to becoming established entries in the lexicon. Examples from the database include *mooseknuckle*, 'large, defined outline of the male/female genitals in tight clothing' and *jeggings*, 'jeans-like leggings'.

The problem of advanced frequency or conventionalization also occurred with lexemes from neologism collections from dictionaries, linguistic journals or word-watcher websites. As mentioned above, lexicographers carefully review potential candidates before they are included in dictionary revisions and updates. Since one of their inclusion criteria is frequency, new words that are added will have proven to be frequent enough so that close monitoring has become impossible. *Social networking*, for instance, was added to the eleventh revised edition of the *Concise Oxford English Dictionary* in 2008, but was by that time already part of everyday English. Although the online editions of dictionaries are updated more frequently and could be a more timely source to select neologisms, the same revision process applies. Thus, *vuvuzela* received an entry in the *Oxford English Dictionary Online* in August 2010[99], but was mainly used during the World Cup two months earlier. Again, if *vuvuzela* had been selected for the present purpose after its inclusion in the OED *Online*, the many hits would not have allowed me to conduct a detailed linguistic analysis. Another approach is chosen by MacMillan publishers, who do not discuss neologisms after they have been included or passed their tests, but continuously compile a collection of new lexemes and weekly present the "Buzzword"[100]. As a result, some of their buzzwords are indeed in their initial stages of diffusion and thus optimal candidates. *Globesity* and *decycling* from my sample were taken from MacMillan's Buzzwords. Frequently, this weekly Buzzword is selected from their Open Dictionary section[101], where users can enter words, not necessarily new ones, which they feel need to be included in the dictionary. As a consequence, many of MacMillan's Buzzwords are indeed buzzwords; fashion words that are in vogue during a particular period for a particular reason, but will not become permanently conventionalized. *Decycling* or *vuvzela*, for instance, belong to this group. Similarly, the "Among the new words" section of the *Journal of the American Dialect Society*, which has quarterly listed neologisms since the 1950s, tends to contain many such ephemeral fashion words. If it is the aim to take a static

99 blog.oxforddictionaries.com/2010/08/dictionary-attack-new-words/. In fact, the OED has a prime collection of neologisms on their *Oxford Words* blog, describing the quarterly updates to the OED *Online*.

100 macmillandictionary.com/buzzword/entries/current-entry.html

101 macmillandictionary.com/open-dictionary/latestEntries.htm

snapshot of the English language at a given time, this approach is of course commendable. If it is the aim to investigate the dynamic conventionalization process, however, one should attempt to compile a balanced sample, where neutral words are included in preference to designer words. Whereas the previous collections are all supervised by professional linguists and lexicographers, a substantial number of word-watching websites are administrated by interested individuals, some like Paul McFedries from Word Spy[102] more famous and authoritative than others. Predominantly these collections feature neologisms coined by the author for humorous purposes or neologisms from jargon or slang. As a result, many of the words the authors call neologisms are not neologisms but nonce-formations.

In order for a word to be included in the present sample, its status as a morpho-semantic neologism[103] (as opposed to a nonce-formation) was the first criterion. Regarding the potential candidates detected by the Discoverer, both via metalinguistic markers and novel grapheme strings detection, this status is often not clear from the beginning. This explains why the NeoCrawler database contains more lexemes than actual neologisms. First, the nonce-formations were filtered out. It is important to stress that they were nonce-formations at the time the sample was assembled; though unlikely, some of them might have exceeded the critical limit in the meantime and begun to diffuse. Thus, all lexemes that occurred only once were discounted. Since a webpage might be stored under various addresses, a nonce-formation can theoretically be found more than once in terms of raw frequency. These pages are exact textual copies with a different layout, format or on a different page within the same domain and strictly speaking do not contain new instances of the lexeme, but identical repetitions and thus, nonce-formations. Appendix 1 on page 241 contains a list of potential neologisms that proved to be nonce-formations and were removed from the set.

Conversely, lexemes that were too frequent were also excluded, because it is debatable whether a word yielding over 1000 pages after a first, unrestricted search with the NeoCrawler, can still be deemed a neologism[104]; in terms of

102 wordspy.com/diversions/neologisms.asp

103 Morphological neologisms were not included, since I assume them to be the product of stylistic considerations and thus not entirely suitable for studying neutral diffusion. Semantic neologisms were discounted because the NeoCrawler is presently not equipped to monitor polysemous words.

104 A second check was conducted using Mark Davies' Google Books Corpus, a 155 billion word corpus compiled from the more than 1.3 million books from 1810 until 2009 from the Google Books database. Accessible after free registration via googlebooks.

overall frequency, these lexemes seem to have diffused significantly. As a corollary, further manual investigation of diffusion into different types of source and fields of discourse is highly problematic and impractical. Not only is the number of pages to be reviewed and classified challenging, but more importantly, Google might not return all the pages due to its quantitative restriction to 2000 pages. The sample of observed occurrences might thus be unnecessarily unrepresentative and inaccurate. Lexemes of this type include *bogof (BOGOF)*, 'buy one get one for free', *earworm*, 'a tune that sticks in your head', *overparenting*, 'the act of overprotecting children' and *unfollow*, 'to stop following someone on Twitter'.

In addition to theoretical and practical selection criteria, several (socio-)linguistic considerations were relevant to the compilation of a diverse set of neologisms. Table 5 presents an overview of the selected neologisms and their various linguistic properties.

*Table 5: Linguistic properties of the neologisms in the sample*

| Linguistic dimension | Class | Amount |
|---|---|---|
| 1) Syntax: parts of speech | countable nouns | 20 |
| | uncountable nouns | 12 |
| | adjectives | 8 |
| | verbs | 3 |
| | interjections | 1 |
| 2) Morphology: word-formation process | compounding | 8 |
| | prefixation | 9 |
| | suffixation | 3 |
| | blending | 23 |
| | unknown | 2 |
| 3) Socio-semantics: field of discourse | business | 3 |
| | computing - Internet | 12 |
| | lifestyle - entertainment | 13 |

byu.edu/. *Diabesity*, *ghost surgery* and *hyperlocal* are attested in the Google Books Corpus; when necessary, qualitative evidence from the GBC will be used. Given the fact that Google Books does not display every page from a particular book, frequency counts obtained from the GBC were excluded from statistical modeling.

| | | |
|---|---|---|
| | politics | 3 |
| | undefined - non-specific | 14 |
| 4) Semantics: noun reference | predominantly abstract | 13 |
| | predominantly concrete | 19 |

Since, at first glance, the neologisms do not seem to be evenly distributed, several mitigating remarks are in order here. Firstly, verbs are underrepresented in the present sample, because they are generally less frequently coined in comparison to nouns and because they are often the product of conversion. Conversion poses an important problem to Google webcrawling; as mentioned above, Google does not distinguish between word-forms or parts of speech. If I were to investigate a new verb like *to twitter,* for instance, Google would also yield instances in which *twitter/Twitter* is used as a noun. Given the pervasiveness of Twitter, further analysis would become impossible. Moreover, two of these three verbs, i.e. *to decycle* and *to robosign*, appeared in the language almost simultaneously with their abstract noun relatives *decycling* and *robosigning* respectively. Although these nominal relatives were also included, they are not listed in the noun row for purposes of clarity. Secondly, not all word-formation processes are represented to the same degree. In line with recent claims, blending seems to be a highly productive word-formation process, especially in those fields such as cyberspace in which creativity, humor and eyecatchiness flourish (cf. Lehrer 1996: 385; Schmid 2011: 220). The original candidate pool from which the selection was made therefore contained a disproportionally high amount of blends. Despite adjustment to compensate for the blending bias, blends still constitute almost 50% of the sample. The relative scarcity of compounding is also due to the exclusion of many synthetic *-ing* compounds, which also appears as a highly productive word-formation process in the data. However, many of them refer to abstractly reified concepts and would have thus distorted the abstract-concrete ratio. Lastly, an attempt was made to discount words from specialist registers or slang and cover a broad range of topics in general, everyday language. This explains the low amount of neologisms from politics and business; many of the recent coinages pertaining to these fields of discourse are only of secondary interest to the majority of the speech community. Whereas some of these lexemes might nevertheless diffuse into the everyday lexicon at a later stage, those that conspicuously represented specialist terminology at the time of selection were excluded and this significantly reduced the presence of neologisms from these fields in the sample. The final list of 44 neologisms is found in Appendix 2 on page 246.

### 3.3.2. The NeoCrawler's socio-pragmatic classification system

As explained in section 2.3, conventionalization in the present study is operationalized not only as overall frequency of occurrence, but also as type of source and field of discourse diffusion. The texts in which the neologisms occur thus need to be classified socio-pragmatically. As mentioned above, Werlich's division into narration, description, exposition, argumentation and instruction (1976) and Beaugrande and Dressler's descriptive, narrative, argumentative, scientific, didactic, literary and poetic types (1981) fail to capture the diversity, fuzziness and dynamism of Internet material.

A finer-grained, quantitative method is proposed by Biber (1988, 1989). His analysis of genres[105] and texts is based on statistically computed co-occurrences of groups of linguistic features, so-called *dimensions*[106]. Only afterwards are issues of functionality and situation-dependence investigated (cf. 1988: 13). Biber thus advocates a linguistically rather than socio-pragmatically driven analysis. In Biber's multi-dimensional analysis framework, six dimensions exist (1988, 1989). These dimensions represent continuous scales of co-occurrence of characteristic linguistic aspects between two endpoints:

1) involved vs. informational production: e.g. telephone conversations vs. official documents
2) narrative vs. non-narrative concerns: e.g. romantic fiction vs. telephone conversations
3) explicit vs. situation-dependent reference: e.g. official documents vs. broadcasts
4) overt expression of persuasion: e.g. professional letters vs. broadcasts
5) abstract vs. non-abstract information: e.g. academic writing vs. telephone conversations
6) on-line informational elaboration: e.g. prepared speeches vs. fiction

In later publications, Biber applies his multi-dimensional approach to texts culled from the Internet (cf. Biber and Kurjian 2007; Grieve et al. 2010) and

105 Biber (1988: 70) distinguishes between "text types", based on linguistic features shared by groups of texts and "genres", based language-external features. However, Biber (1995: 9) replaces the latter with "register". Thus, a register is a variety characterized by situational-functional and linguistic features (cf. Biber and Conrad 2009: 6).

106 For similar, computationally-driven approaches to web genre identification and classification see Santini (2010) and Kim and Ross (2010).

provides a rudimentary comparison of e-mail messages, discussion forum posts and text messages (SMS) (cf. Biber and Conrad 2009: 177-211). Biber and Kurjian (2007) compiled a corpus of roughly 3000 texts from the Google categories Home and Science, grammatically POS-tagged with the Biber tagger (1988, 2006), to identify patterns of shared and different linguistic features along four dimensions: personal, involved narration, persuasive/argumentative discourse, addressee-focused discourse and abstract/technical discourse. Since these dimensions incorporate linguistic characteristics only, no claim is made regarding registers, but only text types. Biber and Kurjian concede that the selected texts are used for a variety of purposes, which are not reflected by the categories set up by Google. As a result, linguistic variation between texts within the two categories was greater than between the categories themselves (cf. 2007: 119). A subsequent cluster analysis revealed four relatively clear text types: informational discourse, persuasive advice, technical discourse and personal narrative (cf. 2007: 121-123). Biber and Kurjian state that a register analysis, considering situational parameters like audience and interactivity, would be more complicated and labor-consuming, because prior to a linguistic analysis, manual coding for register of the individual web pages would be necessary (cf. 2007: 123). Unfortunately, they do not clarify which registers they suspect to be represented in Internet discourse and how they might differ from those in offline language.

In addition, the underlying situational parameters as assumed by Biber (cf. 1988: 28-33) cannot always be applied to online texts, because the necessary information is not available. Although users in discussion fora, for instance, are often openly acknowledged as frequent visitors, administrators or novices (e.g. by the number and color of stars next to the user name, see p. 108), their specific socio-economic background can only be indirectly gleaned from their posts, which are unreliable representations. Thus, the participants' background and the relations among the users can at best be approximated. On the other hand, the traditional set of situational characteristics underestimates the influence of specific factors like the setting and the channel on the language. As Giltrow and Stein (2009: 9) note, the Internet gives rise to "new distance-synchronic forms of communication, new combinations of N-to-N -the number of people speaking and the number of people receiving the communication- and the high speed [...]". Under *setting*, for instance, the time, place and the extent to which they are shared by the participants and the audience are subsumed (cf. Biber 1988: 31). However, unlike traditional distinctions between a letter and a newspaper article regarding the readership the audience of Internet language is by definition infinite. Most content is publicly available to a potentially large number of users.

Even much of superficially restricted content can be accessed if users register with a single click. This implies that users can exploit the degree of sharing personal information for a variety of purposes. Frequently, personal blogs, for instance, are used "for cultivation and validation of the self" (Miller and Shepherd 2004[107]). Whereas traditionally personal letters were destined for one or more particular addressees, some bloggers now divulge sensitive, personal details to an infinite number of readers. It remains unclear how such aspects should be incorporated into the Biberian typology of Internet registers. The present approach therefore distinguishes between personal and professional or "thematic" (Grieve et al. 2010: 320) blogs, i.e. those that are written for a smaller circle of readers sharing a particular passion or interest and those that are written as expert sources of information for a wider audience; this issue will be further explored below.

Closely connected to the audience issue is the type of communication channel that needs to be considered. The traditional dichotomy between speech and writing is increasingly blurred on the Internet due to the various (temporal) constellations of the audience. Morris and Ogan (1996) identify four types of communication in an online setting, depending on the number of participants and the time dimension. The first three instances are asynchronous, i.e. the participants write, read and interact in relayed time. Communication of this type can be one-to-one, as in e-mail, many-to-many as in discussion fora, or a combination. Synchronous communication on the other hand takes the form of one-to-one or one-to-many in chat rooms or games (cf. Morris and Ogan 1996: 42). An Internet genre typology therefore has to consider these subchannels, which will affect and be affected by the language. A new medium like Twitter, for instance, imposing a 140-character restriction on the producer, will need to be distinguished from Internet newspaper articles and blogs, to name but a few, without restrictions on the size of the output.

Based on Dell Hymes' SPEAKING model (1974), Susan Herring developed a "faceted classification scheme" (2007), which convincingly renders the diversity and dynamism of Internet communication. She argues that newer forms of CMD arise through interaction between social-situational and technological influence factors, the so-called "facets" (2007: 10). These facets, constituting dynamic and open-ended sets, are listed in Table 6.

---

107 Available via blog.lib.umn.edu/blogosphere blogging_as_social_action_a_genre_analysis_of_the_weblog.html. No page number available.

*Table 6: Herring's multi-faceted classification scheme for CMD (adapted from Herring 2007: 13, 18)*

| **Medium (= technological factors)** | **Realizations** |
|---|---|
| synchronicity | synchronic vs. asynchronic |
| message transmission: one-way or two-way | one-way: message-by message transmission<br>two-way: message visible to reader during production |
| persistence of transcript | duration of message storage |
| size of message buffer | size of single message, e.g. limitless in e-mailing |
| channels of communication | text, audio, video, graphics |
| anonymous messaging | yes/no |
| private messaging | yes/no |
| filtering | yes/no |
| quoting | yes/no |
| message format | position of new messages, e.g. at the top for blogs |
| **Social situation** | |
| participant structure | one-to-one, one-to-many, etc.<br>group structure<br>degree of anonymity |
| participant characteristics | demographics<br>experience and proficiency with topic and language<br>status |
| purpose | inform<br>entertain<br>develop relationships<br>etc. |
| topic | multiple |
| tone | playful/serious<br>casual/formal<br>etc. |
| activity | game, emphatic exchange, job announcements, etc. |
| norms | netiquette concerns |
| code | language<br>language variety |
| writing system | (language-specific) fonts |

openly marked their posts as criticism on current US politics and started a virtual rally (*Süddeutsche Zeitung*, July 26, 2011[120]).

Returning to the analysis procedure, as mentioned above on page 89, after retrieval from the Web, each page is classified as meta- or objectlinguistic and assigned to a type of source and a field of discourse. Furthermore, its position on the pages is identified as BODY, TITLE or OTHER. The last group includes usage as a CATEGORY collecting posts or articles with similar or related topics, or TAG. Tags are keywords assigned to posts and articles as query-facilitating devices and simultaneously they act as a summary of the content for the user. Some of these, most prominently the hashtags like *#fuckyouwashington* mentioned in the previous paragraph, lead a life of their own in cyberspace. The use of these hashtags to express often emotional aspects and communicate is in the meantime no longer confined to Twitter, where the hashtags originate, but can be found in many other online types of source as well. in In Figure 8, for instance, some ordinary tags are listed directly under the blog post title, which is together with the bottom of the post, their most frequent position. They provide quick links to related content and are therefore not only efficient automatic content-organizing tools, but also advantageous to the user interested in a specific topic. In a blog on digital marketing, for instance, all posts dealing with one particular topic such as search engine optimization are tagged accordingly and returned to the user searching for such posts by either entering the term in the query field or simply clicking on it in one of the posts. These CATEGORIES and TAGS are marked separately, because I assume they reflect a different degree of cognitive status in comparison with the BODY and TITLE occurrences. When a new word is not simply used in a context, which will support its interpretation and meaning, but isolated as a classificatory, metalinguistic, contextless label to facilitate searches, its meaning should be unambiguously known by the users and thus conventionalized to a higher degree. In simpler terms, if the referent of a category or tag is unknown, the category or tag looses its function and becomes useless. If a blogger writing about VIPs, for instance, creates the category BOOBGATE on his/her blog to collect all posts that are related to a famous person revealing too much cleavage in public, he/she assumes that the readers are familiar with this particular meaning and will therefore access the category whenever interest in the Boobgate concept occurs. A category can only serve its categorization function, and justify its existence, if a minimal amount of content or meaning is shared. Due to their different cognitive status and the fact that

120 jetzt.sueddeutsche.de/texte/anzeigen/528255. Retrieved on July 26, 2011.

neologisms that serve as tags or category labels cannot be precisely dated[121], they were excluded from subsequent statistical analysis, but will be discussed for individual neologisms when relevant. Although POSITION affects the individual token and needs to be assessed manually, I decided to take one token for each page and classify it accordingly as body, title or other. Often, only one token was found. Whenever multiple tokens were present on one single page, I classified them according to the position of the majority of tokens. When the word occurred twice in the body of the text and once as title, the page was filed as BODY.

One of the central aims of the present study as mentioned in 1.2 was to investigate the influence of nameworthiness on the conventionalization process, which cannot be captured by means of the classification system described above. The following section will conclude this chapter by discussing an experimental approach to the evaluation of the nameworthiness of neologisms.

### 3.3.3. Operationalizing nameworthiness

In her investigation of the nature and functional basis of constraints on compounding, Downing (1977: 838) remarks that

> the name-worthiness of the category denoted[,] does not serve as an absolute constraint on the formation of the compound, but rather as a constraint on the contextual range within which the compound may be used. Forms which do not denote conventionalizable categories may be used, but they are unlikely to survive beyond the context in which they were originally created.

Extending her observations to other word-formation products, the nameworthiness of the underlying concept or exigencies on the part of the coiner to create a hypostatizing class of things or events is assumed to be a primary propelling factor in the conventionalization process of neologisms. Despite the adoption of the term *nameworthiness* by other linguists, to my current knowledge, no one has attempted to investigate the nameworthiness phenomenon and effect on the diffusion of new coinages empirically. As mentioned in the introduction, the present study fills this gap by including nameworthiness as a diffusion-influencing factor. In order to be able to discuss the degree of influence, the theoretical concept needed to be operationalized, which is not entirely

121 Since diffusion is measured as frequency per month, all occurrences without a clear date were not further considered, because of statistical biasing. They would increase the raw frequency, but not accurately reflect the chronological development of a given neologism.

unproblematic, given the lack of objective, universally-applicable measurements or standards of description. Therefore, I developed a conceptually-oriented questionnaire-experiment which approaches nameworthiness from a quantitative and qualitative perspective. A sample questionnaire can be found in Appendix 3 on page 251.

In the experiment, 40 native speakers of English[122] were asked to give their intuitive opinion on the usefulness of a concept on a numerical scale between 1 and 5, followed by a short explanation of their decision. The concept was not listed as the word-form of the novel lexeme, but represented by its definition. I decided for a conceptual approach because the subjects might be distracted or influenced by the specific word-form in their assessment. Some neologisms like *Boobgate* and *cherpumple* undoubtedly have a humorous effect, which I assume to play a role in people's decisions. Such word-form-guided evaluations of course provide additional clues as to why certain words become established and other do not, but do not directly represent the nameworthiness of the concept. Moreover, a complementary test design would have been required, which was beyond the scope of the present study. The concepts in the present questionnaire consisted of a randomized mixture of novel (the target in line 1), lexicalized[123] (line 3) and non-existing (line 2) concepts. The latter two formed the control groups. Lexicalized concepts are concepts that have been hypostatized and occur as existing lexemes in the language. Non-existing concepts refer to those instances in which the concept is not represented by a lexeme in the language (yet) and were invented for the present purpose. The meanings of the lexicalized and non-existing lexemes were kept as close as possible to the meanings of the neologisms under investigation so as to keep the set semantically contiguous and controlled. As the example of *globesity* below shows, the central semantic properties of concept X, i.e. obesity being a global problem, are reflected in the distractors. The 'global problem' aspect is kept relatively constant, whereas the concept X is varied: in the non-existing condition as *anorexia*, in the lexicalized condition as the earth warming up. Thus, for the target neologism *globesity*, the following test set was developed:

---

122 I am greatly indebted to the students of the University College in London for their cooperation and Kathryn Allan for her hospitality and assistance during the experiments.

123 *Lexicalized* in the present paragraph is used with a different meaning than above in section 2.1.2. Here, it simply refers to the fact that a concept has been expressed in a morphological form in the language.

(1) the idea that obesity has become a global problem (target)
(2) the idea that anorexia has become a global problem (non-existing)
(3) the idea that the earth is warming up (lexicalized as *global warming*)

The two questions relating directly to the nameworthiness were supplemented with two further questions regarding the informants' familiarity with the concept and their possible knowledge of the corresponding lexeme.

In total, 21 neologisms from the sample were tested for nameworthiness. Four different questionnaires were designed, each filled in by an average of 20 native speaker students and staff members at University College London and the Ludwig-Maximilians University in Munich. Save for one, all questionnaires consist of 15 concept sets. Despite extensive efforts to keep the number of neological, lexicalized and non-existing stimuli balanced across the questionnaires, their shares differ, because it proved impossible to create a three-fold set for each neologism. The results of the nameworthiness experiment will be discussed in section 4.2.4. They yield a number of interesting findings regarding nameworthiness and validate the present approach to the operationalization of Downing's nameworthiness concept.

In this chapter I have presented the various procedural steps in my empirical investigation of the conventionalization process of English neologisms. After a detailed overview of existing approaches to the Web-as-corpus, I discussed the problems of using Google as an entry point to the Internet, but also highlighted the advantages for the present study, i.e. its best score regarding quantity, quality and freshness of its index necessary for the close monitoring of neologisms in language. Next, I presented an innovative tool, custom-tailored to the purpose of neolexicology, the NeoCrawler and discussed its merits. As will be shown in the next chapters, despite the project being in its infancy, valuable and interesting results can be obtained. I also addressed the controversial issue of Internet genre typology and suggested an idiosyncratic multi-dimensional, three-level analysis of webpages and tokens based on the intertwining of situational and technological aspects in web language contexts. In the next chapters, I turn to the results and present findings regarding types of conventionalization processes (4.1), diffusion-promoting and -inhibiting factors (4.2) and the semantic and structural development of syntagmatic lexical networks (chapter 5).

# 4. The conventionalization process of English neologisms

## 4.1. The conventionalization continuum

As mentioned in 2.3, the conventionalization process is best conceived of as a continuum ranging from non-conventionalized to topically established lexical items to lexical items that are progressing towards advanced conventionalization. These distinct stages require evidence from long-term monitoring, possibly over the course of a decade or longer. The assignment of the neologisms to various diachronic stages or synchronic statuses along the continuum are thus based on the empirical evidence available in January 2011, when the NeoCrawler retrieved the last results to be included in the present investigation. Some of the English neologisms presented in 4.1.1 and 4.1.2 might yet advance to further stages of conventionalization after their extended period of non-activity that justifies the present classification as non-conventionalized (4.1.1) or topically conventionalized (4.1.2). Similarly, new words that are treated as progressively conventionalized in 4.1.3 and 4.1.4 can become deconventionalized in the future.

### 4.1.1. Non-conventionialization

The most conspicuous candidates for the non-conventionalization stage a) do not occur frequently in objectlinguistic usage, b) do not occur in more than two types of source and c) do not occur in more than two fields of discourse. Before going into detail on the quantitative operationalization of non-conventionalization, it is necessary to emphasize that like many linguistic and extralinguistic concepts the notion of (non-)conventionalization is essentially prototypical. Hence, the three criteria will not be present for all non-conventionalized neologisms or lexical units to the same degree, nor was the frequency threshold of criteria (a) applied strictly. Some lexemes like *roofvertising* presented in detail in the next paragraph are characterized by a low overall frequency (six occurrences) in only one type of source. Other lexemes like *tynonym*, which occurs 104 times in the sample, would seem to be more conventionalized than *roofvertising* on the basis of the overall frequency criteria (a) alone, but upon closer inspection almost all of these occurrences are metalinguistic. Again others like *e-tivity* (51 occurrences) are only found significantly in one type of source, in the case of *e-tivity* in PROFESSIONAL BLOGS.

Based on the available data in the present study the upper limit for the overall frequency for cases of non-conventionalization was set at 150 occurrences, measured as pages retrieved by the NeoCrawler. This number roughly corresponds to 10% of the averaged overall frequency of the three lexemes with the highest frequency, i.e. representing cases of the most advanced conventionalization stage (see Appendix 5 on page 257 for a list of each neologism and its overall and individual type of source frequencies). The quantification of criteria (b) and (c), of the number of types of source and fields of discourse, is a mathematical-statistical one. Given the zero hypothesis of random distribution across the nine types of source in the classification scheme, a type of source is considered significantly available if the number of occurrences exceeds 1/9 of the total frequency of occurrence. For the fields of discourse, numbering 13 in the classification system, slight alterations of the type of source formula were necessary. Firstly, metalinguistic pages were not classified with regard to their field of discourse. These pages therefore need to be subtracted from the total frequency. More importantly, the threshold was doubled, i.e. 2/13, because in view of the stronger conceptual ties between meaning and field of discourse, it requires more effort for the word to exceed its natural semantic domain and spread into others. Thus, occurrence in multiple fields of discourse is assumed to be more indicative of conventionalization than occurrence in multiple types of source. In sum, prototypically non-conventionalized lexemes do not occur more than 150 times and in more than two types of source and fields of discourse in the present data set.

A prototypical case of non-conventionalization is represented by *roofvertising*. *Roofvertising* is a blend of *roof* and *advertising* and refers to the practice of using the roofs of tall buildings as advertising space to increase visibility, for instance, from the air. The first attestation[124] dates from November 2006 from a metalinguistic comment in a professional blog:

(3) Nov 17, 2006. Maps, and MSN Live Maps. This sort of thing is being called "mapvertising" or "*roofvertising*"[125].

In a second occurrence from the same blog in June 2007, *roofvertising* is used as an attention-seeking device in the title, further explained in the body of the text:

(4) "*Roofvertising*" mentioned in the news. Greg Sterling and I were quoted in a news story in yesterday's USA Today by Craig Wilson in an article titled "Shout a message

124 The relevant neologisms in the examples are italicized.

125 naturalsearchblog.com/archives/2006/11/17/kfc-ad-targeting-google-maps-yahoo-maps-and-msn-earth/.

from the rooftops to the world", along with Google Earth's Chikai Ohazama. The article is about how people are increasingly trying to use Google Maps and other online mapping systems to communicate messages or display ads through them. People place the messages on rooftops or other ground surfaces which may be seen via the satellite pix or aerial photos in those interfaces[126].

Despite the absence of an explicit definition, *roofvertising* in (4) is again used metalinguistically. As in example (3), it is not a specific instance or referential application of the concept, but cataphorically summarizes the practice that is described in the paragraph following the occurrence. Additionally, the use of quotation marks in both examples, as well as in all of the other results, highlights the novelty of the word. Overall, a mere six occurrences were found since November 2006, all from professional blogs dedicated to innovative marketing strategies (four hits), one from the filesharing website Flickr as a tag, which was deleted from the sample because of the unknown publication date, and two metalinguistic uses in the same blog. Figure 13 accordingly does not show any increase in frequency and evidences the lack of diffusion, which corresponds to a synchronic state of non-conventionalization in the speech community.

*Fig. 13: New and cumulative pages per month for* roofvertising

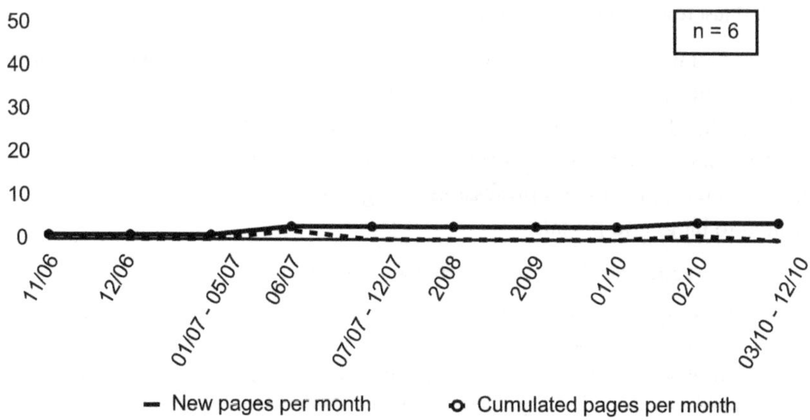


In similar fashion, *preghead*, a blend of *pregnant* and *egghead* to denote a pregnant woman who forgets more than usually, does not display any evidence of

126 naturalsearchblog.com/archives/2007/06/05/roofvertising-mentioned-in-the-news/

progressing or ongoing conventionalization. The first occurrence in the current sample was found in a personal blog in June 2007:

(5) And yet. When I speak with other *pregheads*, or others who have been through the experience, they quickly resound, "But every woman's different! And every pregnancy is different!"[127]

The writer of the blog, a pregnant woman with preghead symptoms (as evidenced by *other* in the first line), shares her experiences and concerns with her audience and for that purpose uses a condensed monolexeme instead of a phrase. Unlike examples (3) and (4), no novelty markers such as explicit or implicit definitions or quotation marks are present. Neither in example (5) nor in example (6) below does the writer assume that the word and its meaning is known to the readers. Since neither of the readers of the blog nor any of the other discussion forum members openly questions or remarks on the word and asks for an explanation, *preghead* might have been understood without further effort, despite its relative opacity. Moreover, both examples come from sources dedicated to exchanging experiences and problems concerning pregnancies. Based on these shared experiences of forgetfulness, it is possible that the members of this microcommunity find the word self-explanatory.

(6) I just realised the original post was from 2008!! *Preghead*!![128]

*Preghead* attained limited topicality (cf. 2.1.3) in February 2010, when scientific reports refuting the 'preghead myth' hit the news, as illustrated in example (7) from the headline of a *Guardian* blog article. In the following days five links to the *Guardian* report, only quoting the headline, are found in health- or pregnancy-focused portals and professional blogs. Overall too, the use of *preghead* is limited to blogs and portals.

(7) I don't care what the researchers say, I was a *preghead*[129]

(8) *Pregnancy Brain*?! Apparently it's a myth?? *Nappy head, Mumnesia, Preghead, Baby brain* there are many names for it and I have a serious case of it this week. I cannot remember anything and keep doing the strangest things. Don't ask me why my sunglasses are in the fridge I have no idea how they got there?![130]

As mentioned in the short passage in (8), synonyms exist, which would suggest that the concept is more established than the 14 occurrences from my sample

127 kendraspondence.com/%3Fp%3D1670/?paged=119
128 babyandbump.com/pregnancy-third-trimester/80314-blocked-nose-sinuses.html
129 guardian.co.uk/lifeandstyle/2010/feb/04/pregnant-women-forgetful-science
130 thebabybubbleblog.blogspot.com/2010/09/pregnancy-brain.html

evidence. Given the fact that most of these hits are found in specialist discourse on pregnancies, *preghead* is likely to be only familiar in pregnancy jargon to the members of this particular microcommunity of pregnant women and therefore not conventionalized in the speech community at large.

Another example of a non-conventionalized neologism is illustrated by the prefixed form *mesofact*. A *mesofact* is a fact that changes over time like the earth's population or the number of mobile phone owners. The word was coined by Samuel Arbesman, a professional from Harvard Medical School in a *Boston Globe* article from February 2010:

(9) Warning: Your reality is out of date. Introducing the *mesofact*. […]These slow-changing facts are what I term "*mesofacts*." *Mesofacts* are the facts that change neither too quickly nor too slowly, that lie in this difficult-to-comprehend middle, or meso-, scale. Often, we learn these in school when young and hold onto them, even after they change.[131]

In addition to Arbesman actively promoting his novel concept in a number of portals, he also writes a blog dedicated to the investigation of such mesofacts, mesofacts.org. However, as Figure 14 shows, most of the 80 occurrences retrieved by the NeoCrawler are metalinguistic definitions or uses by the coiner. *Mesofact* has not become frequently adopted by other writers with reference to new instances.

*Fig. 14: Cumulative pages per month in different modes of usage for* mesofact

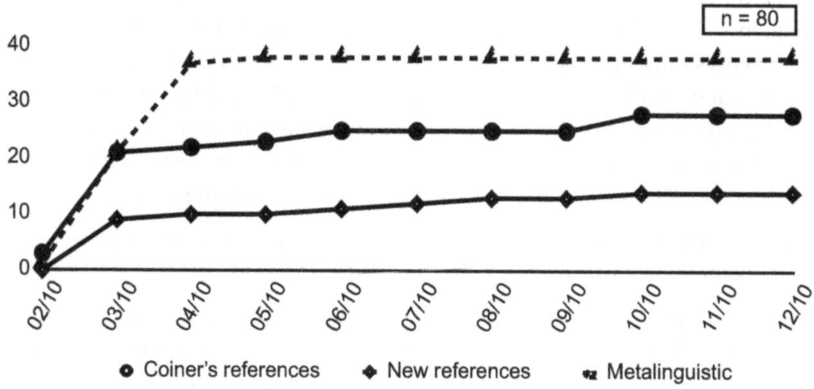


131 boston.com/bostonglobe/ideas/articles/2010/02/28/warning_your_reality_is_out_of_date/

The overall frequency of 80 occurrences within a mere ten months would indicate advancing conventionalization, compared to *roofvertising* and *preghead.* However, upon closer inspection, the distinct usages underlying these frequencies suggest a rather different development. Despite Arbesman's conscious efforts to introduce the concept and the word into the English language as evidenced by the high proportion of pages from his blog, *mesofact* does not catch on. Immediately after the publication of the *Boston Globe* article many websites copy the definition and propel the metalinguistic use forward as displayed in the steep increase in frequency from February to April 2010 in Figure 14. Afterwards the attraction or topicality is reduced and no further metalinguistic mention is made, as evidenced by the dashed curve neatly flatlining. The author himself does continue to publish his invention at regular intervals, mainly only a mention of the word and an explanation, as a small number of other blog authors do, but predominantly in the first four weeks after the original article until the curve quickly flattens, represented by the two continuous lines in Figure 14. Current non-conventionalization is furthermore confirmed by sociopragmatic evidence. The objectlinguistic occurrences are limited to the type of source BLOG.

In some cases, the various lexical units of a polysemous or homonymous lexeme represent different degrees of conventionalization. *Bloglet,* for instance, a suffixation from *blog*, features two lexical units. *Bloglet*$^1$ refers to a short blog entry whereas *bloglet*$^2$, predominantly in plural form (34 out of 36 tokens), is used as a form of address for fellow bloggers or blog readers in blogs. With regard to frequency, *bloglet*$^1$ is attested 515 times, but *bloglet*$^2$ occurs on a mere 26 pages. Both senses only occur significantly in the BLOG category. The frequency development of *bloglet*$^1$ is presented in Figure 39 in section 5.2.1 on p. 193, because it will be discussed in detailed as a case study for the emergence of syntagmatic lexical networks. The first mention returned by the NeoCrawler dates from a personal blog entry in September 2002, as illustrated in example (10):

(10) Oh, and by the way, my little *bloglets*: last night, Evil Rubber Goose Guy was as quiet as a... rubber goose[132].

It is obvious from the sentence that *bloglet* in the present context is not used to refer to the short entry, but to address the readers. The particular syntagmatic pattern with *my* and/or *little* is characteristic of the sense of *bloglet*$^2$, although *little* is also a frequent collocate for *bloglet*$^1$ as I will show in section 5.2.1. Table 7

132 yourcorrespondent.net/2002/09/24/43/

provides the results from a collocational analysis of *bloglet*$^{2}$. As shown in the first column, the particular construction, in which *little* is preceded by a variable kind of modification, often pronominal *my*, elicits the form-of-address-sense, distinct from *bloglet*$^{1}$. For the 34 plural tokens, the following collocational patterns were observed:

*Table 7: Overview of collocation patterns for* bloglets$^{2}$

| Collocates | Raw frequency | Relative frequency |
|---|---|---|
| *X little bloglets:* | 10 | 34% |
| *my little bloglets* | 8 | 27.2% |
| *dear little bloglets* | 1 | 3.4% |
| *lovely little bloglets* | 1 | 3.4% |
| *my X* (other than *little*) *bloglets* *(fellow/darling)* | 2 | 6.8% |
| *my bloglets* | 1 | 3.4% |

The results reveal a relatively strong collocational structure that on the one hand semantically supports the particular meaning of addressing someone and on the other hand lexico-semantically reiterates the diminutive feature that is also present in the suffix. Both *my* and *little* are therefore important and explicit cotextual anchors.

In sum, the non-conventionalized neologisms in the present study are all characterized by low objectlinguistic frequencies in one type of source (save for *preghead*). Metalinguistic uses, when significantly present as for *mesofact*, might yield higher overall frequency scores, but do not necessarily indicate conventionalization of active use. Conventionalization would entail an increasing number of attestations of the word with a growing number of different classes of referents in contexts other than the original coinage context and cotext. The semantic and pragmatic restrictions of the present non-conventionalized neologisms are also evident in the lack of diffusion into different types of source and fields of discourse. Hence, *preghead* is so far only attested in specialist discourse on pregnancies and pregnancy-related issues, *bloglets* in blogs. However, the former exhibited some tendencies towards momentary small-scale topicality after the publication of a scientific study on the matter. Nevertheless, the salience was not widespread enough to propagate the word outside the given microcommunity and instantiate large-scale topicality. The next section will discuss instances of such topicality-induced transitional conventionalization in the speech community at large.

### 4.1.2. Topicality or transitional conventionalization

The term *topicality* is borrowed in slightly altered meaning from Fischer (1998: 16, 172-175, see 2.1.3), who defines the concept as the phenomenon when "a word is used in connection with current affairs for a short period of time" (1998: 16). In the present study, topicality refers to the transitional or momentary conventionalization of lexemes or lexical units under the influence of an increased salience of extralinguistic events, as evidenced by a sudden burst in overall frequency in multiple types of source. This degree of conventionalization is therefore intrinsically connected to what is happening in the world. Fashion or vogue words are almost always illustrations of transitional conventionalization. However, depending on the degree and duration of an item's topicality transitional conventionalization may segue into advanced, and possibly even permanent conventionalization. This development towards permanent conventionalization requires a high frequency of occurrence within a longer time span.

A prime example of topicality is *back scooping*. When US celebrity Heidi Montag said she had had her back scooped and admitted not really knowing what that meant in a talkshow in early April 2010, the word *back scooping* and its morphological variants instantaneously took off. Example (11) illustrates one of the first attestations and contains a comment on the sudden virtual commotion her (and the word's) appearance caused.

> (11) "I had my *back scooped*," Montag said on "On Air with Ryan Seacrest" on Monday. When asked what, exactly, that means, she said, "I actually didn't know. I might be the first one to try it. It carves out your back a little bit." And the Internet was all, *Back scooping*? Is that a real thing?! LOL. Commenters on blogs and celebrity gossip sites pondered together: What is this mysterious procedure?[133] (journalist Melissa Dahl from NBC)

The author does not precisely define the word, but rather describes the reactions from the online speech community, i.e. *and the Internet was all*, whose members initially did not understand the meaning. She even expresses doubt whether the procedure really existed (*is that a real thing?, what is this mysterious procedure?*). A *back scooping* is in fact an ordinary liposuction of parts of the back and hips. From a linguistic perspective, the word's coinage should have been blocked because *back liposuction* already exists. However, the word was created by a celebrity, who did not even know herself what surgery she had had; both her fame and ignorance, evoking mockery, represented two important factors for the lexeme's sudden spread.

This instant diffusion is illustrated by the steep curve in Figure 15.

---

133 nbclosangeles.com/entertainment celebrity/Heidi_Montag_had_her__back_scooped__Huh_-90341534.html)

*Fig. 15: New and cumulative pages per month of* back scooping

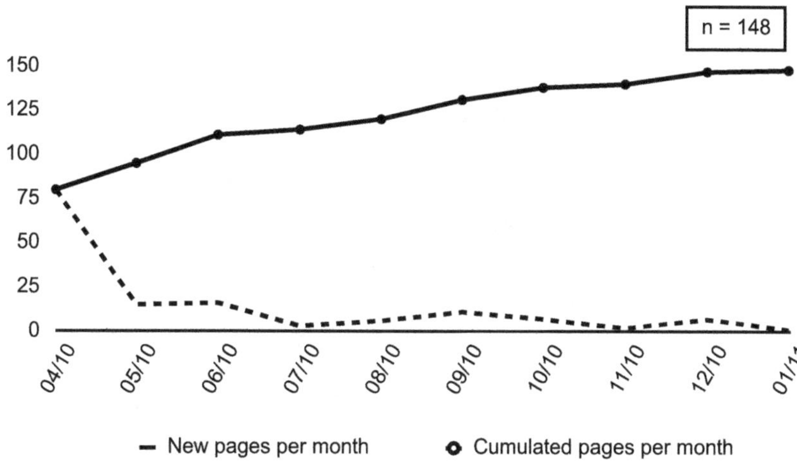


Unlike in a typical diffusion curve, no initial zero or near-zero point is displayed, due to the fact that all occurrences for April were taken together and not separated according to the precise date. It is nevertheless apparent that within the course of a couple of weeks, *back scooping* rapidly increases in frequency. As visible from the dotted curve representing the new pages per month, the drastic decline is also sudden, which is a further typical indicator of topicality.

Strikingly, no real type of source diffusion in the strictest sense takes place. From the beginning, *back scooping* occurs in all types of source, except ACADEMIC WRITING and DISCUSSION FORUM, albeit to different degrees as shown in Figure 16 on the next page. Although only two types of source, PORTAL and BLOG, are significant with respect to frequency, it is interesting to observe the word's occurrence in multiple types of source from the beginning, which underlines the topicality and salience, and might in turn fuel further diffusion. Similarly, the use of *back scooping* is not restricted to the semantic domains of ENTERTAINMENT and LIFESTYLE, to which it inherently belongs, but is also attested in business and general discourse. Figure 16 presents an overview of the types of source attested in April 2010. Admittedly, upon closer inspection, micro-processes of diffusion may be present, in which a novel lexeme originates and is used in one specific type of source prior to spreading to others, but such processes cannot be discussed here due to the decision for monthly interval monitoring.

*Fig. 16: Frequency of* back scooping *in different types of source in April 2010*

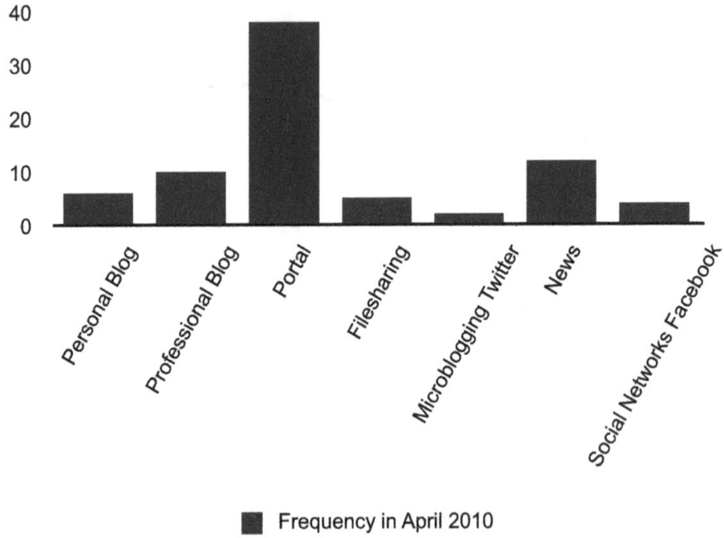


Further evidence of the topicality is found in the referential range of *back scooping* and its word-form variants. Not surprisingly, the word does not emancipate itself from its coinage event. Most instances refer to Heidi Montag. The noun-verb combination *back scooped,* for instance, is preceded in 30 out of 49 occurrences by *her*, with *Heidi Montag* mentioned in the extended cotext. The sentence in (12) contains a similar example, whereas (13) illustrates one of the rare uses with a generic referent in a professional blog providing information on plastic surgery.

(12) *Heidi* had high-praise for the doctor, who had controversially performed ten procedures–including jaw shaving, eyebrow lifting, and *back scooping* on her in one day.[134]

(13) Many women want the perfect hour glass figure and hence they want to undergo breast augmentation, *back scooping,* liposuction, tummy tuck as well as a buttock augmentation one after the other.[135]

134 dramarama.ca/2010/08/man-who-made-heidi-montag-what-she-is-today-killed-in-crash.html, August 2010 (entertainment portal).

135 plasticsurgeryportalca.com/surgical-procedures/body-sculpting-with-cosmetic-surgery/, November 2010.

The case of *back scooping* clearly shows the influence of the coiner, whose creation becomes the subject of topical attention and instantly gains currency. Occasionally, this influence or propagation does not affect the speech community immediately, as is shown by the example of *kindergarchy*. Joseph Epstein, a writer, published an article in the *Wall Street Journal* in November 2007 on the phenomenon that children have acquired a rather powerful and determinative role in society, labeling this phenomenon *kindergarchy*:

(14) For some time in America we have, of course, been living under *Kindergarchy*, or rule by children. If children do not precisely rule us, then certainly all efforts, in families where the smallish creatures still roam, are directed to relieving their boredom if not (hope against hope) actually pleasing them. Let us be thankful that Thanksgiving has not yet fallen to the *Kindergarchy*, as has just about every other holiday on the calendar, with the possible exceptions of Yom Kippur and Ramadan.[136]

*Kindergarchy*, a blend of *kindergarten* and the combining form *-archy*[137], refers to the rule or domination of children in contemporary society or the belief that children's needs and preferences take precedence over those of their parents or other adults. As illustrated in Figure 17, the first article did not trigger diffusion. Only when a similar article by Epstein was published in the *Weekly Standard* in June 2008 did the frequency of *kindergarchy* in Internet discourse suddenly increase.

*Fig. 17: Cumulated pages per month in different modes of usage for* kindergarchy

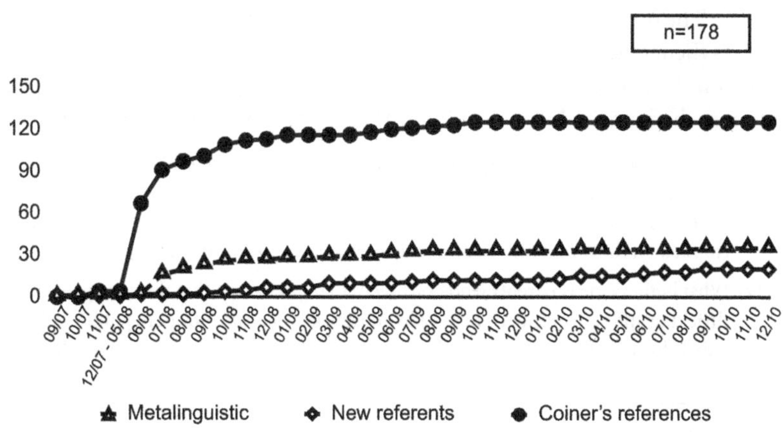


136 online.wsj.com/article/SB119559530489099680.html

137 According to word-formation principles, bound elements cannot be blended. The semantic element 'rule or domination' present in *kindergarchy*, however, does not derive from *anarchy* or *oligarchy*, but solely from the combining form *-archy*.

As already mentioned with regard to *mesofact* in 4.1.1 the overall frequency of 178 occurrences does not accurately reflect the conventionalization process. A fine-grained analysis of these pages revealed that most occurrences following the June 2008 publication are references to Joseph Epstein and the article, as illustrated in (15), taken from a lifestyle-centered portal in October 2008.

(15) US academic Joseph Epstein recently coined the term "*kindergarchy*" in an article for The Weekly Standard magazine referring to a "new world order in which children rule". Although a somewhat extreme explanation for this current cultural trend, our society is becoming increasingly dominated by our children's needs – what they eat, who their friends are, their schooling, what they wear, what they own and, of course, their wellbeing.[138]

Explicit reference is made to the coiner/writer, the source and an explanation of the newly introduced term. Such instances account for 70% of the overall number of occurrences. In fact, they behave similarly to metalinguistic comments, since they do not contain a novel application of the lexeme to a novel class of referents, but copy-paste and adapt explanatory information from other sources. All of these instances were extricated from the purely metalinguistic definitions (from *Word Spy*[139], for instance) that did not name the coiner or the original articles. Two examples of a context in which the scaffolding of the original coinage salience and topicality has disappeared and which accordingly can be interpreted as instances of 'true' conventionalization are presented in examples (16) and (17). The use of quotation marks in the former occurrence, however, further supports the fact that the lexeme is still deemed new and therefore not very advanced on the conventionalization cline yet. A mere 11% of the retrieved pages contain such emancipated, objectlinguistic uses not connected to Epstein.

(16) As our economy and society enters Obama's recession, what effect will it have on the "*Kindergarchy*"? What will happen to the weekend traveling soccer league or the numerous tae-kwon-do schools? What is to become of the restaurants that have counted on the 6 year olds making the dining decisions for the family?[140]

(17) What bothers me is parents who don't seem to mind or care that their offspring are shrieking and screaming (or may I add, hitting, kicking and biting) in public. When kids I don't know do this, I can leave, but my problem is that it's my friends and

138 The original page is no longer indexed by Google. The example is taken from the page in its saved form in the NeoCrawler database.

139 wordspy.com/words/kindergarchy.asp, July 2008. Note that Paul McFedries, the blog writer, incorrectly classifies kindergarchy as a blend of *kinder* and *-archy*.

140 conservativewahoo.blogspot.com/2008/10/what-will-become-of-children-in-down.html, October 2008.

period. In terms of reference, most occurrences, even those after the topicality has disappeared, are strongly linked to the coiner and coinage event, which is a momentary topic of concern to the community. They provide instances of textual and mental copy-pasting without expanding the range to generic or different classes of referents.

Lexemes that have gained currency due to an extralinguistic event and subsequent communicative need may follow any of three conventionalization routes. Often, they will disappear from current usage and depending on the degree of topicality become deconventionalized before reaching full establishment or leaving some traces in the speech community and the speakers' lexicons. Alternatively, they can re-appear as soon as the topic becomes of societal concern again, because identical or similar events occur. Ultimately such repeated periods of topicality can, but do not necessarily lead to advanced conventionalization, which will be illustrated in 4.1.4. Sometimes, topics are intermittently salient because the concept is by definition recurrent, like Christmas trees being more salient in December[146]. This process of repeated topicality of equal or similar intensity, which I have labeled *recurrent semi-conventionalization*, is discussed in the following section.

### 4.1.3. Recurrent semi-conventionalization

In late December 2009, US comedian and humorist Charles Phoenix published a post on his homepage entitled "*Cherpumple.* The turducken of deserts", including a video tutorial on how to make a cherpumple and the recipe[147]. He explains the lexeme as a blend of *cherry*, *pumpkin* and *apple* pie and recalls his underlying motivation:

> (23) The inspiration for the *Cherpumple* came from the typical desert table selection you would find at one of my family's holiday celebrations. Seems there's always cherry, pumpkin, and apple pie and a cake that's a family tradition. It has a layer of spice and a layer of yellow. Since I always want to have a piece of each of the pies and the cake I figured why not make that waaaaaaaay more convenient. So I baked them all together as one and the *Cherpumple* was born.

The title moreover contains an explicit comprehension clue, i.e. *turducken*, which refers to a similar blended dish of a chicken stuffed in a duck stuffed in a turkey.

146 I do not wish to imply that seasonal topicality represents a lower degree of conventionalization altogether. The degree to which lexemes become established depends on the regularity with which salience recurs and the degree of intensity.

147 charlesphoenix.com/2010/10/cherpumple-monster-pie-cake-new-test-kitchen-video/.

Because of the rather irregular phonology and opaque morpho-semantic make-up of the lexeme, which would complicate the comprehension and subsequent accommodation, Phoenix provides the reader with several linguistic and conceptual anchors in the cotext. Given this cotextual support, initial processing is actively facilitated, which may explain why a rather exotic and irregular-sounding word does diffuse considerably, contrary to linguistic expectations. Naturally, precisely its humorous character and famous coiner provoke attention too and cause initial topicality; nevertheless, the lexeme still survives initial topicality, as Figure 19 shows, which is remarkable considering its lack of morpho-semantic transparency.

*Fig. 19: New and cumulative pages per month of* cherpumple

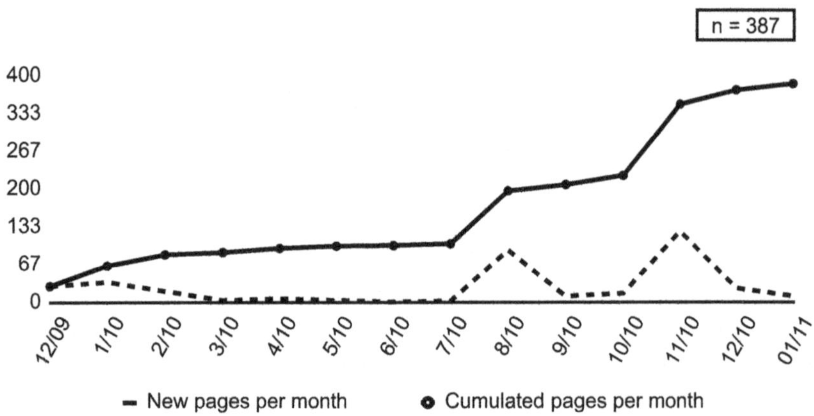


Not surprisingly, directly after its coinage, *cherpumple* slightly increased in frequency during a first period of topicality in December 2009 and January 2010, as illustrated in the frequency graph in Figure 19. However, unlike the examples in the previous section, two further and even higher peaks exist in the curve. The initial diffusion wave, in which the word tentatively spread, was followed by a second wave in August 2010. At the beginning of the winter holiday season *cherpumple* re-appeared, probably because the communicative need re-appeared too. Examples (24) and (25) illustrate occurrences from this period, which seems to be concerned with the planning of the upcoming Thanksgiving and Christmas celebrations, not only in private households, but also in commerce[148].

148 Interestingly, ZDF, one of the German national TV broadcasters, featured a story on Christmas departments opening in Harrod's and Selfridges in London in early

(24) This morning I awoke to hear about a new cakey creature, the *Cherpumple*! The hybrids will not be stopped. (personal blog)[149]

(25) Meet the Chernuttle, the son of the popular *CherPumple* – a godforsaken behmoth of a cake. The ridiculous idea? Bake an entire pie inside a layer of cake. Repeat three times. Then frost and attempt to eat.[150] (food portal)

The last example moreover shows that *cherpumple* forms the basis for further coinages and inventions, which indicates a certain degree of conventionalization and entrenchment. A third increase in usage is found in November 2010, when the holiday festivities are imminent, represented by the last peak in the curve in Figure 19. During this period, the *Wall Street Journal* also featured an article on the cherpumple[151].

(26) The *Cherpumple* is a baking project which involves a lot of pie, cake and engineering.[152] (portal other)

(27) If you are interested in adding the *Cherpumple* Monster Pie to your own Thanksgiving Day dinner table, however, you better start baking now.[153] (social network Gather)

In general, *cherpumple* is mainly used in blogs and portals, although three occurrences were found in newspapers or news sites. Similarly to the instances of transitional conventionalization in the previous section, *cherpumple* is used in multiple types of source from the beginning, so that socio-pragmatic diffusion in terms of text types, again in the strictest sense of crossover of one original type of source into many, is limited. Although metalinguistic definitions are rare, a mere three occurrences were found, *cherpumple* is not often used with new classes of referents. The majority of pages contains either an explanation, a reference and/or link to Charles Phoenix or mentions *turducken*, its closest lexical relative. Whereas in terms of frequency and socio-pragmatic distribution *cherpumple* shows unambiguous signs of semi-conventionalization, it remains

---

August, another illustration of the seasonal salience of the winter holidays (cf. zdf.de/ZDFmediathek/beitrag/video/1402062/ZDF-heute-in-europa-vom-4.-August-2011?bc=saz;saz2;kua246), 4 August 2011.

149 goodiesfirst.com/2010/08/no-fakin-its-a-turcaken.html.

150 biteclubeats.com/2010/08/chernuttle.html.

151 online.wsj.com/article/SB10001424052702304316404575580630406169718.html?articleTabs=slideshow.

152 dailymotion.com/video/xfv5xs_behold-the-cherpumple_news.

153 From juleshan.gather.com, November 23, 2010.

doubtful whether the lexeme can lose its strong associations to its coiner and gain true objectlinguistic currency.

A second case of semi-conventionalization from the sample is *Boobgate*. Rather than conceptualizing one particular event, *Boobgate* carries a generic meaning of a scandal involving some kind of breast-related event. The lexeme thus does not refer to one unique instance of such a scandal, but appears whenever the generic concept of a breast-related scandal arises. As a corollary, the precise nature of the scandal is variable. In the first attestation from the sample, *Boobgate* is used for the controversy surrounding Philadelphia's City Counsel having hired topless dancers for a party in December 1995, as illustrated in (28) from the *Philadelphia City Paper*.

(28) Barnett was one of Rendell's City Council slate back in 1991 when Rendell was running for mayor, but he lost in the primary and more recently was Secretary of Labor and Industry under the Casey Administration. Having just returned from a "several-month" European trip, Barnett was unwilling to offer his take on *Boobgate*. (Mary Frangipanni).[154]

(29) Jackson flap exposes ennui.
I don't know who's to blame for "*Boobgate*" - and I'm not referring to Howard Dean's ability to spend $40 million just to lose a series of primaries pretty badly. (Jonah Goldberg from *Townhall*, a news-centered portal)[155]

The passage in (29) refers to the Superbowl incident in February 2004, when Janet Jackson inadvertedly (or deliberately) bared her nipple, allegedly caused by her energetic choreography. Hence, the first element of *Boobgate* during this period refers to the unwanted and inappropriate showing of breasts and/or nipples in public. *Boobgate* was not the only neologism used with reference to Janet Jackson. US singer Justin Timberlake, who duetted with her during that performance, called the event a *wardrobe malfunction*, which was and is the more popular and widely used synonym, because it is a less direct, euphemistic alternative.

In May 2010, a further celebrity was struck by an instance of *Boobgate*. Rumors were circulating that US politician Sarah Palin had had a breast augmentation. In addition to *Boob* metonymically referring to topless dancers and a nipple slip in previous occurrences, in these instances it refers to the surgical procedure Palin had or had not undergone.

154 archives.citypaper.net/articles/122195/article019.shtml.

155 townhall.com/columnists/jonahgoldberg/2004/02/04/jackson_flap_exposes_ennui/page/full/. Curiously, the same article appears in the *Washington Times*, but without Jonah Goldberg as author.

(30) Another student pointed out how it has been such a long struggle for women's rights in our world, and documented all the progress that we have made, but ended her paper by concluding that our society still doesn't treat women equally (as an example she used the Sarah Palin *Boobgate* controversy). (personal blog entry from July 2010)[156]

(31) Katy Perry's *Sesame Street boobgate* is big news, even making it onto ABC's *Good Morning America* show. In fact, Katy's playpal Elmo and best friend Grover appeared on the morning show to be interviewed by George Stephanopoulos! Elmo assured George that he and Grover were still fans of 'Ms Katy', saying: "We'll have another one. Elmo loves Ms. Katy and we had a good time. (Helen Sanders, *Entertainmentwise* portal)[157]

Example (31) illustrates a further topicality period of *Boobgate*. In September 2010, *Sesame Street* producers decided not to broadcast an episode recorded with Katy Perry, because her dress showed too much cleavage and would upset children and parents. Since Perry was seen wearing a cut-up Elmo T-shirt afterwards, the topic remained in the media and the use of *Boobgate* was reinforced. In November 2010, another Boobgate hit Katy Perry. Allegedly she had asked some photographers to digitally enhance her breasts after an unsatisfactory photo shoot. However, as example (32) shows, the opposite was the case:

(32) Katy Perry on '*Boobgate*'. [...]. Katy Perry took to Twitter late Friday to clarify last week's media reports that the singer's team had asked for a busty shot promoting the VH1 Divas Salute the Troops" TV special be retouched."Silly press check it: I was the one who asked VH1 to tone down my DIGITALIZED image on the poster, particularly the size of my chest," she wrote. (Jem Aswad, *Rolling Stone*)[158]

In addition to personal referents of public character such as celebrities and politicians, *Boobgate* also occurs for more abstract, conceptual phenomena of showing (too many) breasts on film, as in (33) or being flat-chested as in (34). Such examples support the assumption that *Boobgate* functions as a generic placeholder that appears and re-appears whenever applicable.

(33) Next week it looks like there will be more comedy than action. I am already making my sad face as apparently there will be bathing scenes and we know what that means. We had tons of panty shots this week so next week it will be *boobgate*. I wonder if they will be censored though...... (personal blog, August 2010)[159]

156 aconservativeteacher.blogspot.com/2010_07_01_archive.html.
157 entertainmentwise.com/news/55826/Elmo-And-Super-Grover-Support-Katy-Perry.
158 rollingstone.com/music/news/plus-t-i-s-drug-problem-katy-perry-on-boobgate-20101118.
159 tenchithoughts.blogspot.com/2010/08/high-school-of-dead-episode-5.html.

(34) HowardKurtz *Boobgate*: Jack Shafer says NYT piece on women flaunting flat-chestedness and buying modest bras is, uh, inflated. (Twitter, September 2010)[160]

An overview of the various referents of *Boobgate* and their respective frequencies is found in Figure 20, which indicates that most of the classes of referents indeed consist of individuals from the public domain.

*Fig. 20: Relative overall frequencies for the observed referents of* Boobgate

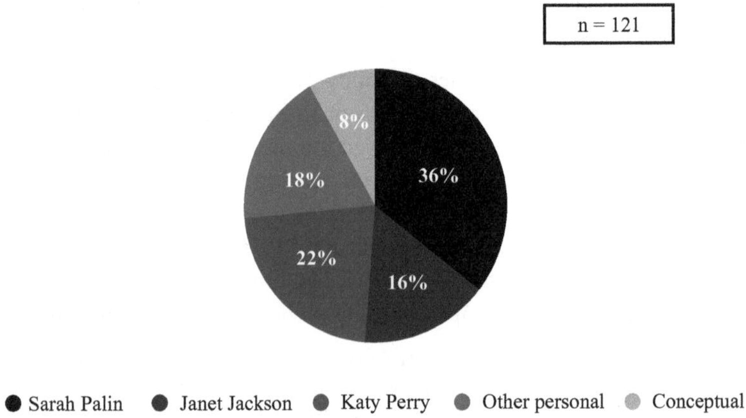


Since the Watergate affair in 1972 the English language has been enriched with many formations ending in *-gate* as the result of a folk etymologically-motivated secretion. *Water* being a clearly identifiable morpheme, it was secreted and *-gate* became imbued with the meaning 'a scandal, usually involving some kind of attempted cover-up' (cf. Schmid 2011a: 94, 167). Originally, *Watergate* was the name of the building where the burglary took place. By means of the place-for-event metonymy, the word came to denote the political scandal. The morphological status of *-gate* is not of concern here (see Nagel 1999 for a discussion). It should be noted, however, that the possible suffix status of *-gate* is debated on various grounds, e.g. restricted paradigm-formation ability and more specific meaning than prototypical suffixes (cf. Schmid 2011a: 167). It does seem highly productive, as evidenced by the many coinages in Algeo's *Fifty years among the new words* neologism dictionary (1991) and some very recent formations like *Foreclosuregate*

160 twylah.com/mattbish/tweets/22799134112.

and *Robogate*[161], *Fortisgate* in Dutch[162] and *Cablegate*[163], which also appeared in German. Moreover, as the analysis of *Boobgate* shows, the meaning is not as specific as assumed, but schematic, i.e. a scandal involving public people, often politicians. Since the precise nature of the scandal is specified by the first element, *-gate* merely constructs a schema in which two rather vague slots are filled: scandal and public figures. In the case of *Boobgate* even the first element is schematic, because it can refer to any kind of activity or event relating to breasts.

Tuggy defines a *schema* as "a pattern, a rough outline, a coarse-grained, less-fully-specified version of a concept which the elaborations render, each in a different way, in finer, more elaborate detail" (2005: 235; cf. Kemmer 2003) and claims that those schemas play an important role in conceptualization, because they enable speakers to compare instances in a structured way (cf. 2005: 234). With regard to word-formation, he says, the schematic relationships abstracted from encountered instances of elaborations also give rise to novel formations of the same schema-type (cf. 2005: 251). In a similar vein, Wilso remarks that schemas arise through habit and repetition and are continually being reproduced and modified depending on the context. Furthermore, schemas arise through interaction, because they rely on collective memory (cf. 1992: 230-231). The recurrent semi-conventionalization of *Boobgate* is therefore not only caused by the extralinguistic events as in the case of *cherpumple*, but also by the cognitive schematicity of its morpho-semantics. Speakers seem to possess a schema for scandals involving public persons that is linguistically realized by the *-gate* suffix. The schema has been constructed on the basis of the salience of the Watergate affair and subsequent novel coinages using the same secretion pattern (*winegate, Volgagate, Fortisgate, Cablegate* etc.). When speakers or writers are confronted with similar events in reality, the comparison processes in the mental lexicon will call up the *-gate* schema and elaborate it according to the particular details of the current context. Upon encountering such a formation involving *-gate*, hearers and readers tap into

---

161 *Foreclosuregate* and *Robogate* appeared in the wake of the robosigning scandal in the US in the summer and autumn of 2010. *Robosigning* will be discussed in 4.1.4.

162 *Fortisgate* occurred in a news article on the Belgian national broadcasting company VRT in September 2011 to refer to a scandal in which politicians were involved in illegally supplying the *Fortis* bank with insider information and consequently slow down the bankruptcy process.

163 *Cablegate* refers to Wikileaks publishing 250 000 cable messages coming from the US State Department in 2010, see e.g. an article from the *Süddeutsche Zeitung* via sueddeutsche.de/politik/wikileaks-julian-assange-das-leck-liegt-in-den-usa-1.1033438.

the same inventory of schematic structures, based on shared experience, and construct the meaning from the contextual combination of *-gate* and its first element.

Recurrent semi-conventionalization is therefore characterized by a series of topicality periods that either arise because the lexeme repeatedly gains salience due to extralinguistic events, or because these extralinguistic events are perceived as similar by the members of the speech community and are conceptualized by an identical lexeme. Like one-off or single periods of topicality, the degree of subsequent conventionalization and entrenchment depends on the intensity of topicality. Given the low overall frequency of *Boobgate*, i.e. 121 occurrences in the sample, it is debatable whether it represents a case of advanced conventionalization. However, given the presence of a productive underlying schema, it may well be that *Boobgate* is already more conventionalized than the frequency evidence suggest. Further research is needed in order to investigate the precise extent of the interplay between frequency and the existence of such schemas. The next section will present some clear cases that are assumed to have progressed towards advanced stages of conventionalization, which I have labeled *adavanced conventionalization*.

### 4.1.4. Advanced conventionalization

A recent case of advanced conventionalization is *robosigning*. The compound with a first element clipped from *robot* refers to the practice of signing important documents, mainly foreclosure affidavits in the US, without evaluating their contents or even reading them. As a result, many homeowners were sent foreclosure notices unwarrantedly and without proper legal validity by mortgage companies and banks. Although the lexeme had been coined by Nye Lavalle, an advocate of consumer rights, as early as 1999, it did not gain currency until a scandal concerning the unlawful treatment of such foreclosures hit the US in August 2010. The subsequent topicality caused *robosigning* and its variant word-forms and morphological relatives to swiftly enter and diffuse through the English language, as illustrated in the frequency curve in Figure 21.

The curve shows a steep incline during October 2010, when reports discussing the practice flooded the news and consumer rights organizations, lawyers and real estate professionals offered advice to potential victims. The subsequent decline was slow; *robosigning* remained a debated issue in November and December 2010 until it no longer yielded a substantial amount of new occurrences in January 2011. Nevertheless, the total amount of 1735 occurrences within a mere five months (in August only one page was found) strongly suggest that the topicality period was intense enough to progress towards advanced conventionalization.

*Fig. 21: New and cumulative pages per month of* robosigning

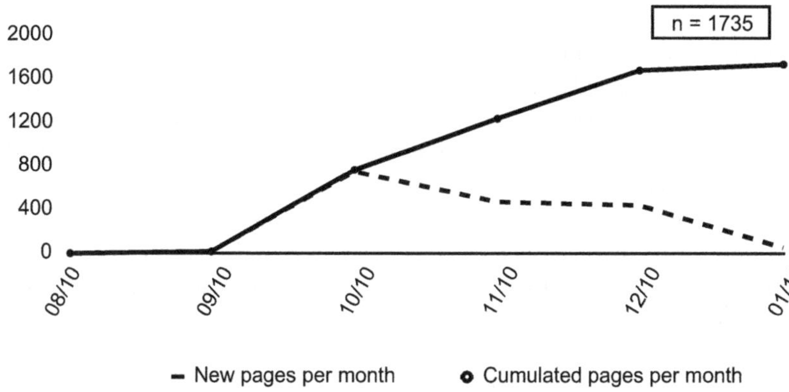


In addition to high-frequency usage, the lexeme *robosigning* also reveals its advanced stage of conventionalization through its appearance in multiple types of source and to a lesser extent also in different fields of discourse, as shown in the pie charts in Figure 22 on p. 138. Illustrations are provided in examples (35) to (37).

(35) "*Robosigning*" allegations are mounting and Sen. Chris Dodd said he will hold a hearing on foreclosure practices November 16. State attorney generals are also investigating and initiating or contemplating fraud suits. Here's more on the prevalence of *robo-signing*. "We started instructing people to pull their documents from the clerk of the court," says Anne Batte, who runs a foreclosure-assistance group in Georgia called Operation Restoration. "And the more we instructed, the more we saw. Nearly every document I have seen has been improperly signed." Bloomberg has an interesting column describing how even a man who had no mortgage had his home foreclosed on due to the *robo-signing*. (Professional political blog, October 2010)[164]

(36) Where's the criminal investigation of bureaucrats, legislators and bankers for the sub-prime mortgage collapse and the *robosign* mortgages? How deep are the lies? (Personal general blog, December 2010)[165]

(37) Everyone in America has heard of *Robosigners* by now. But somehow, in a majority of states (the 27 non judicial foreclosure states), qualms exist about whether this practice is "okay" simply because the matter does not go to court. The clear answer,

164 talkleft.com/story/2010/10/8/131944/906.

165 bruignaboinde.blogspot.com/2010/12/we-have-right-to-know.html.

despite what the banks have said, is no – absolutely not. (Law portal, November 2010)[166]

A graphical representation of the type of source diffusion from August to October 2010 is presented in Figure 22[167]. The first attestation of *robosigning* in the sample stems from an article on a portal, introducing the controversy. The audience size, professionalism of authors and reliability of the information instantiate portals as strong diffusers. Hence, the information is frequently adapted and reposted in both personal and professional blogs. Moreover, the practices are also reported on in established newspapers as soon as they are deemed to be of national importance and the impact of the situation on many citizens has been recognized.

*Fig. 22: Type of source distribution from August until October 2010 of* robosigning

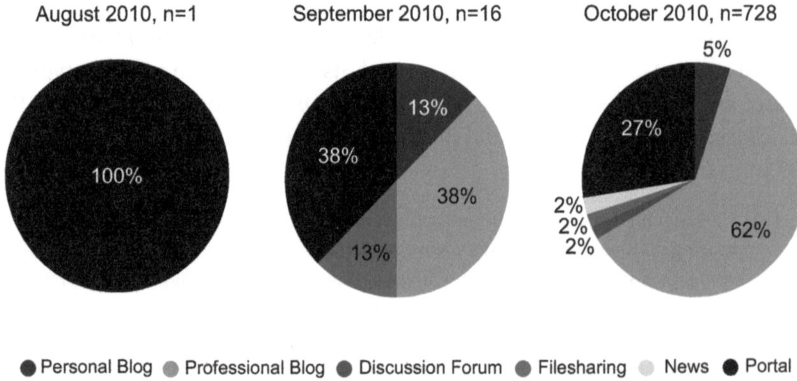


Moreover, the examples (35) - (37) reveal two interesting aspects of advanced conventionalization, albeit in a contradictory manner. Firstly, contrary to the hypothesis regarding orthography in an advanced stage of the institutionalization process described in 2.1.2, *robosigning* is orthographically not fixed. Even within one passage, as illustrated in (35), *robosigning* is spelled in two different ways: the first token is a concatenated instance, whereas the other two are written with a hyphen. In general, however, the hyphenated spelling, which contributes to the morpho-semantic transparency, is preferred, as Table 8 shows:

166 Due to a technical error, the original URL could not be retrieved.

167 Metalinguistic occurrences (36 pages) have been omitted.

*Table 8: Orthography-token frequency distribution for* robosigning

| Orthographical forms | Token frequency |
|---|---|
| *robo-signing* | 1695 |
| *robosigning* | 698 |
| *robo signing* | 249 |

Since a detailed investigation of the chronological distribution of the various orthographical variants was beyond the scope of the present study, it remains unclear whether the increase in currency of usage was accompanied by a standardization, and thus normation (cf. section 2.3), of the spelling alternatives, or whether they continue to co-exist.

Secondly, the lexeme quickly gave rise to the paradigm-formation of lexico-morphological relatives, e.g. *robosign* in (36) and *robosigners* in (37) which is a clear indicator of advanced conventionalization. The process implies that the degree of familiarity or conventionality is substantial enough to provide a cognitive and structural basis for further coinages. This is only feasible if the mental lexicon has been equipped with the necessary lexico-morphological links, in short, if *robosigning* has also attained at least a limited degree of entrenchment. A full list of all attested word-forms and lexico-semantic relatives of *robosigning* and their token frequencies can be found in Appendix 4 on page 254.

Another likely candidate for advanced conventionalization, though not as frequent as *robosigning* yet, is *encore career*. The first attestation from the sample dates from September 2006:

(38) A Nonprofit Leader Builds His *Encore Career*. This all has great potential, I thought. The demographics are compelling. The market is ready-made. The human spirit is there. And my school promises to be financially viable. This could be the *encore career* in public service that I had always entertained but never fully envisioned. (lifestyle portal)[168]

*Encore career* refers to a second career after retirement, usually in the non-profit sector. The compound is often attributed to Marc Freedman, who published a book on the subject in June 2007 and is the person behind encore.org, a website dedicated to providing information on and job opportunities for encore careers. The existence of such an established and acknowledged self-referential website is an important indicator of advanced conventionalization, since it not only supports the hypostatization, but also potentially propels the diffusion

168 philanthropy.com/article/A-Nonprofit-Leader-Builds-His/58529/.

process onwards, because the website founders have actively stimulated discussion around the topic since its launch. The concept became particularly salient in the spring of 2010, when many newspapers[169] published compelling reports on looming labor shortage and the future of retiring baby boomers, who are still in good health and thus capable of embarking on a second career. The frequency development of *encore career* in the sample is shown in Figure 23.

*Fig. 23: New and cumulative pages per month of* encore career

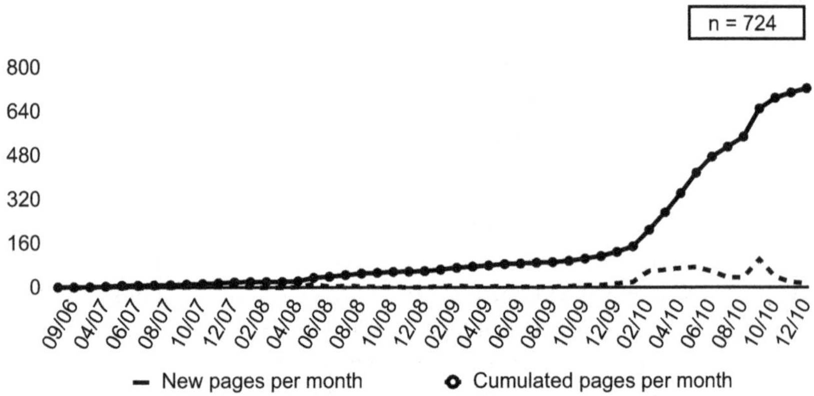


A second peak of topicality follows in October 2010, represented by the second peak in Figure 23, when newspapers, professional blogs and portals report on encore career experiences by individuals, as in a title from *The Boston Globe* in (39), or discuss the development of a branch of business coaching and enterprises specialized in encore careers, as in (40).

(39) Back to work. Many older Americans are finding '*encore careers*'.[170]

(40) Civic Ventures, a non-profit think tank, has taken the lead in advocating that these second careers need to combine "passion, purpose and a paycheck," and the group

169 See, for instance, "Ready for Life's Encore Performances" by Sarah Kershaw in the *New York Times*, March 19, 2010 via nytimes.com/2010/03/21/fashion/21age.html. Interestingly, the title features only the word *encore* without mentioning the entire compound in the text. Whether this occurrence can be interpreted as a first sign of clipping remains a question for further research.

170 boston.com/business/personalfinance/articles/2010/10/31/many_older_americans_are_finding_encore_careers/?page=1.

is offering an online seminar later this month that can help you figure out how to pull it off via *encore careers* in fields like health care, education, non-profits, the environment or government.[171] (professional business blog)

In terms of field of discourse, *encore career* was first used in BUSINESS domains, where the economic advantages were discussed, and LIFESTYLE discourse on retirement. Figure 24 however shows that even before the lexeme became topical, diffusion into other, non-specialized fields of discourse took place. Not surprisingly, the lexeme increasingly occurred in general instances of language, i.e. those not dedicated to a certain subject, particularly significant during the two topicality periods.

*Fig. 24: Field of discourse diffusion of* encore career

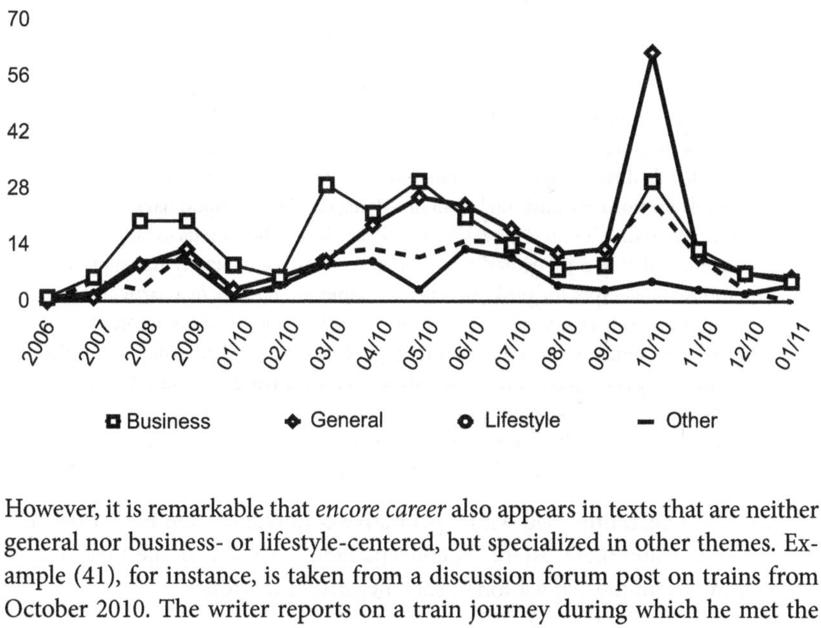


However, it is remarkable that *encore career* also appears in texts that are neither general nor business- or lifestyle-centered, but specialized in other themes. Example (41), for instance, is taken from a discussion forum post on trains from October 2010. The writer reports on a train journey during which he met the conductor, describing him as being in his encore career.

(41) The conductor was also aware and alert. Spying my ship's cap, he asked, "who here was in the Navy?" While I had just been an enlistee, he had been a career man and

171 retirementrevised.com/career/learn-how-to-launch-an-encore-career-at-online-seminar.

after his 20 was now in an *"encore career"* on Amtrak. He was crisp, friendly, and efficient. We thanked each other for our service.[172]

A last instance of advanced conventionalization to be discussed here is *slacktivism*. The blend of *slacker* and *activism*, denotes a form of (sociopolitical) activism that requires little or no effort, especially in the virtual community. Popular examples of *slacktivism* are appeals to post your bra color on social networks like Facebook or to wear purple to support respectively cancer and domestic violence awareness initiatives, or more mundane invitations to sign online petitions. WordSpy notes that the word first appeared in 1995 in a post about an online petition by students from the University of Northern Colorado to protest against government budget cutbacks for arts and cultural institutions. Not until 2001 did the word re-appear (cf. WordSpy entry for *slacktivism*, posted on July 16, 2002)[173]. The earliest attestation in my sample dates from March 2002 from a personal blog post, which refers to an article on Snopes.com, a website collecting urban legends, folk myths and scams.

(42) Also from Snopes.com, a new (at least to me) political term: *slacktivism*: E-petitions are the latest manifestation of *slacktivism*, the search for the ultimate feel-good that derives from having come to society's rescue without having had to actually gets one's hands dirty or open one's wallet. It's *slacktivism* that prompts us to forward appeals for business cards on behalf of a dying child intent upon having his name recorded in the Guinness World Book of Records or exhortations to others to continue circulating a particular e-mail because some big company has supposedly promised that every forward will generate monies for the care of a particular dying child. Likewise, it's *slacktivism* that prompts us to want a join a boycott of designated gas companies or eschew buying gasoline on a particular day rather than reduce our personal consumption of fossil fuels by driving less and taking the bus more often. *Slacktivism* comes in many forms...but its key defining characteristic is its central theme of doing good with little or no effort on the part of person inspired to participate in the forwarding, exhorting, collecting, or e-signing.[174]

*Slacktivism* is currently used with a pejorative connotation. On one of the self-referential websites that exist for the concept, Fred Clark, one of the alleged coiners, comments on the acquisition of such negative undertones:

That's certainly the dominant prevailing meaning of the word, but Clements also digs up another early use that suggests something rather different. A 2000 article in U-Wire, he notes, refers to "television host, filmmaker, author and self-confessed *slacker-activist*

172 rainorders.com/discussion/read.php?4,2298176.

173 wordspy.com/words/slacktivism.asp.

174 bleak.blogspot.com/2002/03/also-from-snopes.html.

(*slacktivist*, if you will) Michael Moore." Whether or not you're a fan of Michael Moore's, he's clearly someone whose idea of activism goes far beyond forwarding e-mails.

That description of Moore gets closer to the original use of the word. I can't say "original" with 100-percent certainty, mind you, since McFedries [the author of Word-Spy] doesn't tell us the context of that 1995 Usenet citation, but as you can see from the scans here, "*slacktivism*" was the title of a seminar series that Dwight and I gave at the Cornerstone Festival in 1995.[175] (June 2009)

Thus, Clark remarks that the originally intended meaning did not contain the connotation of lazy or opportunistic engagement, but *slacktivism* seems to have been imbued with precisely such connotations during the diffusion process. Although the present sample does not contain any more neutrally used instances, an older meaning and use can be assumed to exist.

The present advanced degree of conventionalization is the result of several periods of topicality. The use of *slacktivism* first boomed towards the end of 2009 and continued to simmer with a slightly reduced but still substantial frequency on new pages until the late spring of 2010, illustrated in Figure 25. The lexeme extensively recurred over the course of several months, increasing its currency in the speech community, until a second wave of topicality occurred in the summer and autumn of 2010.

*Fig. 25: New and cumulative pages per month of* slacktivism

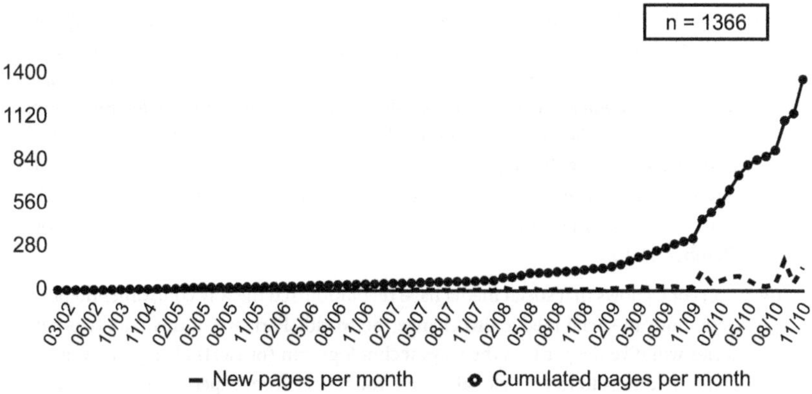


The first wave culminated in a peak in January 2010. At that time, messages widely circulated on Facebook to post your bra color and raise awareness of

175 slacktivist.typepad.com/slacktivist/2009/06/etymology.html.

breast cancer. Consequently, the issue was fiercely debated in various newspapers, portals and blogs, because the effect of such campaigns was supposed to be negligible, as illustrated in (43) and (44), contributing towards the lexeme's negative connotation.

(43) "Here's the thing," wrote NPR's Shereen Meraji, "I changed my status, but I don't know anything more about breast cancer or how to protect myself against it. Is this another example of '*slacktivism*,' virtual activism with no real results?" she asked. (from an article by Carl Franzen on the AOL news portal, January 2010)[176]

(44) Murkier still was what prompted Facebook's bra-color phase. In January, thousands of women posted the color of the bra they were currently wearing, a disclosure that was somehow supposed to support breast-cancer awareness. Never mind that National Breast Cancer Awareness Month is October – this was Internet *slacktivism* at its finest, a pointless gesture that raised no money and took no tangible action. The only people who seemed to benefit were my male friends, who suddenly started posting the Facebook equivalent of a thumbs-up sign on many a status update. (cross-post from a Times article in a professional blog on car insurances, January 2010)[177]

The second phase of diffusion in the autumn of 2010 was not as strongly linked to one particular extralinguistic event like the Facebook buzz. The issue of *slacktivism* was discussed either on a more general level to illustrate the impact of innovative social media platforms or with reference to different instances.

(45) Some were offended by the comedian's mockery of traditional activism, Congress.org's Ambreen Ali reports: Jon Stewart kicked off the three-hour event with a joke about rallies, saying they are not judged by the coherence of their message or the level of engagement. "No, it's colors and signs," he said. Medea Benjamin, a co-founder of the antiwar group Code Pink, didn't laugh with the crowd. She said protests are a hallowed tradition that have helped end wars and give minorities and women rights. "These are things to celebrate and not belittle," Benjamin said, calling Saturday's event "a tribute to *slacktivism*." (professional politics blog, October 2010)[178]

(46) Everyone knows that social media have revolutionized the way companies do business. But can social media also change the world? Part two of this fall's two-part series will dive deeper into the ways technology can (or can't) change the way we create solutions to today's global issues. You'll hear from experts and social entrepreneurs from organizations like Friendfactor, Triple Pundit, and Change.org as we

176 aolnews.com/2010/01/08/great-facebook-bra-update-success-or-slacktivism/.

177 Due to a technical error, the URL could not be retrieved from the NeoCrawler database.

178 craigcrawford.com/2010/10/31/activists-not-thrilled-by-stew/.

address questions of '*slacktivism*,' the strength of online vs. offline relationships and more. (professional business blog, October 2010)[179]

Like *encore career* and *robosigning*, socio-pragmatic diffusion has taken place, so that *slacktivism* occurs in multiple types of source and fields of discourse. Although a fine-grained discussion of this cross-over cannot be presented here, Figure 26a below illustrates the frequency of occurrence in October 2010 distributed across different types of source and Figure 26b the distribution across various fields of discourse. It should be noted that the figures contain occurrences from all types of source/fields of discourse, even if they were not significantly present following the 1/9 rule discussed at the beginning of 4.1. Moreover, the metalinguistic category is also displayed, because October 2010 saw a steep increase in such uses, concomitant with the general rise in objectlinguistic frequency in a variety of types of source and fields of discourse.

*Fig. 26a: Frequency distribution of* slacktivism *across different types of source in October 2010*

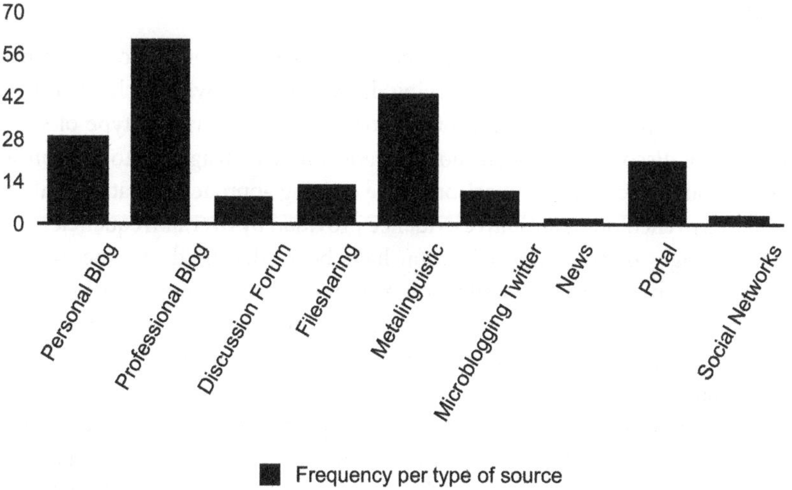


179 blogs.rhsmith.umd.edu/ptmbaaevents/index.php?s=slacktivism.

*Fig. 26b: Frequency distribution of* slacktivism *across different fields of discourse in October 2010*

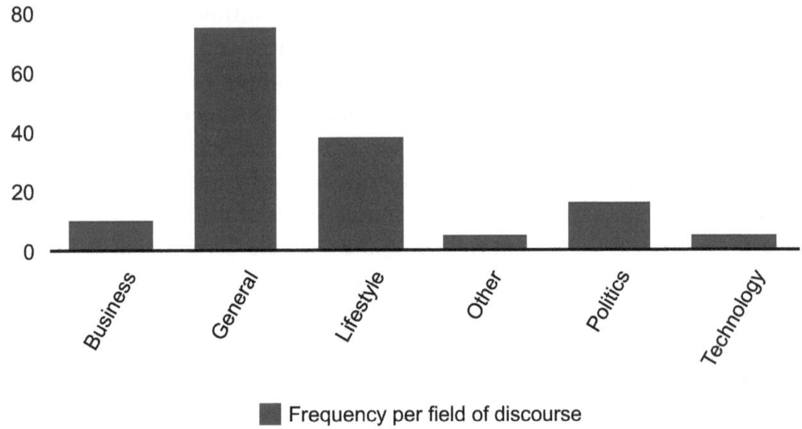


### 4.1.5. Summary

The case studies presented in this section confirm the conception of conventionalization as a continuum of varying degrees with individual characteristics. More importantly, the inclusion of the socio-pragmatic criteria type of source and field of discourse has been shown to add valuable insights into the conventionalization process in comparison to the existing approaches that have almost exclusively relied on quantitative evidence provided by overall frequencies.

Four stages of conventionalization have been identified. At one extreme, instances of non-conventionalization are found. These novel formations did succeed in surviving their one-off coinage events, but did not gain sufficient currency in the speech community to assume even a minimal degree of conventionality. Such neologisms occur infrequently in language at large and are mostly limited to one particular type of source and field of discourse. Sometimes an extralinguistic event sparks the use of a particular neologism and creates a period of topicality. Within this topicality phase, the lexeme's behavior is characterized by a sudden increase in frequency not only within one single field of discourse or type of source, but also by diffusion into other socio-pragmatic discourse types. Typically, this rapid diffusion is difficult to monitor because the cross-over happens within hours and days rather than weeks or months. Whether a novel lexeme will become truly conventional or whether this conventionality is of temporary nature depends on the frequency of occurrence within the topicality period and the salience of the underlying concept, as well as on other factors that will be discussed in the following section. As the examples show, the neologisms are often closely connected to the coiner or the coinage event and are not applied to the full range of classes of potential referents. Since some of these concepts are only seasonally salient, like *cherpumple*, they represent a special case of topicality, i.e. recurrent semi-conventionalization. While the socio-pragmatic diffusion process proceeds similarly to standard topicality, semi-conventionalization is characterized by regularly recurring periods of topicality. A second subtype of recurrent semi-conventionalization is not necessarily connected to extralinguistic regularity, but arises from the cognitive and morpho-semantic schematicity of the lexeme. Since the meaning is underspecified, a single lexeme can realize different, semantically consistent meanings and appear and re-appear in language whenever such concepts become topical. Advanced conventionalization, on the other hand, typically consists of multiple topicality periods, not necessarily following a regular pattern, frequently also during a longer stretch of time. In addition to higher frequency of occurrence, the cross-over into different types of source and fields of discourse is considerably greater than during transitional conventionality.

In the present study, frequency of occurrence in different types of source and fields of discourse have been used as measures of conventionalization. In addition, I propose two further linguistic and extralinguistic indicators of conventionality: the existence of self-referential websites and the presence of morpho-lexical paradigms. It seems probable that the need for such self-referential sources of information only arises when the concept has gained currency. Similarly, the use of a neologism in blog names, nicknames and as content-categorizing labels presupposes a degree of familiarity and salience. Linguistically, advanced conventionalization furthermore crystallizes in the emergence of a full inflectional verb paradigm (for verbs) and the creation of lexically-related lexemes. Such novel coinages on the basis of language material that is rather new itself moreover provide vital evidence of developing entrenchment and support the assumption that entrenchment and conventionalization are intertwined.

Most of the neologisms in the previous section only became topical or conventional under the influence of extralinguistic topicality. Although this result is hardly surprising at all, given the communicative-expressive function of linguistic elements, it might be too reductionist to assume a one-to-one relationship between language and reality. Some events, like Katy Perry's Sesame Street misfortune, for instance, were hotly debated, but not or only temporarily conventionalized as one specific lexeme. Therefore, the following section will investigate several other factors that can propagate or inhibit the conventionalization process of English neologisms and systematically discusses the (non-)extent of their influence.

## 4.2. Conventionalization factors

In the following chapter I will discuss the influence of the various factors that were assumed to promote or inhibit the conventionalization process as presented in section 1.2. In sum, following hypotheses underlie the quantitative and qualitative investigation of the 44 English neologisms in the present study:

- H1: Semantic ambiguity, and/or
- H2: Dominant or disproportionally high use in metalinguistic mode inhibits conventionalization.
- H3: A first or frequent use in more formal types of source and/or
- H4: The authority or prominence of the coiner and first users promotes conventionalization.
- H5: The nameworthiness of the represented concept or its salience in society promotes conventionalization.
- H6: The early development of syntagmatic lexical networks, represented by collocations in the present study, promotes conventionalization.

Given the number of hypothesized factors of influence and the number of neologisms studied in detail, I opted for a statistical model capable of incorporating the entire set of variables in relation to the observed frequency of each neologism and yielding an effect estimate factor for each of the variables. Effect estimate factors with a value of > 1 have a positive effect, effect estimate factors between 0 and 1 have a negative impact. Although a more accurate diffusion model should not only consider overall frequency as the dependent variable, but also the relative frequencies in the various types of source and fields of discourse, the development of such a model proved a more time-consuming and complicated task than anticipated. Regrettably, at the time of writing, work on this advanced model had not been finished yet. Therefore, a simpler generalized linear binomial regression was performed in which frequency provided the single dependent variable. This kind of regression model was considered as the most optimal choice to reflect the intricacies of the data structure on the one hand and the generalizability or predictability of the assumed influence factors[180].

The variables semantic ambiguity (H1) and presence of collocations (H6) were coded binarily, i.e. 0 for the absence of the feature and 1 for any observed presence. A further linguistic variable, synonymy, was also included and coded in identical manner. The variable coiner status (H4) was operationalized as one of the three parameters 'unknown', 'celebrity' and 'professional'; the criteria underlying the distinction are explained and illustrated in the next section. For the frequency-based metalinguistic use (H2) and occurrence in formal types source (H3) variables the relative frequencies in each of the variable parameters entered the model. Lastly, nameworthiness was operationalized as the mean score for each neologism from the experiment. As already mentioned in 3.3.3, such scores were not obtained for each of the 44 neologisms due to the choice for an informant-based method. As a result, the variable was excluded from the present statistical analysis and will be discussed purely in qualitative terms in section 4.2.4.

In addition to testing the six variables in isolation, a number of interactions were also included in the present model. Two mitigating remarks regarding the selection of these interactions are in order here. Firstly, the low number of neologisms in statistical terms entails that the number of observations for many of these interactions was too low to be included, often no observations at all could be collected. Secondly and more trivially, the number of interactions was also restricted due to time concerns, given the number of possibilities for interactions between the six variables. The selection was therefore primarily guided by linguistic intuition and personal interest, e.g. all possible and permissible interaction with coiner status were tested.

The order in which the factors are presented does not correspond to the extent of their influence. The first three sections discuss the social and socio-pragmatic factors 'coiner status', 'formal type of source' and 'metalinguistic usage'. Due to incomplete experimental data on nameworthiness, for which only a selection of 21 neologisms was tested, it was not included in the statistical model and will be discussed separately in 4.2.4. The two remaining sections deal with the structural-cognitive aspects of semantic ambiguity and syntagmatic lexical networks.

180 I am greatly indebted to Johanna Brandt and Shuai Shao from the statistics lab at the Ludwig-Maximilians-University, who developed the model on the basis of the present requirements.

### 4.2.1. Coiner status

As mentioned in H4 above and in 1.2, I assume that coinages by public persons like celebrities and politicians stand a better chance of diffusing and possibly even establishing themselves in the English lexicon than coinages by private persons. In order to test this hypothesis, coiner status was coded as 'unknown', 'professional' and 'celebrity' for each neologism. Initially, a fourth label, 'individual', was applied. However, none of the novel coinages created by individuals in the sample exceeded their one-off occurrence and thus turned out to be nonce-formations. The distinction between 'professional' and 'celebrity' reflects the degree of authority or renown of the coiner on the one hand and the degree of fame on the other hand. The example of Bushisms and Palinisms mentioned in the introduction is a case in point. Bush and Palin are, or were, famous politicians, whose personality and behavior is permanently discussed in the media. When Palin uttered the word *mandation* instead of *mandate*, this slip of the tongue became the topic of public mockery in many blogs and discussion fora. As a result, *mandate* created a sudden, short-lived buzz and diffused, not because the lexeme captured a new political concept or idea, but because it was used by a famous person. The motivation underlying the diffusion and lexical adoption of celebrity-coined versus professional-coined neologisms is assumed to be different. Celebrity behavior, like clothing or make-up, is generally copied because imitation arises from the admiration celebrities arouse in their fans. The use of a new word is part of the entire personality package; it strengthens the admirer's claim to fame and prestige. Experts on the other hand enjoy authority and prestige because of their renown in their particular field. When a professional journalist or computer expert creates a new word, it might become adopted as the standard term of reference for a novel gadget or concept, not because of the surrounding media attention in itself, but because people rely on the expert's assumption that the neologism is the only appropriate and accepted way of denoting the novel entity or event. An overview of each of the neologisms and their parameter realization for the coiner status variable is presented in Table 9 on p. 156.

*Fig. 27: Effect plot for coiner status*

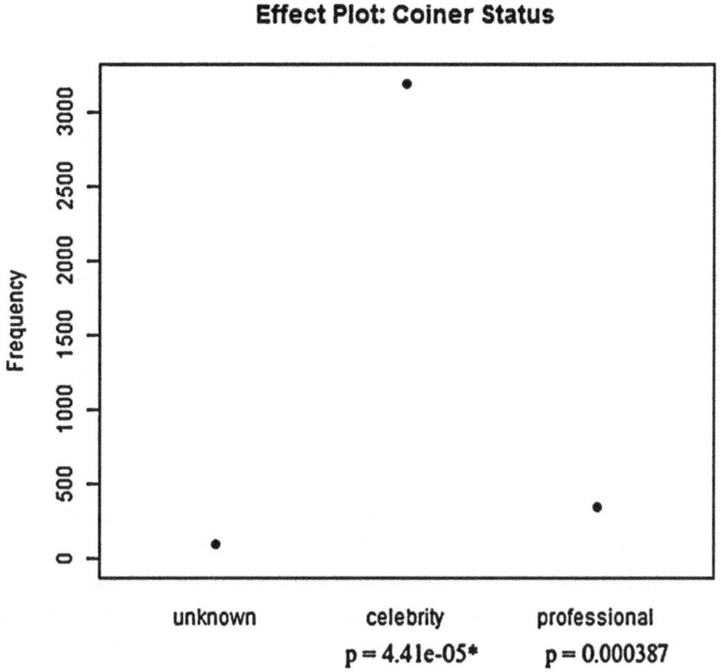


As shown in the effect plot in Figure 27, coiner status 'celebrity' is the most significant factor promoting conventionalization in the current sample[181]. As the 'celebrity' dot in the middle of the X-axis shows, the frequency of neologisms coined by celebrities is generally higher than those coined by professionals and those that appear as anonymous innovations. In addition, the professional coinages also still reveal a diffusion-promoting effect, albeit less markedly than the celebrity-originating neologisms. When the coiner is a famous person, the frequency is multiplied by a factor of 33.69 compared to the instances in which the coiner is unknown. These results explain the moderate diffusion of *cherpumple*,

181 In addition, the interaction between the factors coiner status 'celebrity' and presence of collocations yielded a slightly negative inhibiting effect estimate of 0.05, which was significant. However, since this combination of parameters applied to one single neologism (*back scooping*), the generalizability of this effect should be interpreted with caution. Additional observations are required before any conclusive evidence can be presented in detail.

which is phonologically relatively irregular and semantically opaque, as discussed in the previous chapter, and *back scooping*, for which an established synonym exists. Although the effect estimate for coinages by acknowledged professionals is remarkably lower, i.e. factor 3.65, both parameters of coiner status are highly significant, as the p-values indicate.

Further evidence for the diffusion-fueling effect of coiner status is found in *obesity*-based blends from the health industry, *diabesity* and *globesity*, which are discussed in detail in the remainder of the section. *Diabesity* refers to obesity-induced Type 2 diabetes. In medical jargon and popular scientific medical discourse the lexeme has been in use since the late 1970s, as attested in the GoogleBooks Corpus, from which example (47) was taken. In its early days, its use was mainly restricted to academic discourse. However, *diabesity* started to diffuse into non-academic discourse at the beginning of the 21st century and is now found in a variety of types of source, which are not restricted to a medical context.

(1) There is no such disease as *diabesity*.... *Diabesity* is the combination of diabetes and obesity and they tow together much like Tweedledum and Tweedledee (from Vickery and Fries, *Take Care of Yourself*, 1977: 46).

(2) Type II diabetes particularly afflicts obese individuals. Numerous genes and environmental factors, like sedentary lifestyle, interact to produce a predisposition for diabetes (*diabesity*), making it difficult to tease out individual suspects.[182]

The first non-academic occurrence retrieved by the NeoCrawler, listed in (48), dates from a science portal article from October 2000. Coinage is attributed to two different sources. Some authors[183] name Ethan AH Sims, a professor of medicine, others claim the word has been created by the American Diabetes Association, as mentioned in the following passage:

(3) In fact, diabetes has been so closely linked to obesity that the American Diabetes Association coined the term "*diabesity*" to describe the connection, according to W. Stephen Pray, Ph.D., a professor of pharmaceutics at the School of Pharmacy at Southwestern Oklahoma... (Prevention Magazine Health Books, *Prevention's food and nutrition: the most complete book ever written*, 1996: 155)

Despite these two different opinions it is safe to assume that *diabesity* was coined by a medical professional.

---

182 sciencedaily.com/releases/2000/10/001016074333.htm.

183 See, for instance, the following statement by Scarpa: "The associated symptoms of adult-onset obesity and adult-onset diabetes have been labeled "*diabesity*" by Ethan AH Sims (1980, *Sourcebook on food and nutrition, Vol. 2: part 4*, p. 322).

Until January 2011 785 occurrences were found on the Internet: 165 from scholarly articles and 620 from non-academic sources. The frequency diffusion is presented in Figure 28. The curve neatly shows *diabesity* spreading into general usage. Its use in academic sources did not cease, but from 2000 onwards occurrences in non-specialist discourse steadily increased. The steep cline in 2010 is not caused by one single particular event or article that was passed around in the various types of source and would have sparked a period of topicality, but by a sudden global awareness of the problem.

*Fig. 28: Academic vs. non-academic cumulative frequency development of* diabesity

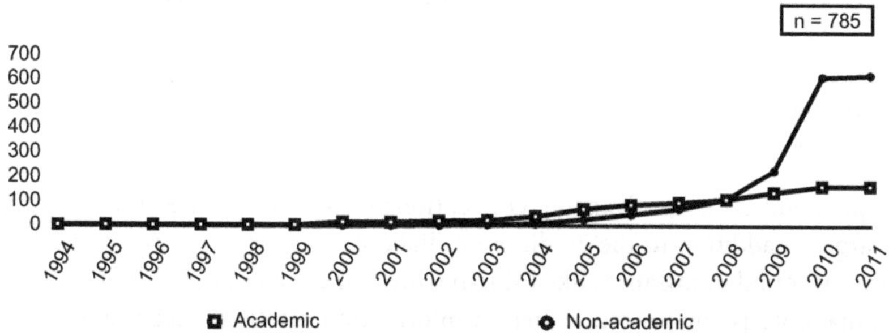


The evidence for *diabesity* advancing into the general vocabulary stems from the socio-pragmatic distribution across different types of source and fields of discourse. Although the neologism first appeared in non-academic sources in 2000, Figure 29 shows that the proper diffusion into non-specialized fields of discourse, i.e. GENERAL and OTHER, did not take place until 2010.

*Fig. 29: Socio-pragmatic field of discourse distribution of new pages per year of* diabesity

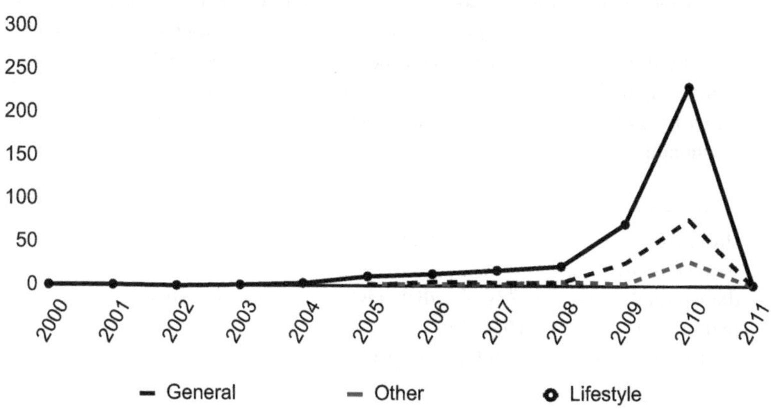

Within the LIFESTYLE category, which includes health-related topics, a further development can be observed. As examples (50) and (51) illustrate, *diabesity* is no longer exclusively discussed in purely medical terms, but increasingly appears in the context of dieting and other health-improving measures that might prevent people from suffering from diabesity.

(4) Make way for *diabesity*. With current projections, one in three Americans will be diabetic come 2050. Adults who sleep six hours or less crave sugar and fat – and take in more. So far, studies show kids getting less than nine hours sleep per night gain weight. (October 2010, professional health blog)[184]

(5) People who want to avoid the *diabesity* epidemic sweeping our country can do so by avoiding aspartame and sucralose. (August 2008, health-centered discussion forum)[185]

(6) Come to "*Diabesity*: It doesn't need to happen to you!" Monday, November 8 from 6:00 pm to 7:30 pm. (November 2010, Twitter)[186]

Another indicator of advancing conventionalization in the speech community at large, in addition to the 46 different diabesity-dedicated self-referential web pages, is found in instances like (52), in which an extralinguistic event concerning diabesity is announced, either an information meeting, a lecture by health professionals or the release of a book.

One source, listed in (53), mentions *diabesity* and *globesity* within one sentence. *Globesity* refers to the idea that obesity has become a global problem and was coined by health professionals at the World Health Organization in a report from February 2001 that warns about the risks of excessive overweight (cf. Quinion 2002 on *World Wide Words*[187]).

(7) In our opinions, Gary Taubes makes a compelling case that much of what we think we know about dieting and weight management is wrong. Given the epidemic of diabetes and obesity ("*diabesity*") in the United States (and globally, "*globesity*"), the healthcare costs associated with these diseases, and new public policies emphasizing wellness and preventive care, patients, doctors and politicians all need to learn and think about what Taubes has to say. (October 2010, health-centered community portal)[188]

---

184 therestdoctor.wordpress.com/2010/10/28/your-kids-new-favorite-bed-partner-102810/.

185 diabetesdaily.com/forum/type-2-diabetes/18789-aspartame-sucralose-3.

186 twitter.com/#!/WFMportlandME.

187 worldwidewords.org/turnsofphrase/tp-glo2.htm.

188 celebritydiagnosis.com/2010/10/food-fight-over-why-we-get-fat/.

(8) I read about *Globesity* and the 10 fattest countries. Most are island nations with over 90% of their populations obese. The U.S. is #8 at 79%. (general personal blog, December 2010)[189]

Similar to the case of *diabesity*, the lexeme does not remain restricted to specialist language, but spreads into general currency, as illustrated in (54). Unlike *diabesity*, however, the increase in frequency in academic and non-academic sources develops simultaneously, albeit to different degrees, as shown in Figure 30.

*Fig. 30: Academic vs. non-academic cumulative frequency development of* globesity

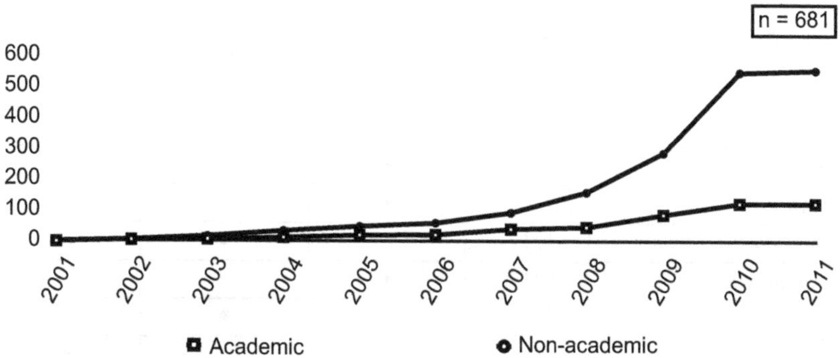


On the basis of their overall frequency and socio-pragmatic diffusion, *globesity* and *diabesity* represent neologisms in an advanced state of conventionalization and therefore illustrate the positive conventionalization effect of authoritative coiner status fittingly. The fueling effect of coiner status is assumed to result from speakers' socio-cognitive and linguistic accommodation processes. In the case of *globesity* for instance, the need in society and language on the part of experts arose to conceptualize the growing number of obese people around the world monolexemically in order to raise awareness for the danger and health risks involved. On the one hand, this holistic conceptualization stresses the fact that such an alarming development exists and fulfills the communicative need of getting the warning across. On the other hand, the concept required a novel lexeme that would not only accurately reflect the underlying concept, but also fulfill the stylistic need of attracting attention and awareness. As a result, health professionals at the World Health Organization coined the blend *globesity*, which effectively

189 fern-ourkoreanadventure.blogspot.com/2010/12/snowfall.html.

reflected their concerns. When speakers were made aware of the social phenomenon, they adopted the term chosen by these experts since they represented the social authority or norm to be acknowledged and trusted. Thus, people conform to new linguistic norms established by professionals to talk about certain events because of the underlying socio-cognitive accommodation process.

In conclusion, Table 9 gives an overview of the coiner status and overall frequency of each neologism, separated into novel lexical units when applicable, in the sample.

*Table 9: Coiner status parameter realization*

| Neologism | Frequency | Coiner status | | |
|---|---|---|---|---|
| | | unknown | professional | celebrity |
| *administrativia* | 41 | • | | |
| *back scooping* | 148 | | | • |
| *bloglet*[1] | 515 | • | | |
| *bloglet*[2] | 26 | • | | |
| *Boobgate* | 121 | | • | |
| *bromosexual* | 941 | • | | |
| *burquini* | 392 | | • | |
| *cherpumple* | 387 | | | • |
| *crapget* | 17 | • | | |
| *cyberchondriac* | 794 | • | | |
| *cyberdisinhibition* | 111 | | • | |
| *decycling* | 20 | • | | |
| *to detweet*[1] | 47 | • | | |
| *to detweet*[2] | 41 | • | | |
| *to detweet*[3] | 19 | • | | |
| *to detweet*[4] | 20 | | • | |
| *to detweet*[5] | 7 | • | | |
| *diabesity* | 785 | | • | |
| *e-tivity* | 51 | | • | |
| *encore career* | 724 | | • | |
| *Eurofascists* | 324 | • | | |
| *facebook official* | 51 | • | | |
| *floordrobe* | 291 | • | | |
| *friendsourcing* | 212 | | • | |

| | | | | |
|---|---|---|---|---|
| *frogurt* | 211 | | • | |
| *ganky* | 92 | • | | |
| *ghost surgery* | 48 | • | | |
| *globesity* | 681 | | • | |
| *grawlix* | 427 | | • | |
| *half-false* | 58 | • | | |
| *halfalogue* | 164 | | • | |
| *hyperlocal* | 1399 | • | | |
| *intexticated* | 913 | | • | |
| *iPad friendly* | 146 | • | | |
| *kindergarchy* | 178 | | • | |
| *meaniac* | 41 | • | | |
| *mesofact* | 80 | | • | |
| *politerati* | 51 | • | | |
| *preghead* | 14 | • | | |
| *radiculous* | 211 | • | | |
| *recombobulation area* | 231 | | • | |
| *robosigning* | 1735 | | • | |
| *roofvertising* | 6 | • | | |
| *slacktivism* | 1366 | | • | |
| *sodcasting* | 76 | • | | |
| *tynonym* | 104 | • | | |
| *tube-free* | 161 | | • | |
| *wellderly* | 608 | • | | |
| *yaka-wow* | 78 | | • | |

Two remarkable aspects of apparent counter-evidence for the promoting effect of coiner status emerge. First, some neologisms coined by an authority or celebrity do not seem to indicate that conventionalization is taking place. The lexemes *cyberdisinhibition, to detweet*[4], *e-tivity, mesofact, yaka-wow* and *tube-free* are all of relatively low frequency, i.e. less than 150 occurrences (or only slightly above in the case of *tube-free*). Certain linguistic and extralinguistic factors and their interactions such as semantic ambiguity in the case of *detweet*[4] or name-unworthiness in the case of *tube-free* and *mesofact* might be assumed to override the fueling effect of the coiner status. However, such explanations may result from idiosyncratic, neologism-specific developments rather than generalizable effects tested in the current model and require further research.

A second kind of apparent counter-evidence is represented by neologisms with a moderate to high frequency whose coiner is unknown. Lexemes belonging to this category are *cyberchondriac, Eurofascists, wellderly, radiculous, floordrobe, bromosexual* and *bloglet*[1]. Whereas the same idiosyncratic interactions of factors of influence as in the first category of counter-evidence should be posited, a closer inspection reveals a remarkable pattern for the latter four. *Radiculous*, a blend of *rad* ('awesome', 'cool') and *ridiculous*, *floordrobe*, a blend of *floor* and *wardrobe*, *bromosexual* and *bloglet*[1] can be characterized as colloquial expressions found in close-knit networks. These networks are both social and linguistic in nature. They represent online communities in which members of a similar socio-economic background in the widest sense exchange ideas and are associated with different speech styles. Such online networks can be seen as the 21st century continuation and development of Milroy's social networks (cf. 1980; Gruzd and Haythornthwaite 2011: 167). It is important to note that I am not concerned here with the introduction of lexical innovation into these networks, nor with their norm-retaining or norm-changing behavior with regard to sound changes like Milroy. The point to be made here concerns the diffusion. In spite of the fact that the coiner is unknown, neologisms like *bromosexual*, which predominantly occurs in discussion fora and social network sites consisting of multifarious dense and weak ties between the members, show signs of advancing and advanced establishment in their microcommunities. Although network density has not been considered as a factor of influence in the present study, it might also provide an explanation for the marginal promoting effect of type of source on the conventionalization process, which will be discussed in the following section.

### 4.2.2. Type of source

In addition to coiner status, the medium in which the neologism appears has been assumed to positively influence the diffusion and lead to conventionalization, as represented by H3 mentioned at the beginning of 4.2 and in 1.2. The type of source is presumed to catalyze establishment in two ways. Firstly, the formality of the type of source traditionally correlates with the audience size (cf. Schmid 2011a: 75). Thus, newspapers not only establish a norm in the form of a novel expression, but also provide large-scale exposure. Depending on the number of readers who actively adopt the neologism, expanding diffusion circles arise until the lexeme has become established and is familiar to the majority of the members of the speech community. Secondly, formal sources such as newspapers function as normifying authorities in the coinage process. When a novel expression is required, professional journalists and editors appeal to their experience and skills in order to create a new lexical item that will accurately capture the concept in a linguistic form that can be easily understood by the readers. As a result, the accommodation process on the part of the reader, motivated by prestige and norm adoption, has been shown to fuel diffusion in the previous section.

The regression model yields a slightly promoting and statistically significant effect of the formal type of source NEWS. Remarkably, the effect estimate factor of 1.11 is low (p= 0.041267*). Neither the factor type of source PORTAL, nor any of its interactions with other variables, contribute any information to the generalizability and predictability requirements of the model, as represented by the AIC[190]. In view of this neutral effect within the current model, type of source PORTAL cannot be considered as a factor of influence on the conventionalization process.

A first explanation for the minimal effect of occurrence in news sites and the absence of an effect of occurrence in portals might relate to the method. As mentioned in 2.3 and 4.1, diffusion in the present study is not only operationalized as overall frequency, but also as relative frequency in the various types of source. Since these relative frequency scores represent the total frequency in a particular type of source observed during the entire monitoring period, they might not accurately reflect the influence of type of source on the conventionalization process but indicate its development. The occurrence in more formal texts might not be the initial trigger of diffusion, but a consequence thereof. When a neologism starts to diffuse, the likelihood that it will be picked up by the media generally increases, which might in turn fuel further diffusion.

This process can be illustrated with the help of the example *encore career*. Figure 31 on the next page shows the chronological frequency distribution of *encore career* since its first attestation retrieved by the NeoCrawler. The grey curve, representing the NEWS category, does not appear until 2010, when the word has already occurred much more frequently in blogs and portals. In order to investigate whether formal types of source should be considered as an indicator rather than a trigger or propagator of conventionalization, a meticulous description of monthly frequencies in all types of source is required to accurately capture the minute details of the diffusion process, which was beyond the scope of the present study. Moreover, as mentioned above, a second statistical model that

190 The AIC, *Akaike's Information Criterion,* provides a measure of goodness-of-fit of a particular statistical model in a selection of statistical models that seem equally applicable (Akaike 1974).

incorporates type of source as a dependent variable can provide further insight into this issue.

*Fig. 31: New pages per year in different types of sources for* encore career

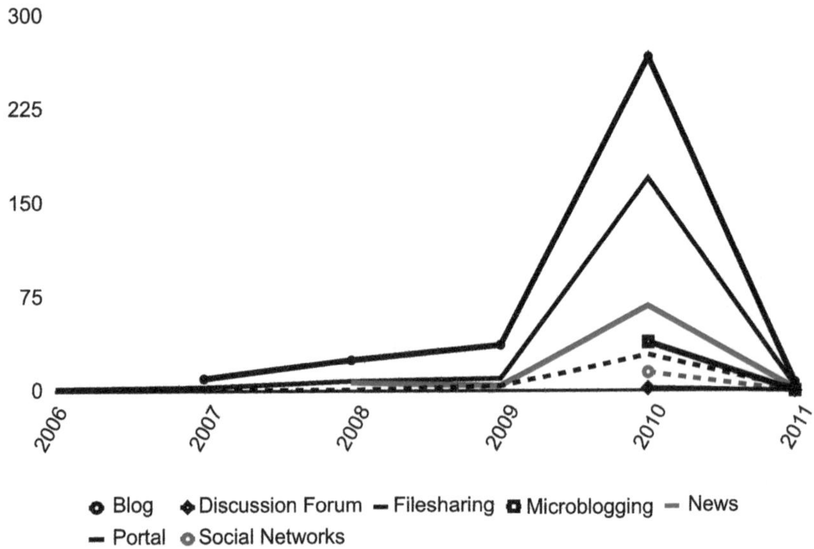


Appendix 5 on p. 257 lists the frequency with which each neologism or novel lexical unit occurs in the different types of source. Significant frequencies, i.e. those exceeding the random distribution expectations, are highlighted in bold. Although many neologisms in advanced stages of conventionalization are characterized by frequent occurrence in more formal types of source, the numbers for the NEWS category are relatively low in general. Of the 1399 overall occurrences of *hyperlocal,* for instance, a neologism originating in and pertaining to the media, a mere 60 stem from newspapers, whereas 445 are found in portals. Given the socio-pragmatic and socio-economic similarities to print newspapers (see 3.3.2), online portals are to be positioned towards the more formal extreme of the style continuum, only slightly less formal than newspapers. They represent "equivalents of traditional media institutions" (Androutsopoulos 2007: 289). However, they do not constitute a homogenous category in themselves. Some smaller-scale community portals are not staffed by professional writers and journalists or use more casual, colloquial language. Moreover, as shown in 3.3.2, not all blogs are private rants or diary-like reflections. Rather, they provide factual expertise. Professional blogs of this kind too could be considered as formal texts. As a result, the distinction between formal and informal online types of source becomes even more blurred than in traditional classifications of written discourse. Therefore, a second explanation for the marginal effect of formal types of source on the conventionalization process might be methodological in nature. The fuzzy and questionable division between formal and informal speech styles merits further research within the CMD framework and might yield a finer-grained continuum than the gradation imposed on the current data. Given the peculiarities of the CMD medium in many linguistic, social and cultural respects, it remains questionable whether the traditional interpretations and definitions of the notion of formality can be applied to the same extent as in offline language, which would necessitate a rethinking and rephrasing of such style-related hypotheses.

Virtual reality is not only linguistically structured differently from face-to-face interaction, but also socio-economically. Two important developments that are relevant for the diffusion process will be briefly addressed, but will need to be considered in future research on diffusion of lexical innovations in more detail. The first aspect concerns the flexibility with which virtual communities[191] appear and disappear. Deterding describes virtual communities as follows, "VC (Virtual Communities) sind hoch dynamische Gebilde, die binnen kürzester Zeit Konventionen ausbilden, reproduzieren, herausfordern und transformieren" and thus defines such virtual communities as highly dynamic constructs that develop, reproduce, challenge and transform conventions within a very short period of time (2009: 118, my translation; cf. Castells 2000: 386, 389). They are changeable and loose structures of membership, easy to join and leave, unlike offline communities (cf. Kneidinger 2010: 45-46). Such virtual communities are, for instance, found on discussion fora, portals or among blog readers. Since they are not geo-spatially-bound or restricted by socio-economic background, they provide a broader platform for exchanging content than offline communities enable. Moreover, the number of online communities a user actively or passively belongs to tends to be higher than in offline reality, partly because of the available technological tools, partly because they constitute more voluntary assemblies with less severe sanctions and different norms (cf. Kneidinger 2010: 46). As a consequence, the exposure to novel ideas or linguistic items is increased due to the number of members and their different social and professional backgrounds.

191 A detailed overview of the concept of "virtual community" can be found in Rheingold (1994: xv ff.).

In addition, the diffusion of such items stands a better chance due to the temporary density within and openness towards other communities. Fringe members of one particular community, whether permanent or temporary, pick up an innovation, either from a more established member, i.e. the "opinion leaders" (Valente 1995: 33; cf. Friemel 2008: 830) or from other fringe members and carry it into other virtual communities they belong to. In other words, the flexibility to join and leave as one may creates a substantial network of weak ties that have been attributed a diffusion-enhancing role. Moreover, the emergence of online social networks like Facebook or MySpace and to a certain extent also microblogging services[192], have caused such weak ties to be maintained and intensified. In contrast to virtual communities, however, online social networks occupy an intermediate position between online and offline communities (cf. Kneidinger 2010: 48). They continue existing offline ties and extend them to online communication and are only marginally complemented by new, exclusively online ones (cf. Kneidinger 2010: 48, 54-55, 59; Autenrieth and Herwig 2011: 213; Gruzd and Haythornthwaite 2011: 167). In her study on the functions and nature of relations within Facebook, Kneidinger concludes that the medium is predominantly used to maintain strong ties and actively strengthen weak ones by keeping the community members permanently updated on the daily lives of less intimate acquaintances (cf. 2010: 112-113, 131). Since weak ties have been claimed to constitute diffusion-promoting and -reinforcing channels (cf. 2.3), it can be assumed that their growth and intensification in online social networks and virtual communities[193] positively contribute to the conventionalization of novel linguistic

192 Originally, microblogging platforms like Twitter were designed to post momentary reflections and preoccupations. However, they quickly developed into a platform of academic exchange and news aggregation (cf. Autenrieth and Herwig 2011: 212-214). The exchange of content was facilitated and enhanced by the implementation of technological tools like the retweet button and the use of hashtags to organize content according to topic (e.g. *#obama*) or attitude (e.g. *#iambored*). These two features increase the distribution and diffusion of posts and reinforce their visibility outside the circle of immediate followers (cf. Autenrieth and Herwig 2011: 221-22, 225).

193 Although not all blogs are accompanied by a virtual community that reads and discusses all of the members' posts, a remarkable indication of the community character of blog audiences is illustrated by *bloglet*[1] in section 5.2.1. This kind of less conspicuous online community might explain the high frequency of the novel lexeme. The precise extent of community dynamics in blogs deserves further research.

items[194]. For example, the establishment of *bromosexual* in social networks and discussion groups mentioned in the previous section and explained in detail in 5.2.3 might be the result of the intensity of accommodation between online community and social networks members[195]. As the socio-pragmatic distribution in Appendix 5 shows, in addition to frequent occurrences in blogs, *bromosexual* predominantly appears in the informal DISCUSSION FORUM and SOCIAL NETWORK categories. A further case in point is represented by *radiculous*. As mentioned in the previous section, in spite of the coiner being unknown, its frequency indicates small-scale conventionalization. The individual frequencies for each type of source in Appendix 5 again indicate that the lexeme is mainly used in densely structured online communities and networks. These examples show that the lack of a positive effect of formal types of source might be caused by the emergence of flexible, dense online networks of weak ties that continue and expand their offline counterparts.

Finally, from a cognitive perspective, the failure to ascertain a strong promoting effect of formal type of source occurrence might be related to the insufficient frequency and duration of exposure. As mentioned above, a single exposure to a novel lexeme is claimed to be sufficient to leave a tentative trace in lexical memory, which instantiates entrenchment and facilitates subsequent retrieval. This in turn is assumed to have a positive influence on diffusion. However, such studies were conducted in a controlled environment in which the attention of the participants was exclusively focused on the stimuli under scrutiny. In natural environments, speakers are confronted with a steady influx of words to be recalled from and processed in memory. In addition, other cognitive abilities like sensory-motor functions are active simultaneously. These concurring activities in ordinary everyday situations might claim a greater share of cognitive energy than required in artificial lab conditions. As a result, a novel expression, especially without metalinguistic markers, might not even be recognized or attract attention upon the first encounter[196] and require further, immediate exposure. Such continuing

194 Mair (2011) noticed that *mzungu*, Swahili for 'white person' and predominantly used in East and Southern Africa, unexpectedly spread on a discussion forum in his Corpus of Cyber-Jamaican/Jamaican English due to active promotion by its introducer, which was an established user of the forum (cf. 231-233).

195 Sebba (2007) discusses the construction of identity in virtual communities of Ali G fans, who perform their identity through adaption of his speech style, which he assumes to be an exclusively online performance (cf. 375).

196 More importantly, its position within the entire online domain should be considered. Probably only a minority of readers spells a newspaper from front to back; the

exposure typically takes place when an extralinguistic event causes one or more periods of topicality. As mentioned in 4.1.2, the intensity of short-term topicality determines the extent of the long-term conventionalization. In the case of *back scooping*, for instance, of which 89 of the 147 occurrences in objectlinguistic use are found in formal types of source, the period of topicality in the wake of Heidi Montag's confession was short. After the hype had faded out, the lexeme did not re-appear in discourse, despite its frequent use in newspapers and portals. A word like *politerati* on the other hand, referring to the class of political decision-makers in Washington, is also predominantly found in formal texts (37 out of 51 occurrences in objectlinguistic use). However, these occurrences are spread over a longer period, as illustrated in Figure 32 and do not result from topicality. The peak towards the end of 2010 consists of discrete references not connected to one particular event.

*Fig. 32: New pages per month in the categories NEWS and PORTAL of* politerati

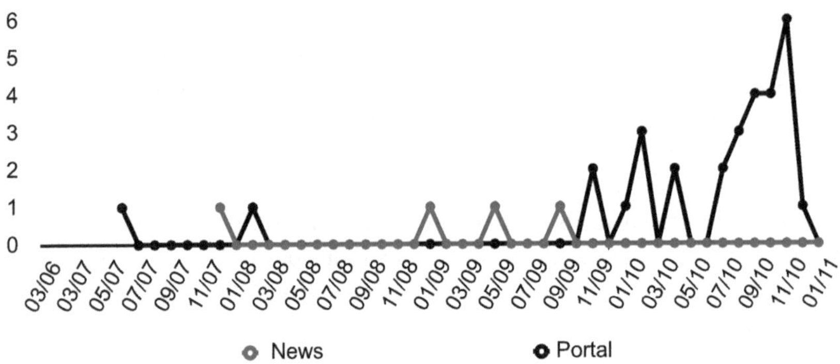


Thus, the observed effect (or lack of effect) of formal types of source on the conventionalization process might have a cognitive cause. When newspaper or portal articles do not promptly follow up on a particular topic for which a neologism was coined or used, the original single exposure might fall short of generating a trace in lexical memory that is robust enough to activate storage, similarly to the weakening of mental traces of lexemes that have not been actively used for an extended period of time (cf. Langacker 1987: 59).

majority will tend to focus on topics of interest in the various sections or headlines. Since online newspapers and portals provide even more information, it is likely that the position of the neologism contributes to or diminishes its visibility.

### 4.2.3. Metalinguistic usage

The linguistic abilities of speakers do not only allow them to retrieve, create and use lexemes to refer to extralinguistic objects and events, but also to refer to linguistic structures themselves. Within the metalinguistic awareness research paradigm, extensive research has shown that these abilities develop in childhood and facilitate the acquisition of reading comprehension skills (cf. Kamhi and Koenig 1985: 199; Nagy and Anderson 1995) and vocabulary (cf. Nagy 2007). As a corollary, speakers can appeal to their metalinguistic awareness skills when confronted with novel linguistic items, in their mother tongue or in a foreign language, and improve comprehension. In addition, metalinguistic comments often provide explicit explanations which reduce processing effort. Correct understanding in turn is a prerequisite for initial entrenchment and conventionalization. Therefore, the presence of metalinguistic comments on neologisms, at the same time as increasing their salience, should have a positive effect on their diffusion (cf. Schmid 2011a: 75). However, as mentioned in 1.2, it can also be assumed that substantial metalinguistic usage has an inhibiting influence on conventionalization. This hypothesis is based on an observation by Metcalf. He claims that

> a word shouldn't call attention to itself [...]. If it does attract notice, chances are it will be rejected. If, however, it is unobtrusive and sounds familiar even if it is not, those who hear or see it are more likely to think it's something they have missed rather than something missing from the language. (2002: 144)

Moreover, if such neologisms succeed in escaping the attention of lexicographers and new-word experts, they stand an even better chance (cf. Metcalf 2002: 144, 185-186).

The results from the statistical analysis contradict Metcalf's claims. A statistically significant fueling effect of metalinguistic usage was observed, albeit marginally (effect estimate factor 1.01, p=0.032851*) and substantiate Schmid's assumption with regard to the positive diffusion-promoting effect of metalinguistic usage (cf. 2011: 75). The effect is represented by the upward sloping continuous line in Figure 33. The interactions in which metalinguistic usage was tested parallel the results regarding interactions discussed above. The interaction of metalinguistic usage and the presence of collocations yielded a slightly inhibiting effect (effect estimate factor 0.11, p=0.000323 ***), illustrated by the downward sloping dotted line in Figure 33. Again, the combination of these parameters only applied to *detweet*[1] and *intexticated*. As mentioned above, more observations of this type are needed to provide conclusive evidence so that the significance of the influence of this interaction should be treated with caution.

*Fig. 33: Effect plot for the metalinguistic usage (in percentage) and metalinguistic usage x collocation factor*

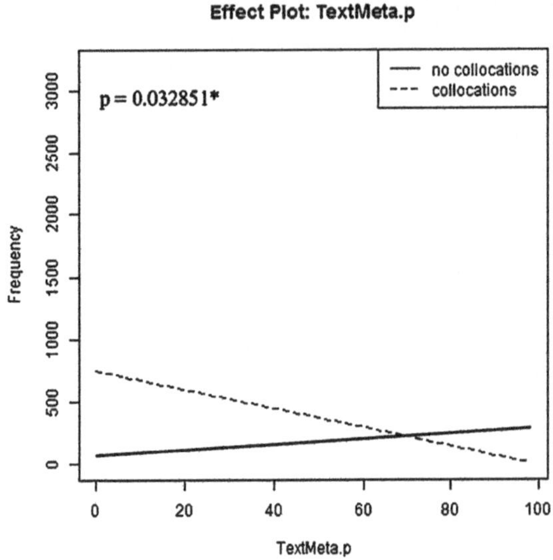


The promoting effect is assumed to result from the cognitive metalinguistic awareness abilities, the explicit comprehension clues contained in such metalinguistic comments and the temporary salience. The extent of the effect is not directly apparent in the data, which are seemingly randomly distributed. Table 10 lists the individual percentages of meta- and objectlinguistic occurrences for each neologism and lexical unit.

*Table 10: Mode of usage percentages*

| Neologism | Frequency | Mode of Usage % | |
|---|---|---|---|
| | | metalinguistic | objectlinguistic |
| *administrativia* | 41 | 2 | 98 |
| *back scooping* | 148 | 0 | 100 |
| *bloglet*[1] | 515 | 2 | 98 |
| *bloglet*[2] | 26 | 0 | 100 |
| *Boobgate* | 121 | 0 | 100 |
| *bromosexual* | 941 | 5 | 95 |
| *burquini* | 392 | 2 | 98 |
| *cherpumple* | 387 | 1 | 99 |
| *crapget* | 17 | 6 | 94 |

| | | | |
|---|---|---|---|
| *cyberchondriac* | 794 | 20 | 80 |
| *cyberdisinhibition* | 111 | 19 | 81 |
| *decycling* | 20 | 10 | 90 |
| *to detweet*[1] | 47 | 2 | 98 |
| *to detweet*[2] | 41 | 45 | 55 |
| *to detweet*[3] | 19 | 5 | 95 |
| *to detweet*[4] | 20 | 35 | 65 |
| *to detweet*[5] | 7 | 0 | 100 |
| *diabesity* | 785 | 4 | 96 |
| *e-tivity* | 51 | 0 | 100 |
| *encore career* | 724 | 1 | 99 |
| *Eurofascists* | 324 | 0 | 100 |
| *facebook official* | 51 | 0 | 100 |
| *floordrobe* | 291 | 18 | 82 |
| *friendsourcing* | 212 | 6 | 94 |
| *frogurt* | 211 | 9 | 91 |
| *ganky* | 92 | 0 | 100 |
| *ghost surgery* | 48 | 38 | 63 |
| *globesity* | 681 | 20 | 80 |
| *grawlix* | 427 | 89 | 11 |
| *half-false* | 58 | 0 | 100 |
| *halfalogue* | 164 | 99 | 1 |
| *hyperlocal* | 1399 | 1 | 99 |
| *intexticated* | 913 | 45 | 55 |
| *iPad friendly* | 146 | 0 | 100 |
| *kindergarchy* | 178 | 20 | 80 |
| *meaniac* | 41 | 22 | 78 |
| *mesofact* | 80 | 48 | 53 |
| *politerati* | 51 | 0 | 100 |
| *preghead* | 14 | 0 | 100 |
| *radiculous* | 211 | 2 | 98 |
| *recombobulation area* | 231 | 18 | 82 |
| *robosigning* | 1735 | 2 | 98 |
| *roofvertising* | 6 | 17 | 83 |
| *slacktivism* | 1366 | 28 | 72 |
| *sodcasting* | 76 | 34 | 66 |

| Neologism | Frequency | Mode of Usage % | |
|---|---|---|---|
| | | metalinguistic | objectlinguistic |
| *tynonym* | 104 | 93 | 7 |
| *tube-free* | 161 | 1 | 99 |
| *wellderly* | 608 | 26 | 74 |
| *yaka-wow* | 78 | 56 | 44 |

Some neologisms in advanced stages of conventionalization such as *grawlix*[197] and *intexticated* are frequently found in metalinguistic usage, others such as *bloglet*[1], *burquini, cyberchondriac, encore career* and *hyperlocal* hardly occur. Some of the non- or less conventionalized novel lexemes such as *halfalogue, mesofact* and *tynonym* frequently occur in metalinguistic mode, others like *preghead* and *politerati* exclusively occur in objectlinguistic usage.

The case of *halfalogue*, i.e. an overheard cell phone conversation, represents a striking example that would support Metcalf's claim. Its establishment process (or lack thereof) will be discussed in 5.2.3. *Tynonym* falls into the same category. *Tynonym* or *t9onym*[198] is an example of erratic predictive texting, i.e. the practice of words in text messages being suggested or completed by dictionaries and spell-checkers on a cell phone. Thus, a *tynonym* is a word suggested by the T9 function in the text message interfaces. These suggestions arise from identical key combinations: *book* appears when *cool* is intended, *rejected* when *selected* is intended. In February 2008, David Crystal created a buzz around *tynonym*, when several newspapers reported on his research into a new kind of slang arising as the result of predictive texting, as illustrated in example (55) from *The Daily Telegraph*.

(9) Children are inventing a whole new verbal language based entirely on the predictive text function they use to send messages on their mobiles. They are replacing words they mean with the first alternative that comes up when typing a message. So if you hear your teenager describing something as "book", then it means it is "cool" - because book is the word that first comes up when you type cool into your

---

197 *Grawlix* should be treated with caution. It seems doubtful whether it indeed represents a case of progressive conventionalization, since the percentage of objectlinguistic occurrences in relation to the overall frequency is very low, particularly when compared to *intexticated*.

198 In addition, the synonyms *textonym, txtonym, adaptonyms* or *cellodromes* exist, though none of them has gained currency.

phone using predictive text. If they exclaim "zonino!" then it means "woohoo!" and when they refer to someone's "nun" they mean their mum. [...]. David Crystal, a linguistics expert at Bangor University, said the language is known as textonyms, or *t9onyms* (pronounced *tynonyms*). "Playing with language isn't new, kids have been doing it since at least Victorian times," he said. "It shows incredible ingenuity and, believe it or not, a high degree of literacy on their part. And don't worry if you find it confusing. There's little chance many of these words will be incorporated into our language. They'll likely fall by the wayside." Despite this the Oxford English Dictionary is said to be considering putting "book" into the dictionary. (Richard Alleyne, February 5, 2008)[199]

(10) Which made me think of a new word I've made up: *Tynonym*. I googled it and found only two hits, both of which I think is [sic, dk] just spelling errors. *Tynonym*: Definition. So what is a tynonym? It's a word that you get as a suggestion on your mobile phone when you spell a word with T9 on. (professional technology blog, November 2006)[200]

(11) Cell phone update. at Linkstew Says:
And speaking of *t9onyms*, how did Dewitt not coin that phrase when he wrote his class T9 Synonyms [...]. (private blog, March 2007)[201]

However, examples (56) and (57) show that the word and especially the concept is older. The entry from Oyvind Solstad's blog, listed in (56), seems to ascertain that he was the coiner. No further references that corroborate his claim are found in other sources. Moreover, as early as January 2005, professional blogger Clinton DeWitt, referred to in (57), published an article on his blog about T9 synonyms and how to automatically extract all the possible substitutions[202].

The frequency development in both modes of usage in Figure 34 disproves the assumption that an increase in metalinguistic discourse instantiates an increase in objectlinguistic usage. Despite two topicality periods, the first one due to the reproduction of a Wikipedia entry on predictive texting, the second one in the wake of Crystal's use with regard to his research, *tynonym/t9onym* did not catch on. Although the non-establishment of *tynonym* and the generally low numbers of metalinguistic comments for neologisms in advanced stages of conventionalization in the sample seem to tally well with Metcalf's claims, the statistical results present evidence refuting such claims.

199 telegraph.co.uk/news/uknews/1577676/Predictive-text-creating-secret-teen-language.html.

200 brilliantdays.com/tynonym/.

201 linkstew.org/2007/03/cell-phone-update/.

202 blog.unto.net/t9.

*Fig. 34: Cumulative pages per month of* tynonym *in meta- and objectlinguistic usage*

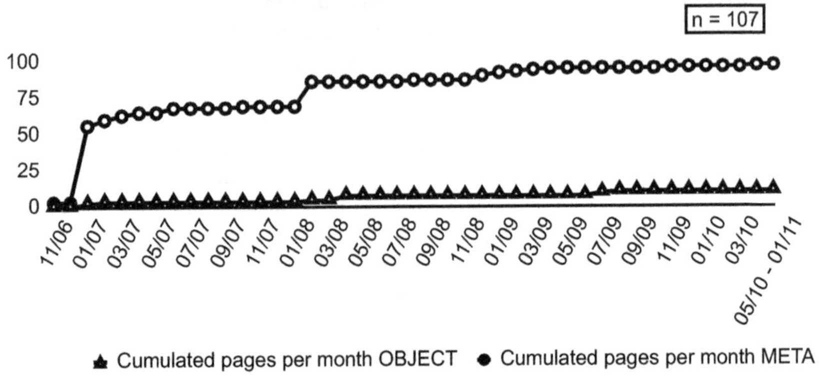


In conclusion, the positive effect of metalinguistic usage cannot readily account for the conventionalization behavior of all the neologisms in the current sample. Additional neologisms and possibly an improved method for describing metalinguistic usage are required. On the one hand, input of monthly frequency instead of an overall frequency into the regression model, as suggested in the previous section, might reflect any causal interactions between the two modes of usage more accurately and yield more conclusive evidence on the precise extent of influence of these modes. On the other hand, a possibly more significant effect might also crystallize if the data are classified on token-level instead of on page-level (see 3.3.2). Given the vast amount of data in the present study, manual token-level classification was an impractical enterprise and the need for an automatized mode of usage analysis arises.

Before presenting the results on two structural aspects of neologisms that were assumed to exert an influence on their conventionalization process, a final accommodation-driven factor, nameworthiness, will be discussed in the following section.

### 4.2.4. Nameworthiness

Lexical innovation operates at the crossroads of social and linguistic motivations and concerns. Frequently, the need for a new lexeme, sense or word-form arises from a naming need in response to a change or innovation in society (cf. 1.2). The study of diffusion and conventionalization should not neglect extralinguistic aspects. In contrast to many linguistic phenomena that can be directly observed, described and quantified, however, many social factors are less tangible and are largely invisible. Since words stand for concepts, the durability, pervasiveness and salience of the concept itself are assumed to contribute to the establishment of their linguistic realizations. Metcalf compares the connection between concepts and words to dogs and their fleas, "[i]f the dog is healthy, so is the flea. If the dog dies, so does the flea - unless it's able to find another dog" (2002: 162). The extent to which fleas are kept alive after the death of their hosts depends on the durability and salience. The Cold War, for instance, dominating post-war history for many decades, has ended, but *Cold War* still survives in language, whereas *Benigni moment*[203] has disappeared (cf. Metcalf 2002: 162-163). Salience or durability are elusive concepts, both on the social level of the speech community and the cognitive level of the individual lexicon. How should these concepts be operationalized? Whereas the salience and lifetime of lexemes can be attested by means of their frequency in synchronic and diachronic corpora, the salience of a concept involves more than counting its specific linguistic form because it is an essentially social artifact. Moreover, the pervasiveness of a given concept does not entail that the corresponding lexeme will be adopted by all or most of the members of the speech community and set up mental traces leading to storage. The accommodation process is not only affected by the objective frequency or intensity of exposure to an innovation in society, but also by the subjective need of the individual to adopt it and/or talk about it. In other words, novel concepts must be nameworthy to become conventionalized (cf. Dowing 1977).

The influence of the nameworthiness of the underlying concepts, not all of which represent social innovations (e.g. *preghead*), on the conventionalization of English neologisms was investigated in an experiment, described in detail in 3.3.3. A sample questionnaire is attached in Appendix 3 on p. 251. Subjects were asked to rate the usefulness of the given definition[204] (questions a and b), indicate familiarity (question c) and provide the corresponding lexeme (question d). In order to probe into the variety of concerns that might take effect, 'usefulness' was not specified further. Thus, the participants were encouraged to appeal to their individual intuition without being restricted by a predetermined situation or occasion.

Figure 35 on the next page presents a comparison between the nameworthiness scores of 15 of the 21 targeted neologisms and their semantically contiguous established lexemes. As mentioned above, subjects did not receive the lexeme, only its definition, i.e. a description of the underlying concept. Since for some of the targets no semantically related conventionalized candidate exists,

203 *Benigni moment* "refer[s] to Roberto Benigni's exuberant behavior at the 1999 Oscars when he received the Best Actor award" (Metcalf 2002: 163).

204 Definitions were taken from metalinguistic comments and online dictionaries such as *Urban Dictionary* when available.

e.g. *Boobgate, encore career, intexticated, slacktivism* and *tube-free*, definitions for such potential words were made up (see Appendix 3). They are excluded from the comparison in the figure. Moreover, an attempt was made to include relatively young lexemes in order to minimize a potential bias regarding familiarity with and durability of the underlying concept. However, some control words such as *septuagenerian, booklet* or *oligarchy* fail to meet this requirement. Control words and targets as used in the present study are listed in Appendix 3 on p. 251.

*Fig. 35: Comparison of nameworthiness scores for novel and established lexemes*

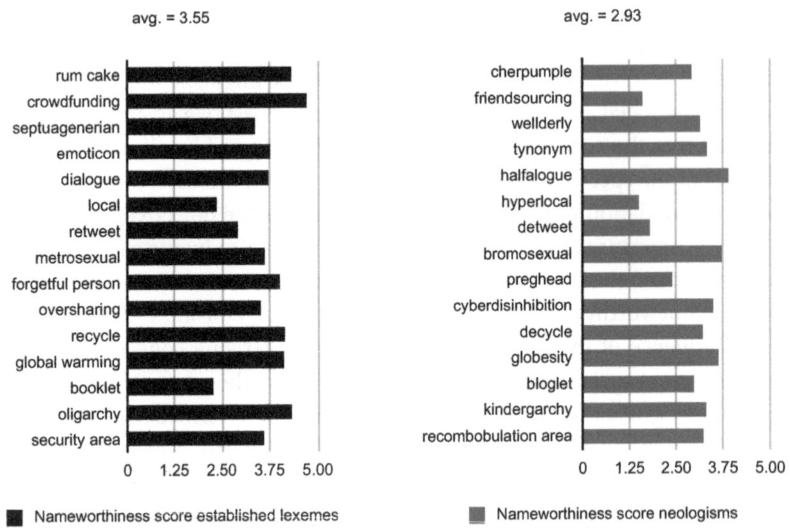


As reflected by the average, conventionalized words were deemed more nameworthy than neologisms. With the exception of *retweet* and *booklet*[205], subjects consistently indicated that the definitions were useful, i.e. scores > 3.5, illustrated by the shorter horizontal bars in Figure 35. For these definitions, the majority of subjects were also able to provide the correct lexeme. These results tally well with the hypostatization effect discussed above. Speakers familiar with a particular lexeme are aware of the existence of an underlying concept that is holistically stored. The fact that a distinct entry has been set up in lexical memory seems to justify and

205 The low usefulness scores for *local* and *hyperlocal* are assumed to result from the relatively abstract definition given (see Appendix 3).

is justified by the perceived need on the part of the speaker. When such a lexical entry is not present yet, however, the concept is generally judged less useful[206].

Within the neologism category, no correlation between conventionalization stage and nameworthiness could be observed. Among the three highest ranking neologisms regarding nameworthiness, only *bromosexual* represents a noteworthy degree of conventionality among the subjects, as illustrated by the lexico-semantic related responses in Table 11 below. Conversely, some of the more conventionalized neologisms such as *wellderly*, *slacktivism* and *intexticated* are found towards the middle or bottom of the list. *Halfalogue* and *bloglet*[1], for instance, score higher than their established counterparts. Thus, despite the subjective nameworthiness of certain concepts, their linguistic realization does not necessarily become conventionalized.

*Table 11: Nameworthiness scores and responses for the target neologisms*

| Target lexeme | Frequency | Average score | Responses |
|---|---|---|---|
| *halfalogue* | 164 | 3.90 | *by-listening; eavesdropping (3); ear-wrigging; snippet (6)* |
| *bromosexual* | 941 | 3.72 | ***bromance** (9); best friend; friend* ***bromo**; homosocial; buddy (2)* |
| *sodcasting* | 76 | 3.68 | *music-bombing; unthoughtful; blaring; annoying; disturbing; anti-social; jerk with loud music; noise pollution; sound pollution* |
| *globesity* | 681 | 3.63 | ***global obesity**; obesity pandemic; obesity epidemic (3); obesity problem; epidemic; globalised obesity; obesitism;* ***globesity*** |
| *cyberdisinhibition* | 111 | 3.49 | *e-expression; embarrassment; stupidity; idiocy; technological distancing; weakness; webhonesty; cyber-parapraxes; digi-drunk* |
| *encore career* | 724 | 3.47 | *planning; second job after retirement; OAP; re-employment; gero-job/golden age career; paid hobby; hobby* |
| *tynonym* | 104 | 3.32 | *auto-correct;* ***predictive texting** (3); spell check; texting; ignorance; prediction (2)* |

206 One could argue that the level of conceptual specificity plays a role too. However, a concept like emoticon or metrosexual received higher usefulness scores than booklet or security area.

| Target lexeme | Frequency | Average score | Responses |
|---|---|---|---|
| *kindergarchy* | 178 | 3.30 | *brat; paediocracy; child overrule; infantocracy; child centric; filiocracy; spoiledness; kidocracy* |
| *recombobulation area* | 231 | 3.22 | *baggage claim (7); security check; check in lounge; baggage reclaim; baggage collection* |
| *decycle* | 20 | 3.21 | *anti-recycle (3); recycling; waste; deliberately waste; pollute; unenvironmental; recycling refusal* |
| *wellderly* | 608 | 3.15 | *long life; senior; senior citizens/elders; elderly; healthy/useful; healthy living; OAPs* |
| *slacktivism* | 1366 | 3.12 | *lazy (4); activist; non-profit organization; lazy activism; passive; armchair/plastic activist* |
| *bloglet*[1] | 515 | 2.97 | *microblog (3);* ***bloglet****; blog; tweet (2); blog post; blogpiece; post; short blog* |
| *intexticated* | 913 | 2.95 | *texting (4); textaholic; careless/multi-tasker; phone-a-lolhic; driving distraction;* ***intexicated****; dangerous driving* |
| *cherpumple* | 387 | 2.92 | *thrifle; layer cake (2); gateaux four-seasons cake; cherry-pumpkin-apple-cake;* chumple cake |
| *preghead* | 14 | 2.40 | *silly; baby brain (3); hormone-induced confusion; scatty* |
| *tube-free* | 161 | 2.08 | *napkin; paperless; wipes; garbage; tissue (4); unrolled toiletpaper; sheets; loose* |
| *Boobgate* | 121 | 2.07 | *exposing; rumor; revealing; leaked pictures; inappropriate; crazy; gossip; nip-slip; flash* |
| *detweet*[2] | 41 | 1.80 | *sign out (5); sign off; log off; log out* |
| *friendsourcing* | 212 | 1.60 | *chatting; surfing the web/the net; retrieve-communicate; research (2); gather info; being nosey; email* |
| *hyperlocal* | 1399 | 1.50 | *beneficial; outside; news; area/vicinity; top story; live* |

The absence of a correlation between nameworthiness and conventionalization cannot be readily accounted for. A variety of reasons could play a role. Firstly, nameworthiness judgements in this study were evoked by an onomasiological description of the concept rather than by the linguistic word-form in order to mitigate influence by the latter. Since speakers encounter the emerging symbolic association between concept and form, one might argue that the precise morphological form also positively or negatively contributes to the nameworthiness of a novel concept. Therefore, the lack of advancing conventionalization of *halfalogue* and *sodcasting*, which represent nameworthy concepts according to the subjects, might arise from their relatively odd word-forms. *Bromosexual* and *globesity* on the other hand do not seem to be affected. Secondly, in addition to the orthographic and phonetic realizations, morpho-semantic transparency should be considered. Although *halfalogue, sodcasting* and *globesity* are all blends, they differ with regard to transparency. When subjects were asked for the word corresponding to the definition, only the latter elicited a correct monolexemic answer. This indicates that it seems the preferred and most transparent form. Moreover, the responses for *bromosexual* show that an association to its morpho-semantic parent *bromance* exists, which is assumed to pave the way, both in terms of nameworthiness and morpho-semantic acceptability, for the progressing establishment of *bromosexual* on micro-community level. As a result, a follow-up experiment with a semasiological design is required to investigate these assumptions. Lastly, confounding effects of other variables cannot be excluded, but could not be investigated due to the incomplete observation set for the nameworthiness variable.

In addition, the motivations for assigning a specific score, as explained by the informants in question c, result from highly individual issues of perception and utility, reflecting the strong cognitive component involved in the nameworthiness notion. The results of the elicitation test indicate that speakers' judgements are governed by three broad types of communicative concerns, summarized in Table 12 on the next page for the three most and least nameworthy definitions. The first type reflects the degree of societal utility. When asked to explain the usefulness or uselessness of a given definition, speakers referred to the salience of the extralinguistic referent in society. They reported having encountered these concepts in everyday life and described them as common, recognized and topical phenomena. As a result of the relative ubiquity of the referent, speakers expressed the need to have a lexeme at their disposal to allow them to talk about it in the speech community. A second socially-motivated cause arises from the degree of personal utility. The objective, societal usefulness of concepts can be overridden by subjective, individual perceptions and needs to be located more on the cognitive side. A first aspect of personal utility concerns the degree of identification. Speakers generally assigned higher scores to definitions of concepts they could personally relate to. Thus, one person judged *Boobgate* as useless, because he or she claimed not to be interested in celebrities. The personal utility concern is particularly apparent for *Boobgate* and *detweet*[2] illustrated in

Table 12. Similarly, some of the subjects found *tynonym* superfluous, since they have a Blackberry device. Moreover, an emotional aspect is involved. The definition of *sodcasting,* for instance, evoked strong connotative responses reflecting speakers' attitude towards the concept. A substantial number of subjects found the definition useful, not only because of the ubiquity of the phenomenon in society, but because they were personally affected. Many speakers described the phenomenon as 'obnoxious' and 'annoying'. Lastly, the degree of holistic utility or informativeness, reflected by the succinctness and expressivity with which the concept unites the individual meaning components, seems to be a concern on the part of the speakers. Such concepts represent holistic units of information and associations and are therefore the primary means of categorizing and describing the world in all its different and diverse aspects. When a concept accurately reflects an extralinguistic event or phenomenon by containing the kind of information and the degree of informativeness speakers perceive as necessary or beneficial for communicative purposes, its nameworthiness increases. In their judgements, speakers rely on knowledge about the categorization of events, objects and ideas to decide on usefulness. Although the majority of informants judged *globesity* to be nameworthy on the basis of the specificity and clarity with which it classifies the phenomenon, one speaker said that there is 'no need to coin a specific word specifically linking obesity and global problem'. Speakers exhibit a sensitivity towards the informativeness or specificity with which concepts holistically represent meaning. However, as mentioned above, the linguistic realization of a given concept might still be rejected if it is too opaque or morphophonologically irregular.

*Table 12: Types of utility responses*

| Target lexeme | Responses | Utility type |
|---|---|---|
| ***halfalogue*** | • it happens a lot<br>• recognized/common phenomenon<br>• relevant to everyday life | societal |
| | • no relevance to me<br>• not interesting<br>• interesting<br>• amusing | personal |
| | • informative<br>• describes quite clearly the situation<br>• fairly explanatory of the action<br>• clear, detailed<br>• explains the concept well | holistic |

| | | |
|---|---|---|
| ***bromosexual*** | • I know someone to whom it may usefully be applied<br>• I don't think I care | personal |
| | • specific<br>• description makes sense | holistic |
| ***sodcasting*** | • actual phenomenon<br>• I know it happens<br>• recognizable situation<br>• my students do it all the time<br>• new phenomenon people might want to refer to<br>• useful to have a word for it | societal |
| | • obnoxious<br>• annoying<br>• I can relate to it, identify with it | personal |
| | • clear<br>• conveys, describes meaning well<br>• detailed and succinct<br>• specific | holistic |
| ***Boobgate*** | • this is often seen in the media<br>• I'm normally watching this on television | societal |
| | • irrelevant in my life<br>• not important to me<br>• interesting to see what famous people do in public or private<br>• I'm normally watching this on television | personal |
| | • informative<br>• detailed<br>• not depicting anything | holistic |
| ***detweet***[2] | • never used Twitter<br>• people sign out when they leave the computer anyway<br>• I don't ever log off<br>• I don't know much about Twitter<br>• I am not a member of Twitter | personal |
| | • understand what's being done<br>• action is understood anyway | holistic |
| ***friendsourcing*** | • source of information<br>• it's an everyday thing | societal |
| | • can relate to the meaning<br>• I engage myself in this thing<br>• I don't use the Internet a lot for this | personal |
| | • gives a brief idea of what's going on | holistic |

It is important to note that speakers use these strategies simultaneously. Some subjects, for instance, stated that despite the informativeness or topicality in society of a specific item, they do not feel personally affected by it.

On the basis of these findings it can be assumed that the degree of nameworthiness influences the degree of accommodation that fuels or inhibits conventionalization. On the one hand, the extent to which a speaker perceives the need to have a word at hand to discuss shared or personal experiences determines the readiness to adopt a certain innovation. On the other hand, the cognitive-linguistic functionality or utility also feeds into this process. When the need in society arises to discuss novel events or concepts, the degree to which their meaning and morpho-phonological forms are able to integrate the various components into a clear, classificatory, informative and expressive holistic structure influences speakers' communicative concerns and their potential accommodation behavior.

In the following sections I will discuss two structural-linguistic factors, semantic ambiguity and the presence of collocations, that are assumed to influence the conventionalization process of neologisms. As mentioned in H1 in section 1.2, I assume semantic ambiguity, i.e. the existence of multiple senses for the same neological word-form, to exert a negative influence of the conventionalization process. In contrast, the presence of collocations is hypothesized to influence the conventionalization process positively, reflected in H6 in 1.2. Both factors provide a contrast to the socio-economic, socio-pragmatic and socio-communicative aspects discussed in the previous sections, because they reflect cognitive processes in lexical memory rather than social or socio-cognitive accommodation processes in the community. First, issues relating to semantic ambiguity are discussed in 4.2.5 before introducing the role of collocations in 4.2.6, which is then explained in more detail in chapter 5.

### 4.2.5. Semantic ambiguity

Semantic ambiguity is used here as a cover term for the association of one novel word-form with multiple related and/or unrelated senses[207], i.e. polysemy and homonymy. The motivation to assume an inhibiting effect is derived from comprehension difficulties on the part of the recipients, especially with regard to homonyms. As mentioned in 2.1.2, semantic ambiguity is typically reduced in the course of diffusion as part of the lexicalization process. Both production and

207 Naturally, semantic neologisms (cf. 2.1.1) are also instances of semantic ambiguity. However, since at the time of writing the NeoCrawler was not able (yet) to detect and monitor such cases, they were excluded altogether.

comprehension benefit from semantic unambiguity in neologisms. The writer or speaker increases the successful interpretation of his or her communicative intent by the reader or hearer, who in turn requires less cognitive effort during the comprehension process. However, psycholinguistic studies that have investigated the influence of semantic ambiguity in lexical decision and naming tasks, i.e. in controlled settings in isolation, have observed a facilitatory effect[208] (cf. Kawamoto et al. 1994; Hino and Lupker 1996; Pexman and Lupker 1999). According to Hino and Lupker (cf. 1996), who did not distinguish between polysemy and homonymy, the processing advantage arises from multiple representations in lexical memory that enhance the semantic feedback to the orthographic forms serving as cues in the experimental tasks. All available meanings are rapidly activated before a selection process, possibly constrained by the specificity of the context[209], the lexeme frequency[210] and frequency of the individual meanings, elicits the appropriate meaning (cf. Seidenberg et al. 1982; Duffy et al. 1988; Piercey and Joordens 2000; Klepousniotou and Baum 2005). Studies that do distinguish between homonymy and polysemy have confirmed the processing advantage of polysemous words, but discovered an inhibitory effect of homonyms (cf. Pexman and Lupker 1999; Rodd et al. 2002). Since homophones activate distinct orthographic forms, discrimination occurs earlier than for polysemous words, which slows down processing (cf. Pexman and Lupker 1999). However, these claims result from lexical decision and naming tasks, in which the subjects are presented with isolated words. In text comprehension tasks, which are more similar to encountering words in everyday life, ambiguous lexemes yielded a processing disadvantage (cf. Rayner and Duffy 1986). Moreover, in contrast to the targets employed in the psycholinguistic experiments, the different senses in the present study are by definition novel and not or not firmly stored in lexical memory. It remains unclear to what extent a processing advantage or disadvantage might arise when no representations are available, or only weakly present.

In the present model semantic ambiguity[211] exerts an inhibiting influence of effect estimate factor 0.87, which is not statistically significant (p= 0.717754). In spite of its non-significance in isolation, the negative effect of semantic ambiguity supports the claims by Rayner and Duffy (1986) regarding the processing disadvantage of semantically ambiguous lexemes in text comprehension. Further

---

208 A detailed discussion of such studies can be found in Hino et al. (2002).

209 On the effect of context see Dixon and Twilley (1999).

210 See Lichacz et al. (1999).

211 An additional sense was postulated if it occurred in more than five individual occurrences.

evidence of the negative effect is provided by a significant interaction between semantic ambiguity and professional coiner status, which yields an inhibiting effect of factor 0.11, represented in Figure 36. Thus, the fueling effect of professional coiner status[212] in isolation is overridden when the neologism is semantically ambiguous. Again, this result should be treated with caution due to the low number of observations. Furthermore, it should be noted that no distinction is made between polysemy and homonymy in the present sample, since such decisions are necessarily based on diachronic evidence which is insufficiently available, if one wants to avoid the fuzzy discussion regarding the definition of polysemy, vagueness and related concepts in cognitive approaches (see Taylor 2003; Tuggy 1993, 2006; Tyler and Evans 2001; Evans and Green 2006 for an overview of the problematic status of polysemy).

*Fig. 36: Effect plot for coiner status x semantic ambiguity*

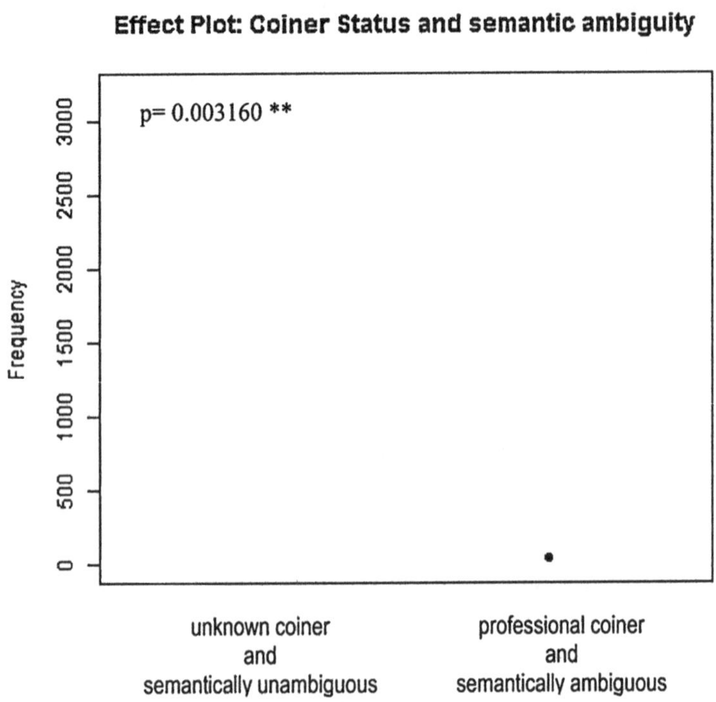


212 No observations in the sample exist for the potential interaction between celebrity coiner status and semantic ambiguity.

A remarkable case of semantic ambiguity in the sample is represented by *detweet*, which I will now discuss in detail. The lexeme *detweet* exhibits a broad range of different senses, which have arisen from different senses of the *de-* prefix[213] and the base *tweet*. As Table 13 shows, five senses, found to be occurring with varying degrees of frequency, have been attested in the data from the NeoCrawler.

*Table 13: Overview of lexical units of* detweet

| Lexical unit | Overall frequency | Meaning | First attestation |
|---|---|---|---|
| *detweet*[1] | 47 | to delete a tweet (after posting) | May 2008 |
| *detweet*[2] | 41 | to sign off from Twitter | September 2009 |
| *detweet*[3] | 19 | to unfollow (another Twitter user) | March 2009 |
| *detweet*[4] | 20 | to pass along a tweet with disapproval | February 2009 |
| *detweet*[5] (mainly passive) | 7 | a tweet or user account being removed by the Twitter authorities | March 2009 |

The most frequently found sense, resulting from the ablative use of *de-*, is illustrated in (58). It represents the first attestation from May 2008, retrieved from a music portal. In this sense, *detweet*[1] can be paraphrased as 'to remove a tweet'. It is apparent from (59) that the intended sense in this example is not to delete a tweet, but to sign off from Twitter. Hence, *de-* is used as a negation of *to tweet*.

(12) Can you delete your twitters? yup, login to twitter.com, then select the trashcan by the tweet you want *detweeted*. (my 1000th answer!!!)[214].

(13) I can't be on here longer than 10 mins…I start neglecting the ANIMATE loved 1's in my life while Tweeting, ReTweeting… need to *DeTweet*. (August 2009, microblogging Twitter)[215]

A third attested meaning also uses the negative *de-* prefix, but with a different meaning of the base. *Tweet* in this sense does not refer to 'a post' or 'to post something on Twitter', but to 'to follow the posts of another Twitter user'. Thus, in example (60), the writer explains the reason for removing someone from his

213 It is unclear whether *detweet*[1] and *detweet*[5] are the result of prefixation or of blending with *to delete*. For now, they are treated as prefixations.

214 Due to a technical error, the original URL could not be extracted.

215 twitter.com/#!/BROADWizzAY/status/3133242073.

follower's list. It is important to note that a lexicalized and established lexeme *to unfollow* which is synonymous with this sense exists. This potential sanctioning or blocking effect of established synonyms is discussed below. The fourth meaning is explicitly defined by the coiner, Craig Danuloff, as an antonym of *retweet*, 'to pass along a tweet'. Despite his extensive efforts to promote the use of his coinage, *detweet*[4] is mostly found in metalinguistic comments.

(14) I've only ever *detweeted* one person, and that was because she was making a zillion random posts a day that were pretty much content-free.[216] (December 2009, personal blog)

(15) So I'm going to just *De-Tweet* it in the same way people Re-Tweet stuff. I hope to start a trend. The *DeTweet* Defined: DeTweet (AKA: *De-Tweet* or DT) = Passing along the tweet of another with some degree of disapproval. It can range from strong (that's a lie) to mild (there are exceptions or conditions). (professional business blog, February 2009)[217]

The least frequently found meaning represents a semantic narrowing of *detweet*[1]. In these occurrences, it is not the Twitter user who deletes his or her tweets, but rather the Twitter administrators. Moreover, *detweet*[5] is also used with a part-whole metonymy of *tweet*, which does not refer to the actual post, but to the user who suspends his/her account or whose account is suspended. This meaning became topical in August 2009 when NBA player J.R. Smith decided to leave Twitter after some offense caused by his tweets. Almost at the same time, Twitter suspended the account of a businessman who had been abusing the medium to raise money for one of his dubious activities. These instances are exemplified in (62) and (63).

(16) *Detweeted.* One of my tweets disappeared today. It wasn't a latency issue – sometimes text tweets to Twitter appear several hours later or never appear at all. This tweet was in my stream long enough to receive a reply and to be referenced in another tweet before it went missing. I didn't delete it, and I've never experienced or heard chatter about spontaneously combusting tweets before, which led me to wonder if Twitter administrators deleted it because they considered it offensive. (general personal blog, March 2009)[218]

(17) In the End, Rawman Was *Detweeted.* 7 days after the first negative Tweet, Rawman left a flurry of quotes from Mother Teresa & Gandhi and then, presumably, deleted his page. His thousands of tweets disappeared instantly. Rawman was *detweeted.* (general portal, August 2009)[219]

---

216 slave2tehtink.livejournal.com/.

217 clickequations.com/blog/2009/02/introducing-the-detweet/.

218 suttonhoo.blogspot.de/2009/03/detweeted.html.

219 everyjoe.com/articles/franchise-founder-loses-twitter-food-fight/.

Although the senses of *detweet*$^{1}$ and *detweet*$^{5}$ are semantically connected, no firm evidence exists that the semantic specialization of the latter is caused by or temporally derived from the former, neither from a diachronic nor from a cognitive perspective. The label of polysemy should therefore be assigned with caution. The relationship of these two meanings to *detweet*$^{2}$ and *detweet*$^{3}$, which are polysemous due to the polysemy of the base, can be assumed to be homonymic as a result of the homonymy of the prefix *de-*. The frequency diffusion of the distinct meanings in Figure 37 shows that, at the time of writing, *detweet* has not become significantly conventionalized. However, the oldest meaning, i.e. *detweet*$^{1}$, seems to win out as the preferred meaning. This development is a very recent one. When working on the paper published as Kerremans et al. (2012), the meanings 'to unfollow' and 'to sign off' prevailed in the available data until April 2010, which led us to conclude that "the latter meaning will become fixed for reasons of language economy, as *unfollow* has already become conventionalized in the meaning in question, which might make a new word-form for the same concept redundant" (Kerremans et al. 2012: 89). This example pointedly shows how rapid diffusion can take a different course.

*Fig. 37: Cumulative frequency development per assigned meaning of* detweet

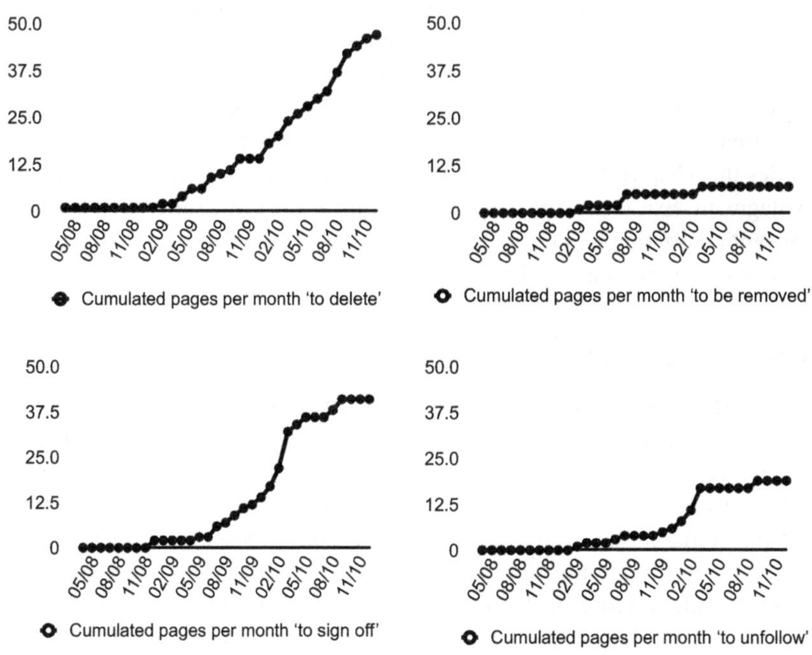

A further lexico-semantic factor tested in the statistical model is synonymy. The claim that established synonyms exhibit a negative influence on the conventionalization process is based on sanctioning (cf. Langacker 1991: 162; Schmid 2007: 121) or "blocking" (Aronoff 1976: 43; cf. Bauer 1983: 87-88; cf. Fischer 1998: 178-179) principles. However, sanctioning has also been attributed a positive effect, because in contrast to blocking, which pertains to the creation or production of new words, sanctioning applies to the establishment process in the minds of speakers and in the speech of the community. Schmid (2007: 121) points out that

> [i]f the way to establishment of novel structures in the repertoire of individual speakers and in the lexicon and grammar of a language [i.e. their conventionalization, dk] is paved by similar structures that are already well entrenched, their entrenchment (i.e., of these novel structures) will be facilitated in turn.

Thus, the coinage of novel linguistic items might be prevented by the existence of established synonyms, but if coined, their conventionalization and entrenchment can be expected to be fostered by this presence.

The synonymy factor does not have a significant effect on the conventionalization process, neither in isolation nor in interaction with other variables. Since inclusion of synonymy did not improve the generalizability and predictability of the regression model, the factor was removed altogether. Hence, neither the blocking constraint nor the facilitation or inhibition through sanctioning can be proven to influence the conventionalization process of neologisms.

A final lexico-semantic factor of influence, the presence of collocations, concludes this chapter. Since the next chapter will discuss the emergence of such syntagmatic lexical networks and their cognitive-linguistic function during the conventionalization process in detail, the next section will be limited to a brief presentation of the statistical results.

### 4.2.6. Syntagmatic lexical networks

Syntagmatic lexical relations are relations of structural co-occurrence. They consist of sequences of lexemes that frequently recur together with different degrees of compositionality, idiomaticity, adjacency and mutual expectancy (cf. Schmid 2003). Within this continuum, collocations occupy an intermediate position between random, loose and flexible combinations of lexemes and structurally and semantically fixed idioms. Thus, speakers can vary the adjective preceding *eggs* to a wider extent than the adjective preceding *moon* in the phrase *once in a blue moon*. However, *eggs* will immediately call up an associative set of specific adjectives like *foul*, *rotten*, *fresh* or even *Easter*, because these combinations are stored together to a certain degree as a result of their frequent co-occurrence (cf. Schmid 2003: 252-253). It is precisely this "balance between the welcome reduction and processing load" (Schmid 2003: 255) and the retention of semantic and structural flexibility that is assumed to promote the conventionalization of neologisms. Not only does the recurrence facilitate individual entrenchment, but more importantly, I assume collocations to serve as crucial cotextual anchoring points aiding comprehension and therefore to have a promoting effect on the conventionalization process, as already mentioned in H6 in 1.2.

The hypothesized promoting effect of collocations is confirmed by the statistical analysis. With an effect estimate factor of 15.35, it is the second strongest fueling factor observed in the present model, as shown in Figure 38.

*Fig. 38: Effect plot for collocations and other syntagmatic lexical patterns*

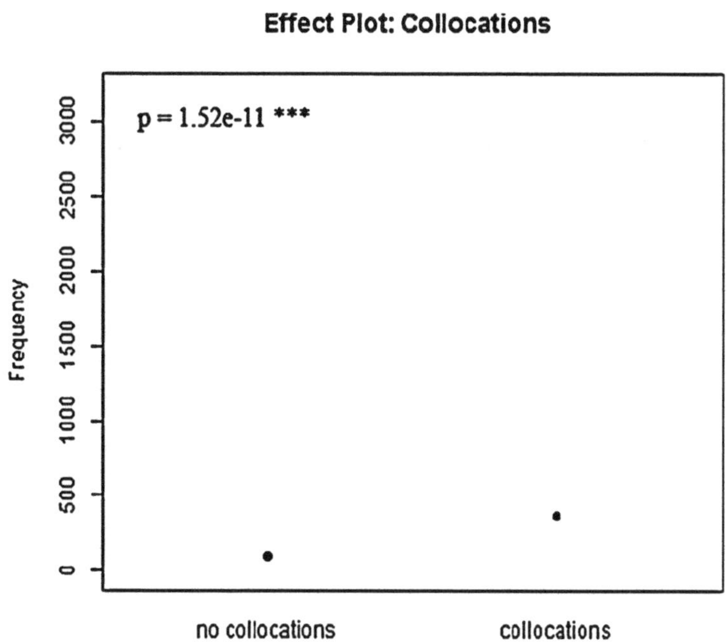


As noted above, my aim was not only to study the potential influence of collocations on the conventionalization process, but also to investigate the nature of their influence and their development during the conventionalization process. This issue is explored in detail in the following chapter.

# 5. Incipient lexical networks in the conventionalization process of English neologisms

As mentioned in the introduction, the aim of the present study is twofold. In addition to empirically investigating several linguistic and extralinguistic aspects that have been assumed in prior studies to influence conventionalization, a second major goal is to investigate the emergence of lexical networks during the conventionalization process. More specifically, the present chapter will describe the development of syntagmatic lexical associates[220], i.e. collocations (sections 5.2.1 and 5.2.2), and other syntagmatic usage patterns (5.2.3 and 5.2.4). Moreover, the promoting effect of collocations[221] during conventionalization presented at the end of the previous chapter will be discussed in detail in (5.3). First, a brief theoretical overview is in order.

## 5.1. Collocations as syntagmatic lexical relations

Even for laymen it is apparent that the assembly of words in sentences is not a random chaining of lexical items combined by means of grammatical rules, but often follows predictable patterns. Thus, when people want to convey that the butter has turned bad, they will use *rancid*, when the eggs have turned bad, however, they will use *rotten*. Indeed, in the OEC *rancid* is a much more frequent collocate for *butter* than *rotten* (T-scores of 6.40 compared to 1.94), whereas *rotten* seems to be the most frequent collocate expressing 'badness' for eggs (T-score

220 Although paradigmatic associates are also considered as important cotextual clues to meaning, they are beyond the scope of the present paper. *Recombobulation area*, for instance, is in almost half of the occurrences in metalinguistic use found together with the antonymic lexeme *discombobulate*; in instances explicitly referring to the introduction of such an area at Milwaukee airport, antonymic associations by means of *discombobulate* are found in almost a third of the cotexts. For preferred grammatical-semantic word-forms that crystallize during conventionalization, see the case of *detweet* in Kerremans et al. (2012: 85-89).

221 Due to brevity concerns, I will use *collocation* as a hyperonym for *collocations*, which involves recurrent co-occurrence of two lexical items, and *collostructions*, as introduced by Stefanowitsch and Gries to refer to the recurrent co-occurrence of lexical items and grammatical constructions (cf. Stefanowitsch and Gries 2003: 209-214).

of 17.15). Accordingly, English possesses different, but semantically related semi-fixed expressions *rancid butter* and *rotten eggs*. Such predictable sequences of adjacent lexemes that frequently and recurrently co-occur are called collocations (cf. Firth 1951/1957; Sinclair 1991; Stubbs 1995; Herbst 1996; Lipka 2002; Schmid 2003)[222].

These multi-word lexical chunks illustrate Sinclair's *idiom principle* (1991: 110), which maintains that speakers possess a substantial number of more or less prefabricated phrases that seem to operate as one slot-like unit, although they are decomposable. The idiom principle explains cases like *rancid butter*, in which the open-choice principle (Sinclair 1991: 109-110) would allow any kind of semantically appropriate adjective to occur as a premodifier for *butter*. It is important to note that unlike the examples used here, collocates do not need to be directly adjacent. As Schmid remarks, "discontinuous collocations" (2003: 242) like *keep_promise* (where the gap can be filled in by *a, my, your* etc.) also abound in language; in corpus queries a preferable window span of four or five words should be used (cf. Stubbs 1995: 29). Evidence from empirical studies by Sinclair (1991: 70ff.) and Stubbs (1995) moreover indicates that the range of collocates for a given node, i.e. the head word under scrutiny in a collocation (cf. Sinclair 1991: 115), consists of semantically compatible lexemes. In his study on collocational patterns of *cause*, Stubbs shows that 80% of the collocates represent negative concepts, 18% neutral concepts and a mere 2% are positive, like *cause him to smile* (cf. 1995: 28). He concludes that *cause* is used in rather pejorative constructions, which is surprisingly enough not listed in the dictionary despite its negative examples (cf. 1995: 27). Collocation nodes thus often attract a set of particular lexical associates loaded with positive or negative associations, so that the collocation at large evokes certain positive or negative associations, also known as semantic prosody. The precise meaning of collocations stretches across a multi-word unit and is frequently non-compositional to the extent that the meaning conveyed is not purely denotational but has acquired connotational features precisely through the collocation in its entirety.

A further defining characteristic of collocations consists of the frequent recurrence of their co-occurrence (cf. Schmid 2003: 238-242). Recurrence is difficult to quantify and several thresholds have been proposed, e.g. "more than once" in a one million corpus (Kjellmer 1982: 26), three attestations in a 25 million

222 See Bartsch (2004) for an overview of the different definitions that have been used in linguistics.

corpus (cf. Clear 1993: 277) or three to five occurrences straight (cf. Stubbs 1995: 40; Evert 2008: 1215, 1244). In the present collocation analysis with the AntConc concordancer, where total size for each of the neologism corpora is unknown, I have taken the standard of three occurrences, similar to the predefined settings in the OEC, except in cases where the neologism node occurred with a frequency of less than 100.

Frequency of recurrent co-occurrence, however, also implies predictability or mutual expectancy (cf. Firth 1951/1957: 195; Hoey 2005; Schmid 2003: 243, 244; Herbst 1996: 389). Native speakers are readily able to complete *rancid* with *butter* or *to commit* with *a crime* or *suicide*, because they have encountered these recurrent combinations repeatedly during exposure to language. Language users cannot only predict which collocates will precede or follow, but will also expect these lexemes to appear. One of the reasons for this kind of expectancy or predictability arises from the associative ties that have been set up in the mental lexicon; this issue will be further explored below. Predictability and expectancy can be quantified objectively with the help of simple association and more advanced statistical measures. Fortunately, in his encompassing overview of such measures Evert remarks that despite some minor inaccuracies, simple association measures are often sufficient to determine the collocativity of word pairs (cf. 2008: 1230-1231). Simple association measures, reflecting the relationship between observed and expected frequency, fall into two categories: those that measure the attraction strength between lexemes, like MI (cf. Church and Hanks 1990: 23) and $MI^3$ (cf. Oakes 1998: 171-172) and those that provide information on the significance of co-occurrence like T-score and log-likelihood[223] (cf. Evert 2008: 1228; McEnery and Hardie 2012: 51)[224]. There does not seem to exist one specific measure that can be universally and uniformly applied to all kinds of purposes, because each of these measures, irrespective of their effect size or significance character, is prone to deficits (cf. Evert 2008: 1236). The effect size measures, for instance, tend to overestimate the attraction strength between word pairs of low frequency and thus become unreliable when such low-frequency data are concerned (cf. Evert 2008: 1226, 1234, 1237-1238). Evert claims that in general the log-likelihood measure provides the most accurate information of all the significance measures; however, it does not distinguish between positive and negative association

223 The log-likelihood measure is described in detail in Dunning (1993).

224 For a detailed discussion and comparison of the available statistical measures see Evert (2008). Briefer surveys can be found in Hunston (2002: 70-75), Baker (2006: 101-103) and Hoffmann et al. (2008: 149-158).

scores (cf. 2008: 1227, 1229). Since the present study is concerned precisely with the positive significance of recurrent co-occurrences of novel lexemes, I have opted for measurement of collocation strength with the T-score, which delivers the most accurate information for low-frequency data (cf. Evert 2008: 1229; Barnbrook 1996: 97).

As a result of the assumed "direct proportionality" (Schmid 2003: 244) between frequency of recurrence and mutual predictability or expectancy, collocations are gradient phenomena (cf. Herbst 1996: 385). At one end of the continuum we find "free combinations" or "accidental, syntactically motivated co-occurrences" (Schmid 2003: 245) that are rare and consequently hardly predictable and therefore cannot be considered collocations at all. At the other extreme, we find lexical or lexico-grammatical combinations that almost always co-occur and possess a maximum of predictability, like *at sixes and sevens* (cf. Schmid 2003: 247). Such examples are better known as idioms, because they constitute non-compositional and syntactically rigid combinations of lexemes. Schmid suggests that true collocations, also located towards the 'fixed' extreme of the continuum, are more transparent than idioms and can thus be clearly separated (cf. 2003: 246-249).

Despite their difference regarding the degree of transparency, idioms and collocations share several functional aspects. Firstly, collocations are used to achieve textual cohesion (cf. Halliday and Hasan 1976: 287). However, Herbst remarks that their view of collocation is a broad one, based on typical lexical association in a similar textual and extralinguistic context rather than mutual expectancy or predictability of lexemes; the likelihood that lexemes such as *path, steep, climb, coast* and *sea* will co-occur in a text on coastal walks is not a language-internal given, but determined by the topic and its extralinguistic realization (cf. 1996: 379, 381). More importantly, evidence from children's language acquisition and language impairments like Wernicke's aphasia indicate that collocations are not mere linguistic strategies to ornament discourse, but represent cognitive principles of lexical storage (cf. Schmid 2003: 251 for examples). Collocations are cognitively profitable for speaker and hearer, because it requires less effort to retrieve entire chunks from memory than to assemble and compute an utterance word by word. Given the predictability of collocates, hearers will need less effort to complete the construction as soon as the first part has been recognized and speed up comprehension (cf. Schmid 2003: 251; Hoey 2005: 7-8). These effects of reduced processing effort and increased automatization do not only affect online language processing, but also long-term storage in lexical memory. Since collocates frequently co-occur, they are also retrieved and activated together; consequently, they are entrenched together.

However, unlike idioms, collocations are only partially entrenched (cf. Schmid 2003: 253), because the majority of them are still to a certain extent compositional and transparent. Full entrenchment yields gestalts, i.e. multi-lexemic, non-compositional units that are processed as a single chunk (cf. Langacker 1987: 59). Consequently, the individual elements are cognitively backgrounded. Intertwined with this decrease of salience, the entire unit becomes enriched with semantic, pragmatic and/or conceptual content not contributed by the parts so that compositionality is reduced or even lost (cf. Langacker 1987: 59; Schmid 2003: 253). As a result, Schmid remarks, such gestalt units tend to undergo semantic specialization, which restricts "their applicability, and hence also their frequency." (2003: 253). In *black coffee* and *strong tea*, although these are conventionalized expressions stored together, the semantic material added by the parts can still be disentangled and exchanged without effort. Collocations are therefore deemed to be partially entrenched, which

> seems to be cognitively advantageous in that it strikes the balance between the welcome reduction of processing load achieved by chunk-like storage and retrieval, on the one hand, and the less welcome narrowing of the range of applicability caused by complete idiomatization. (Schmid 2003: 255)

As mentioned in 1.2, I assume that the presence of collocates will have a positive effect on the diffusion process of the node lexemes which they accompany because of the twofold cognitive potential. Firstly, as mentioned in the quote by Schmid, the complexity of cognitive processing and retrieval is reduced. Secondly, the fact that collocates constitute formal cotextual anchoring points aids the comprehension of novel lexemes and lexical units and reduces any ambiguities in the range of possible interpretations evoked. I will return to the functional issue of cotextual anchoring in detail in section 5.3. In the following sections I will first investigate the emergence of collocational networks during conventionalization and present evidence of their fostering role during this process.

## 5.2. The emergence of syntagmatic lexico-semantic networks

In the following section I will discuss three kinds of syntagmatic lexico-semantic patterns: collocations in the narrowest sense, i.e. recurrent co-occurrences of two directly adjacent lexemes (5.2.1 and 5.2.2), broader, semantic-pragmatic usage patterns, including a case of idioms in 5.2.3 and comprehension-aiding, explicit explanations following the neologism (5.2.4). I will start with evidence from the neologisms *bloglet*[1] and *hyperlocal* that corroborates the abovementioned assumption that collocations slowly arise during the conventionalization process, when the neologism becomes increasingly frequent.

### 5.2.1. Gradual emergence

*Bloglet*[1], like its polysemous sense variant *bloglet*[2] discussed in chapter 4.1.1, is a suffixation consisting of the base *blog* and the diminutive suffix *-let*. It refers to a short blog entry. The first attestation of the lexeme in my sample dates from December 2001, as illustrated in example (64). The actual date of coinage and the coiner are unknown.

> (64) I was thinking. What are all these *bloglets* for? Here's some of the ways it seems like we use it: Communicating with the blogmass (including Cecily's contacting Kerne through it, and other untypical short-term messages; also, formal happy birthdays, Johnny-style discussions on Profound Matters, and direct questions, to specific people or the blogmass at large. I also wonder whether talking on a *bloglet* is different, in important ways, from email or in-the-flesh; because we know there's others listening, but it's our blog, so whatever appears on it is understood to be with respect to ourselves. We can get personal that way, without feeling like wet blankets.) [...]. (personal blog)[225]

A total number of 515 pages were found which included *bloglet*[1] between its first attestation in December 2001 and January 2011. In addition, *bloglet*[1] frequently occurs as a blog name, e.g. *Bloglet, the little friendly blogger*, *Liz's Bloglet* and *Romantic Snacks Bloglet*[226]. No less than 28 different blog names with *bloglet* exist in the sample. Moreover, *bloglet*[1] also features prominently as a category label (46 different instances) on blog pages, redirecting readers to a collection of blog posts that are less lengthy and informative. Since neither these blog names nor uses as a category can be easily assigned a specific date but belong to the blog at large, they were removed from the chronological frequency development, presented in Figure 39. However, these two kinds of usage are clear indicators of advanced conventionalization, since they both rely on the meaning being familiar to the readers in order to make sense. Not surprisingly given its referential range, *bloglet*[1] in objectlinguistic use is predominantly found in the BLOG category of types of source (491 pages) with rare occurrences in discussion fora (13 pages) and a single mention on the microblogging platform Twitter, and in the general field of discourse (505 pages). A mere ten pages contained instances of metalinguistic use. The frequency curve

225 m14m.net/m14m/search?query=metafilter&username=haberdash.

226 See bloglet.burntout.net/, m14m.net/liz/bloglet-archive-2009302122541.php and improve-your-romance.com/romance-blog.html. At a furtive glance, the second bloglet belongs the same Internet domain as the first attestation. It is therefore likely that some of these blog writers were inspired by already existing bloglets when creating a name for their own blog.

in Figure 39 shows a steady increase in frequency until 2010, when the lexeme seems to have reached a state of stagnation in terms of frequency diffusion.

*Fig. 39: New and cumulative pages per year of* bloglet[1]

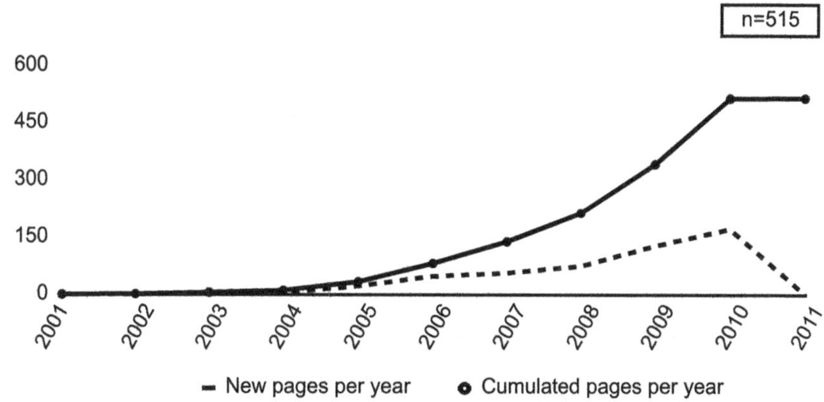


The eleven tokens of the singular form between the first attestation and December 2004 all occurred without a premodifier. Of the 16 tokens in 2005, three were premodified: twice with *humble*, once with *little*[227]. A similar pattern is observed for the period 2006 - 2008. Although only a minority of tokens (13) is preceded by an adjective, this adjective is mainly *humble* (2) or *little* (8). In 2009, a total of 25 premodified tokens replicated the findings for previous occurrences. *Humble* precedes four times, *little* ten times. In the data from 2010 and 2011 the collocation with *little* is strengthened further: of the 19 tokens, *little* premodifies *bloglet*[1] in twelve occurrences. Interestingly, lexico-semantic associates *mini* and *wee* are also observed once each. *Humble* is found in a mere single instance. The plural tokens reveal an identical pattern. The premodified occurrences show a strong tendency to use *little*. Of the 17 tokens found with an adjective, almost half are used with *little*. The collocation *little bloglet/bloglets* is illustrated in examples (65) and (66); an example of *humble bloglet* in (67).

(65) I've also added on my sidebar a *little bloglet* that shows everything tagged in my library as "currently reading". Yes, as you might suspect, these are the books I am currently reading. (October 2005, personal blog)[228]

---

227 Given the low counts of premodified instances of *bloglet*[1], a manual collocation analysis was conducted without statistical measures.

228 listeningtomyself.blogspot.com/2005/10/30-weeks.html.

(66) It has been a comment-tastic week on my *little bloglet* - from help after the sleepover from hell to the heartfelt enough is enough.. And of course we met the new addition to our family in the form of Pixie (who is currently playing to the old lady cat's tail! Trust me, she is as wild as she is cute!) and we rounded off the week with a great product review (July 2010, personal blog)[229]

(67) I think I may have confused or annoyed a number of mega-uber value readers with my post on the arrival of the Memphibian blog. Make no mistake, it is not supplanting this *humble bloglet*, but during the first couple of weeks I had to ensure I had seeded enough content there to give it a life of its own. (October 2009, personal blog)[230]

Summing up the gradual emergence pattern of the collocational network for *bloglet*[1], the adjective *little* is already found in the very first premodified instances of the lexeme, but only becomes a stable and significant collocate during the concomitant conventionalization process of the node neologism, as evidenced by the increase in frequency of occurrence.

A gradual development of collocations or strengthening of preselected lexical companions, or incipient collocates, also arises during the conventionalization process of *hyperlocal*, which will be discussed first. *Hyperlocal*, an adjective prefixation by means of the degree-denoting prefix *hyper-*, refers to the immediate surroundings, mainly applied to instances of news or journalism. The word-form *hyperlocal* is recorded as early as 1969 in mathematical and photography-related documents from the Google Books Corpus, as illustrated in example (68) from the 1971 issue of the *Canadian Journal of Mathematics*:

(68) Note that Theorem 3.3 could have been stated in terms of *hyperlocal*-connectedness, for any admissible metrizable topology r, because of our Theorem 4.4. in the appendix. (Borges 1971: 762)

The current meaning of referring to the immediate surroundings is not attested in the Google Books Corpus before 1990, when a book by Steve Redhead on developing globalization was published, quoted in (69). A similar entry is found in the 1997 book *The skin of culture: investigating the new electronic reality* by Derrick De Kerckhove. Whereas example (69) shows that *hyperlocal* is not specifically used for news coverage, but more general cultural aspects, example (70) already contains a reference to the word's semantic specification.

(69) The context of such *hyper-local* initiatives pitted against and within the global development of the cultural industries is extremely important. (Redhead 1990: 74)[231]

229 mostlyyummymummy.com/2010/07/03/weekly-round-up-2/.

230 eurotelcoblog.blogspot.com/2009/10/that-was-week-that-was.html.

231 The full book title is *The end of the century party: youth and pop towards 2000.*

(70) The demand for *"hyper-local"* news, even in media-dense New York, the nation's No. 1 market, is just too potentially lucrative to ignore. (*The Hollywood Reporter* vol. 320, 1991: 270)

This rather general use of *hyperlocal* is also found in publications by the architect Rem Koolhaas and business documents relating to optimizing marketing on the Internet. Simultaneously, as illustrated in (70), *hyperlocal* acquires a semantic specialization by means of the lexeme *news* during the 1990s. Between 1990 and 1999 the Google Books Corpus yielded 20 hits containing *hyperlocal* in this specific sense, mostly from academic books on digital journalism and popular magazines. Although one source claims the term was coined by *The New York Times* in July 1997 or *The Chicago Tribune* in December 1998[232], the earlier attestations from the Google Books Corpus clearly refute such claims. Therefore, the coiner remains unknown.

As shown in Figure 40, the first attestation in the present sense in the NeoCrawler sample dates from March 2004, when *hyperlocal* is used in a title to announce the introduction of a news aggregator dedicated to local news. Due to the author's mention of *local news* and *my home town*, it becomes apparent that *hyperlocal* is used for news coverage of the immediate neighborhoods, illustrated in (71).

(71) *Hyperlocal* news aggregator. Topix.net is officially launching today. This is a Google News-like aggregator with a twist: the ability to drill down to local sources such as advertiser type freebie papers. It'll generate custom RSS feeds as well. Local news is one of the very few things keeping me a subscriber to dead tree newspapers. I'm going to give the results for my home town a try and will report here on the comparison over time. (professional blog)[233]

Between the first attestation in March 2004 and April 2010[234] the NeoCrawler retrieved 1399 pages from the Internet, shown in Figure 40, supplemented with 118 pages from academic and popular books and journals. In addition, *hyperlocal* is also frequently used as a domain or blog name or in user or website profiles, e.g. *HyperLocal Real Estate, hyperlocal.co.uk – The Home of Hyperlocal* or *HelloMetro.com – Get connected. Get hyperlocal*[235].

---

232 owenyoungman.com/2010/12/02/local-fourth-sees-a-hyperlocal-future-part-i/.

233 due-diligence.typepad.com/blog/2004/03/hyperlocal_news.html.

234 Due to the massive amount of fresh monthly data, manual classification became impossible after April 2010.

235 See hyperlocalrealestate.wordpress.com/, hyperlocal.co.uk and hellometro.com, which functions as a portal for a wide range of hyperlocal communities.

*Fig. 40: Cumulative pages per month of* hyperlocal

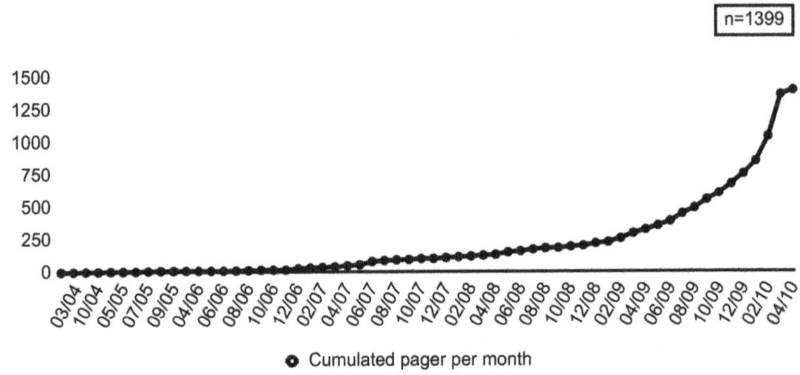


The advanced conventionalization status of *hyperlocal* is not only evidenced in the high frequency of occurrence and the existence of self-referential pages, names, category labels etc. that were not included in the page count, but also in the variety of types of source in which it is found. As Figure 41 shows, *hyperlocal* is predominantly found in blogs, which seem to be the preferred medium for covering news events on a smaller scale because, unlike established print newspapers, they are more cost-effective and often address a smaller audience. Moreover, many bloggers themselves start up hyperlocal blogs in which they report on local events from their community or neighborhood. Such instances of participatory journalism have become popular and often also successful in the digital age, as the example of the *Huffington Post* shows (see 3.3.2).

*Fig. 41: Type of source distribution of* hyperlocal

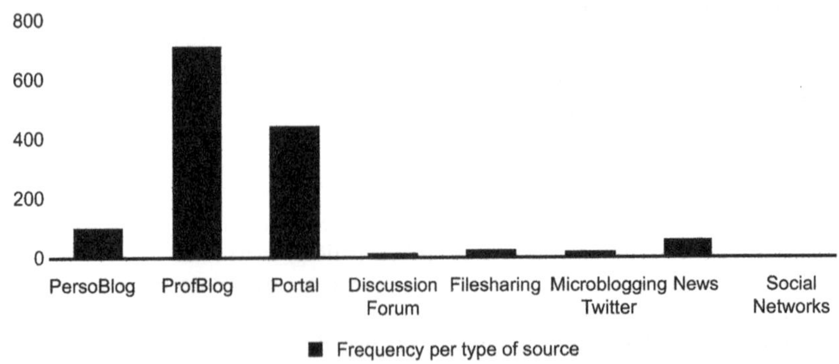

The emergence of *hyperlocal* as a new concept in (digital) journalism is also reflected in its distribution across fields of discourse, illustrated in Figure 42. On the one hand, *hyperlocal* frequently occurs in specialized discourse dedicated to the concept, its development and various realizations in the media business, which is reflected in the LIFESTYLE-MEDIA, SELF-REFERENTIAL and BUSINESS scores. On the other hand, *hyperlocal* is also significantly used in general discourse: approximately 25% of the pages belong to the general domain of non-specialized topics. In sum, frequency, field of discourse and type of source diffusion clearly indicate that *hyperlocal* has progressed considerably towards conventionalization.

*Fig. 42: Field of discourse distribution of* hyperlocal

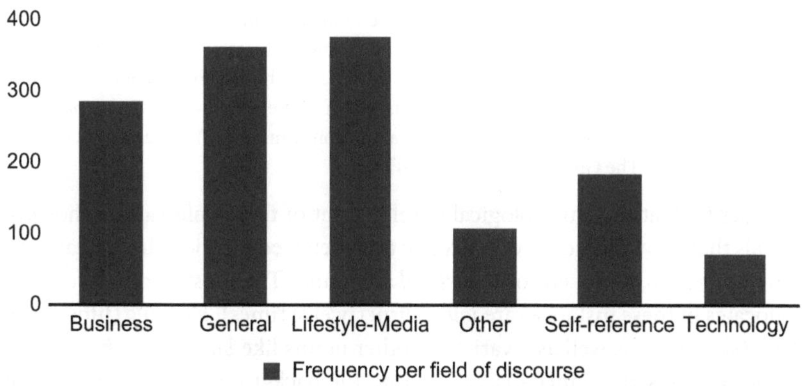


Turning to the emergence of collocational networks for *hyperlocal*, I will start with some examples from the data. In the two attributively used instances of *hyperlocal* in (72), it is once used as a premodifier of *journalism* and once of *sites*. The second occurrence in (73) repeats the combination with *news* found in the first attestation, whereas the first occurrence refers to its presence in the blogosphere. The last example contains two more abstract co-occurrences with *newswire* and *content*. Although the referential range is restricted to the media domain, the examples show that *hyperlocal* occurs with a varied set of head nouns across different types of source and fields of discourse. Save for *newswire* and *blogging*, which is more often found as the morpho-lexical variant *blog*, these nouns represent the five most significant collocates for *hyperlocal*. The collocation analysis for all 10,119 tokens, 9861 forms of *hyperlocal* and 258 of *hyper-local* yielded *news* as the top collocate for the first position to the right

(T-score of 37.28), followed by *sites* (23.98), *blog* (18.05), *journalism* (16.23) and *content* (13.37).

(72) The American Journalism Review reported last year that Gannett and several other large companies were going to embrace *hyperlocal journalism* through a myriad of new sites. Gannett and others believe *hyperlocal sites* can engage more readers and generate more traffic. I agree that *hyperlocal* could bring back fleeing readers and even expand into new territories. (general personal blog, August 2007)[236]

(73) I've been interested in the *hyperlocal blogging* movement since I started blogging. Once you have your own printing press, you start thinking about what you might write about the place you live. And I've written about school sports, little league heroics, contentious local issues, and a host of other *hyperlocal news* over the years. (business page of the *The Faster Times* news portal, December 2009)[237]

(74) New York Times strikes deal with *hyperlocal newswire*. The NYTCo's local content efforts are getting a quick boost from *hyperlocal newswire* Fwix. In a sense, the deal with Fwix can buttress the NYTimes.com's New York metro area blogs program, The Local, which it began last year. The deal enables the distribution of Fwix's technology and *hyperlocal content* across any of NYT's Regional Media Group properties, as well as other properties such as Boston.com and NYTimes.com. (media page from The Guardian, March 2010)[238]

A closer look at the chronological development of these collocations, however, reveals that *news* did not always occupy this preferred position. In the data from 2004 until 2006, 87 tokens of *hyperlocal* are found. The most frequent recurrent collocates in these instances are *journalism* (twelve times), *blogging* (nine times), *news* (six times) as well as a variety of other nouns like *bloggers, web, website or media*, whose significance disappears into the background during the advancing conventionalization process. An overview of the collocational profile development, ranked according to T-score, is given in Table 14[239]. When *hyperlocal* gains widespread currency, the combinatory frequency with *news* increases and strengthens this particular collocation: after rankings of places 2 and 3 in 2007 and 2008, it moved to the first place from 2009 onwards. Moreover, the collocational strength of *hyperlocal news* becomes apparent from the T-scores, which are almost twice as high for *news* as for the other collocates. As the data from

---

236 patthorntonfiles.com/blog/2007/08/01/how-not-to-do-hyperlocal/.

237 the fastertimes.com/venturecapital/2009/12/08/cnn-and-outsidein-hyperlocal-goes-mainstream/.

238 guardian.co.uk/media/pda/2010/mar/18/new-york-times-hyperlocal.

239 Lexemes with a T-score of less than 2 are deemed not significant and are not shown (cf. Barnbrook 1996: 98).

2007 and 2008 show, the differences in significance between the highest-ranked co-occurring lexemes are negligible.

*Table 14: Overview of collocates for* hyperlocal *between 2007 and 2010*

| Year | Total amount of tokens | Collocates on 1R | T-score |
|---|---|---|---|
| **2007** | 684 | *sites*<br>*news*<br>*journalism*<br>*web* | 5.76<br>4.85<br>4.33<br>2.63 |
| **2008** | 776 | *blogging*<br>*blogs*<br>*news*<br>*blog*<br>*blogger*<br>*journalism*<br>*sites*<br>*bloggers* | 5.63<br>5.33<br>4.96<br>4.74<br>4.11<br>3.88<br>3.58<br>2.72 |
| **2009** | 4240 | *news*<br>*sites*<br>*journalism*<br>*site*<br>*blogs*<br>*blogging*<br>*content*<br>*blog*<br>*media*<br>*web*<br>*websites*<br>*bloggers*<br>*lawyers*<br>*website* | 28.52<br>16.80<br>10.58<br>9.48<br>9.00<br>8.81<br>8.52<br>8.30<br>7.40<br>6.66<br>6.43<br>6.16<br>5.80<br>4.88 |
| **2010** | 4378 | *news*<br>*blog*<br>*sites*<br>*blogs*<br>*site*<br>*blogger*<br>*journalism*<br>*blogging*<br>*websites*<br>*content*<br>*website*<br>*web* | 27.41<br>14.32<br>14.26<br>9.80<br>11.33<br>8.05<br>7.64<br>7.25<br>6.73<br>6.36<br>7.95<br>5.49 |

*Hyperlocal* moreover establishes collocational networks of variable strength in different types of source. Both in the BLOG and NEWS category *news* and *sites* are the most frequent collocates. However, the remainder of the collocate list differs in its make-up and order of significance. In the BLOG category, the almost type-of-source-inherent collocates *blog(s), blogger(s)* and *blogging* occur more frequently as head nouns and consequently constitute stronger, more significant networks than in the NEWS category. *Blog(s)*, for instance, is found in 442 out of 6189 instances, amounting to 7% in the former category, whereas this percentage decreases by half in the latter category. Therefore, *blog(s)* appears as the third strongest collocate for occurrences of *hyperlocal* in blogs, but in the news sources it is ranked from place nine downwards. Since collocations serve as linguistic means of achieving coherence and facilitating comprehension, such socio-pragmatic differences in collocational strength and collocate-selection in different types of source are not surprising (cf. Schmid 2003: 252).

The most significant collocates for *bloglet*[1] and *hyperlocal* arise from a set of preselected lexical companions that these neologisms co-occur with during the initial stages of conventionalization. When the novel lexemes become more frequent, the syntagmatic set of lexical items might be expanded, as shown in Table 14, but simultaneously specific combinations gain significance and recur more frequently than others until firm collocational patterns are established. Thus, frequency of occurrence of the neologism seems a prerequisite for the formation of collocations during the conventionalization process. This does not entail that high-frequency neologisms will automatically construct strong collocations; they simply stand a better chance because the frequency requirement has been fulfilled. Although space does not permit me to provide a detailed presentation of the potential emergence of lexical networks for the lower-frequency neologisms in the study, the majority of them do not develop or have not yet developed any significant syntagmatic lexical networks. Examples of this kind are *mesofact* (total frequency of 80), *ganky* (total frequency of 92), *preghead* (total frequency of 14) and *iPad friendly* (total frequency of 146). One notable exception, *bloglet*[2], was presented in 4.1.1. However, when the frequency requirement has been met, collocates might also be present during the initial stages of conventionalization. This phenomenon, which I have named *instantaneous emergence*, is discussed in the following section.

### 5.2.2. Instantaneous emergence

In March 2007, a young woman posted the following passage on her personal blog:

(75) Also on my way home while driving and speeding, i was texting(i know shame shame) but i was texting jdubb;) and then when i get home there was a thing on

the news called "*driving while intexticated*" talking about driving and texting. Long story short, i'm never texting and driving EVER again. It scared the hell out of me. the news talked about a little boy that got hit on his bicycle because someone was texting, and ill be damned if i hit anybody let alone, a little kid all because i was texting. (general personal blog)[240]

The blog writer, who had just been engaged in an activity she only later heard being described as *driving while intexticated* on the news, reiterates the exact phrase as previously heard, although she herself expressed the concept linguistically differently as *while driving, i was texting, texting and driving* or *driving and texting*. The mental and linguistic copy-pasting of the established construction *driving while intoxicated* seems the cause for the phrase *driving while intexticated* rather than only *intexticated*[241], a blend of *intoxicated* and *texting*, in isolation to diffuse, although the first attestation in the sample, a metalinguistic explanation from January 2007, uses the latter. Since the blog mentions a news broadcast, it is likely that the term had been in use prior to the NeoCrawler's first retrieved hit. In July 2007, the concept and/or the matching phrase features in several newspaper articles. One such article from the *Fall River Herald News*[242] is commented upon in a blog entry given in (76). TV broadcasts too dedicate time to the topic, as referred to in the personal blog entry in example (77). The mental and linguistic copy-pasting addressed above is explicitly explained in example (76) and will be discussed in detail in section 5.3.

(76) There's a new phrase in the English language. You're familiar wit [sic] "driving while intoxicated". Well, here comes "*driving while intexticated*" as seen in the Fall River Herald News today. (general personal blog)[243]

(77) This new type of "*DWI*" is claiming lives across the country. Here is a story [from Associated Press] about a fatal crash in New York that may have been a result of this new phenomenon – young people trying to read and answer text messages as they drive. Here is a story a Minneapolis TV station did on this subject. If you are

240 jennadbaby.livejournal.com/2007/03/15.

241 It should be noted that another sense of *intexticated*, i.e. 'sending text messages while being drunk', is observed in the sample, but is altogether rare and only found on a mere five pages.

242 "Driving while intexticated: Teens have gotten so used to text messaging, they're doing it behind the wheel." (July 16, 2007, heraldnews.com/archive/x1769860913). A follow-up article was published two days later, heraldnews.com/archive/x2144990533.

243 moeissuesoftheday.blogspot.com/2007/07/bullish-day.html.

the parent of a text-messaging teen (or if are one yourself [sic]), you should address this TODAY. (general personal blog)[244]

Blog entries of this kind increase the exposure of the audience to novel concepts and lexemes and promote conventionalization.

The remarkable topicality peak in November 2009 in Figure 43 on the next page, which represents the chronological frequency development of *intexticated*, is caused by the lexeme becoming one of the Oxford New American English Word of the Year 2009 finalists. As a consequence, a sudden increase in metalinguistic usage is observed. The majority of retrieved pages for November 2009 contain instances of definitions, paraphrases of *intexticated* and comments on its inclusion on the Word of the Year list, as illustrated in (78). In October 2010 *The Daily Telegraph* published an article on a collection of new words recently included in the Collins Dictionary, including *intexticated*[245].

(78) Which leads us neatly to the American Oxford Dictionary's Word of the Year shortlist, which, in an example of terrifying cultural serendipity, this year contains the word '*intexticated*': the condition of being distracted by texting while driving. Sadly it was pipped at the post by 'unfriend' - possibly more useful but not quite as clever. (professional lifestyle blog)

Although the metalinguistic discourse certainly increases familiarity among the members of the speech community, further conventionalization does not seem to benefit from this hype, since the frequency does rise, but rather tentatively and not to the expected degree. This semi-arrested conventionalization might also be caused by the existence of a semantic competitor, *texting while driving*. Unfortunately, quantitative data from the NeoCrawler for this competitor was not available at the time of writing, so that this claim needs to be investigated further[246].

244 sfosterstar.blogspot.com/2007_07_01_archive.html.

245 "Dictionary hung up on economic downturn", October 28, 2010, see dailytelegraph.com.au/news/world/dictionary-hung-up-on-economic-downturn/story-e6frev00-1225944541079.

246 Two anecdotal remarks seem to confirm these assumptions. When I presented a part of this research at the ISLE conference in Boston, native speakers from the audience told me they had not encountered *intexticated* before, but were familiar with *texting and driving*. During the same trip I picked up some teen magazines for my niece at the airport. One of the headlines read "Selena Gomez [a famous teen idol, DK] says no to *texting and driving*".

*Fig. 43: New and cumulative pages per month of* intexticated

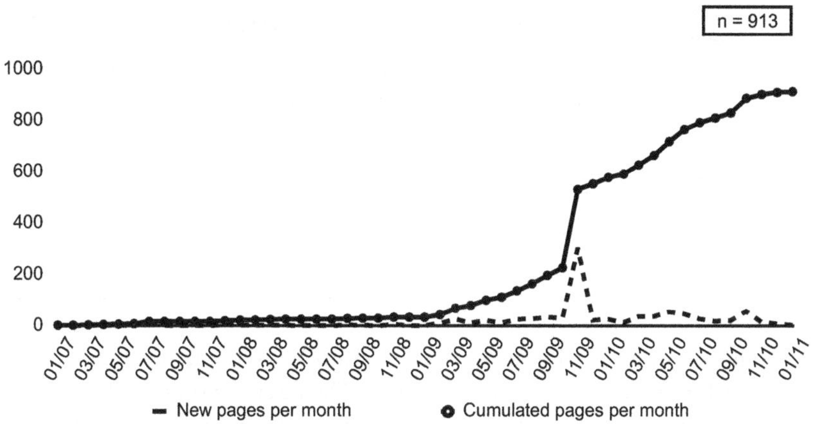


The main point here is that unlike the cases mentioned in the previous section, *intexticated* is preceded by *driving while* for over half (59%) of the 34 object-linguistic tokens during 2007 and 2008, while no other significant collocates were observed. In metalinguistic use, the phrase occurs in only twelve of the 479 token instances. The collocational ties to *driving while* are thus the result of objectlinguistic use in widespread texts like newspaper articles and broadcasts. As Table 15 shows, this pattern is gradually loosened during the following years. In 2009 the phrase occurs 121 times, accounting for 38% of the tokens. In 2010, this percentage is reduced to 27%. Concomitantly, the phrase is syntactically and lexically modified to the extent that other verb forms are found, e.g. *drive while intexticated*, and the *while* is elided, yielding *driving* and *drive intexticated*.

*Table 15: Collocational profile for* intexticated

| Year | Amount of tokens | Collocates 1L | T-score (raw F) | Collocates 2L | T-score (raw F) | Collocates 1R | T-score |
|---|---|---|---|---|---|---|---|
| **2007** | 18 | *while* | 3.02 (10) | *driving* | 3.05 (10) | – | – |
| **2008** | 16 | *while* | 3.02 (10) | *driving*<br>*drive* | 2.78 (8)<br>1.70 (3) | – | – |
| **2009** | 313 | *while*<br>*driving* | 12.00 (145)<br>4.16 (18) | *while*<br>*driving*<br>*drive* | 12.21 (150)<br>11.84 (141)<br>4.45 (20) | *driver*<br>*driving* | 5.09<br>3.78 |

| Year | Amount of tokens | Collocates 1L | T-score (raw F) | Collocates 2L | T-score (raw F) | Collocates 1R | T-score |
|---|---|---|---|---|---|---|---|
| **2010** | 313 | *while*<br>*drive*<br>*driving* | 10.25 (106)<br>4.45 (20)<br>4.28 (19) | *while*<br>*driving*<br>*drive* | 10.54 (112)<br>10.31 (107)<br>5.73 (33) | *driving*<br>*drivers* | 3.51<br>3.45 |
| **ALL** | 650 | *while*<br>*driving*<br>*drive* | 16.64 (278)<br>6.19 (39)<br>5.18 (27) | *while*<br>*driving*<br>*drive* | 17.00 (290)<br>16.53 (274)<br>7.93 (63) | *driver*<br>*driving*<br>*drivers* | 5.37<br>5.22<br>4.23 |

In addition, *intexticated* is starting to be used attributively and function as a pre-modifier for *driving* and its lexical variants. The lexeme has gradually emancipated itself from its initially strong cotextual ties and acquired morpho-syntactic and lexical flexibility to the extent that *intexticated* is now imbued with additional semantic features, i.e. [+ DRIVING]. As a result, *intexticated* has become lexicalized and is used with the *driving* component incorporated into its form without formal cotextual realization.

A further case of instantaneous emergence of collocational networks in the data is presented by the phrase *tube-free toiletpaper*. As mentioned in 2.1.2, in October 2010 Kimberly-Clark released tube-free toiletpaper, i.e. toilet paper that is not wrapped around a tube, as part of their Scott household necessities line. No instances of *tube-free* in other contexts had been retrieved by the NeoCrawler prior to October 2010. Similarly to the case of *intexticated*, linguistic and mental copy-pasting from the earliest occurrences in different types of source, as illustrated by the examples (79) to (81), has caused the entire phrase to gain currency, frequently in connection with a mention of the manufacturer as shown in the following examples:

(79) Who says progress is dead? Kimberly-Clark, the paper giant, has introduced a *tube-free* roll of toilet paper, hailed as the biggest advance in toilet paper in a century. The new *Scott Naturals Tube-Free toilet paper* is being tested at Wal-Mart and Sam's Club outlets in the Northeast. (business section of the *LA Times* newspaper)[247]

247 From the article "Consumer Confidential: Shorter commercials, sweeter toy rewards, tube-free toilet paper", October 27, 2010, latimesblogs.latimes.com/money_co/2010/10/consumer-confidential-media-commercials-tv-toys-rewards-kimberly-clark-toilet-paper-tubes.html.

(80) "Roll with it: Scott's *tube-free toilet paper*". [...]. But what about *tube-less toilet paper rolls*? Impossible you say? Watch out, George Costanza, because soon shoppers will be able to purchase just that: *toilet paper rolls sans cardboard tubes.* USA Today is reporting that on Monday at Walmart and Sam's Club stores across the Northeast, Kimberly-Clark will introduce *tube-free loo rolls* through the Scott Naturals brand. I first blogged about Scott Naturals back in August 2009 when Kimberly-Clark launched the recycled content brand, giving the company's sullied environmental reputation a boost. Well, it seems that K-C is on an, ahem, eco-roll with news of *Scott Naturals Tube-Free toilet paper.* The "*tube-less* technology" behind the toilet paper is, not surprisingly, hush-hush. (lifestyle discussion forum, October 2010)[248]

(81) Kimberly-Clark rolls out *tube-free toilet paper*: http://goo.gl/53zj9 [link to USA Today article, DK[249]]. What will my kids use for a toy telescope now??? (microblogging Twitter, November 2010)[250]

Example (79), from an established newspaper, contains the phrase *Scott Naturals Tube-Free toilet paper*, indicating that the unit functions as a brand name for the new product. Example (80) shows more linguistic variation. Although it was posted on a discussion forum dedicated to music lyrics, the passage is an exact copy of an article by Matt Hickman, originally published on the *Mother Nature Network* portal[251]. A couple of days later, *Forbes* also featured the article[252], thus increasing exposure and triggering further diffusion. Hickman not only reiterated the brand name phrase created by Kimberly-Clark marketing strategists, but varied it with *tube-less* and *loo rolls* in order to meet stylistic demands and provide cotextual clues to facilitate comprehension. Lastly, example (81), illustrating the Twitter potential for diffusing novel ideas and words on a large scale with a single mouse-click, copies the exact title of the *USA Today* article, in which the established *tube-free toilet paper* is used.

Figure 44 presents the chronological frequency development of *tube-free* since its first attestation in October 2010 as found by the NeoCrawler's Discoverer module. After an initial diffusion initiated by Kimberly-Clark's launch of the product, *tube-free toilet paper* was discussed in several newspapers and portals, which often simply reprinted the newspaper article or slightly adapted it. Since the product was not received with great acclaim, the amount of new pages

248 illestlyrics.com/board/contest-interesting-story-vt19018.html

249 "Kimberly-Clark rolls out tube-free Scott toilet paper", October 27, 2010 content.usatoday.com/communities/greenhouse/post/2010/10/kimberly-clark-tube-free-toilet-paper/1#.T084khzN7i9.

250 indoorairnerd.com/category/twitter-updates/page/2.

251 mnn.com/your-home/at-home/blogs/roll-with-it-scotts-tube-free-toilet-paper.

252 forbes.com/2010/11/01/toilet-paper-environment-technology-scott.html.

containing instances of the neologisms gradually decreased: in October 2010, 125 new pages were retrieved, in November 2010 this number dropped to 33.

*Fig. 44: New and cumulative pages per month of* tube-free

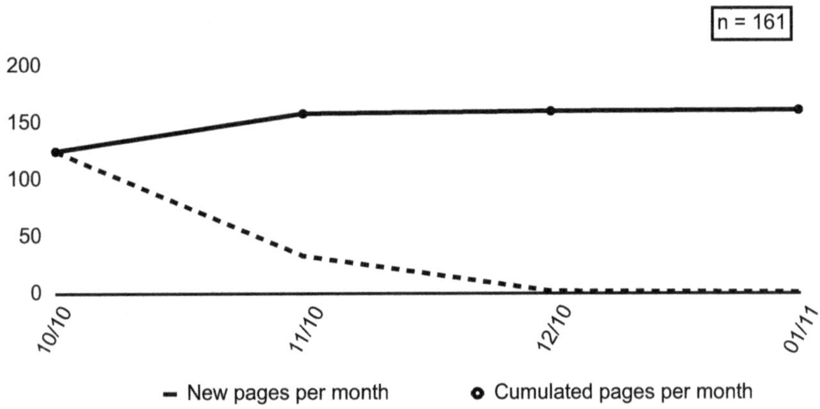


Although significant cross-over into different types of source has taken place in this short period, the evidence from the overall frequency does not indicate advanced conventionalization. Rather, the number reflects a typical topicality pattern. An investigation of the linguistic cotext provides additional support. In almost half of the 488 tokens of *tube-free*, *Scott Naturals* or *Scott* precedes as contextual anchors that tie the neologism to an explicit event, in this case the brand. Thus, decontextualization has not taken place: *tube-free toilet paper* might have become hypostatized as a distinct mental category, but mostly in connection with the specific manufacturer or brand that created the product, which is frequently explicitly present in the cotext. As shown in the overview of its post-positioned collocates in Table 16, the only noteworthy collocates are *toilet paper* and *bath tissue*.

*Table 16: Collocational profile for* tube-free

| Word-form | Token amount | Collocates *1R* | T-score (raw F) | Collocates 2R | T-score (raw F) |
|---|---|---|---|---|---|
| ***tube-free*** | 488 | *toilet*<br>*bath* | 17.83 (323)<br>6.66 (45) | *paper*<br>*tissue* | 17.18 (301)<br>6.86 (48) |
| ***tube free*** | 90 | *toilet*<br>*bath* | 7.82 (66)<br>3.23 (11) | *paper*<br>*tissue* | 7.71 (65)<br>3.01 (10) |

A detailed collocation analysis of the individual months resembles the pattern of *intexticated* with regard to the weakening of the collocational cluster. Whereas in October 2010 70% of the tokens with a postmodifier were followed by *toilet (paper)*, this figure sank to 53% for the data from November 2010. However, *bath tissue* did not emerge during this cotextual emancipation, but was present, to a less significant degree, from the beginning. The example of *tube-free toilet paper* moreover shows that when such semi-fixed syntagmatic phrases are an intrinsic part of the initial diffusion cotext of the neologism, the frequency prerequisite posited in the previous section can be overridden. In sum, collocational patterns also emerge instantaneously within novel syntagmatic lexical networks, either as the result of pattern-copying from already established semantically, morpho-lexically and/or conceptually related constructions, as in the case of *driving while intexticated/intoxicated/X* or as the result of embedding in a semi-fixed phrase structure as in *tube-free toiletpaper, toilet/bath tissue.*

In addition to collocations, a variety of other syntagmatic lexico-semantic and lexico-pragmatic networks, summarized as *syntagmatic usage patterns* in the following section, can be observed in the data from the present sample. Syntagmatic usage patterns of this kind are found in a wide range from explicit, modifying explanations to semantic preferences in the selection of head nouns accompanying neologism adjectives to lexico-pragmatic usage clues and idioms.

### 5.2.3. Other syntagmatic usage patterns

In view of the fact that neologisms strongly rely on the cotext for their interpretation and comprehension, one of the most evident and frequent types of syntagmatic patterns consists of explicit explanations or definitions that modify the neologism. Although collocations also serve the purpose of clarification (see section 5.3), the type discussed here applies to multi-word phrases that are not necessarily tied as strongly to the neologism as pure collocates. Moreover, during continuing diffusion, these metalinguistic explanations tend to be reduced, because the neologism has acquired a sufficient degree of familiarity to be able to occur without cotextual support. One example of such syntagmas with a metalinguistic function from the sample pertains to *halfalogue.*

*Halfalogue*, a blend of *half* and *dialogue*, was coined by Cornell scientist Lauren Emberson, who co-authored a paper investigating the emerging phenomenon. She found out that people (in)advertedly listening to incomplete telephone conversations were more distracted and had more difficulty concentrating on other tasks than people who had been listening to entire dialogues. The first attestation, given in (82), dates from May 2010, when results of the study were made public:

(82) Ever wonder why overhearing a cellphone conversation is so annoying? American researchers think they have found the answer. Whether it is the office, on a train or in a car, only half of the conversation is overheard, which drains more attention and concentration than when overhearing two people talking, according to scientists at Cornell University. "We have less control to move away our attention from half a conversation (or *halfalogue*) than when listening to a dialogue," said Lauren Emberson, a co-author of the study that will be published in the journal Psychological Science. "Since *halfalogues* really are more distracting and you can't tune them out, this could explain why people are irritated," she said in an interview. (general section of *The Globe and Mail*)[253]

After the original press release and interview by Reuters, several other newspapers and blogs featured the article in the ensuing months. However, the lexeme did not become topical until September 2010, when the research article was published in *Psychological Science*. An example is given in (83).

(83) It's not just you. Other people's phone conversations are annoying, and now there's proof. The results of a study published in this month's Psychological Science journal suggest people get more distracted by overhearing others talking on a phone than by regular conversations. Why? It's all about the "*halfalogue*". That's the term the researchers gave to the half of a dialogue that people hear when someone else is having a conversation on a phone nearby. And it's that *halfalogue* that does your brain in. (technology section of a news portal, September 14, 2010)[254]

Afterwards, the use of *halfalogue* faded out, consistent with the results from transitional conventionalization discussed above. As shown in Figure 45, the frequency only increases marginally until peaking during the topicality period in September and October 2010 before suddenly decreasing again.

253 theglobeandmail.com/news/technology/annoyed-by-cellphones-scientists-explain-why/article1576908/.

254 news.com.au/technology/proof-mobile-phone-conversations-are-annoying/story-e6frfro0-1225922427710#ixzz1nswg3VNg

*Fig. 45: New and cumulative pages per month of* halfalogue

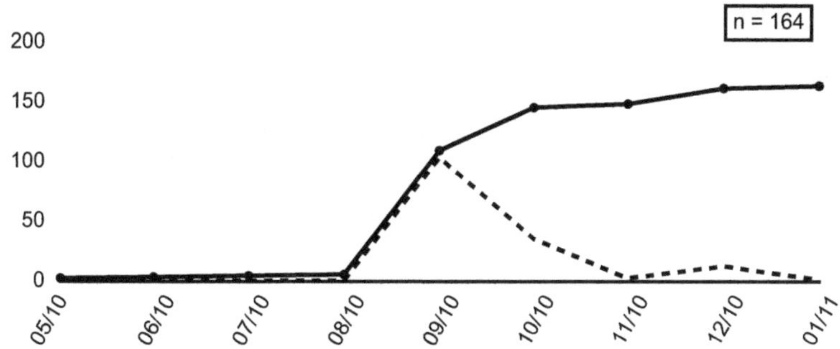


Remarkably, the sample pages retrieved by the NeoCrawler contain only two pages from October 2010 on which *halfalogue* is used objectlinguistically, as illustrated in example (84). The cotext provides semantic clues like *cheap mobile, fellow traveller* or snippets from a woman's talk, but the neologism is not explicitly defined.

(84) A minute to go, the thirty second whistle then peace shattered by tinny rap on a cheap mobile. My new fellow traveller answers it. "I just fucking made it. You'll never guess what he asked me to do for him". Oh, I am pleased. I now have to endure a *halfalogue*. Not only is 'fucking' being used to qualify every adjective. She has bent the rules of the English language to contract it into a noun. (general personal blog)[255]

Of the 271 singular tokens in the *halfalogue* corpus, 267 are used metalinguistically. In addition to the numerous instances in which quotation marks set the lexeme apart as novel, the adjacent cotext contains multiple references to explanatory words like *overheard* (T-score 9.34), *cell* (9.78) *phone* (10.07) and *conversation* (9.99), corroborating the claim that *halfalogue* is predominantly used metalinguistically. The frequent occurrence in explanatory, commentative metalinguistic usage therefore gives rise to the systematic recurrence of a set of paraphrases and glosses, which become part of the syntagmatic lexical network of the neologism.

In some cases, neither significant collocates nor explicit explanations are present as syntagmatic usage patterns, but a tendency to select certain semantically appropriate head nouns from a wider range of semantically possible lexemes arises. The novel adjective *facebook official*, for which the acronym *FBO* also

255 andrewck.co.uk/?m=201010.

exists, is first attested in November 2010 in a cartoon title "It's not official until it's Facebook official"[256], which is given in Figure 46.

*Fig. 46: Cartoon illustrating* facebook official

The cartoon humorously captures the idea that information, an event or change, can only gain significance and truth if it has been posted on Facebook (or other social networks). The author posting the cartoon on *Gizmodo*, a technology portal, describes the new trend as follows:

(85) You can show me all the legal documentation you want. You can line up notary publics out the door. But unless I see it in a news feed item or a profile update, it's invalid. Now if you'll excuse me, I've got to update my status to make it quite clear that I'm pre-qualified for extremely generous mortgage terms.

---

256 gizmodo.com/5688388/its-not-official-until-its-facebook-official. Cartoon originally published on thedoghousediaries.com/comics/uncategorized/2010-11-12-8410034.png.

Since the lexeme was still in its infancy at the time of writing, no firm statements regarding its conventionalization can be made. However, the curve points slightly upwards, which indicates tentative diffusion in terms of overall frequency. From a socio-pragmatic perspective, this trend is confirmed: although the majority of pages are blogs, 31 personal and eight professional ones, the neologism also appears in portals (nine pages) and also, interestingly, in discussion fora, social networks and on Twitter.

*Fig. 47: New and cumulative pages per month of* facebook official

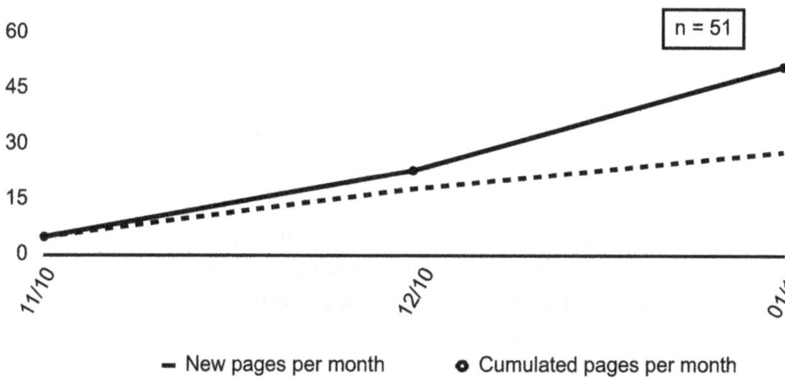


As the following examples show, not every subject matter functions as the referent of *facebook official.* Whereas the cartoon referred to legal matters, most instances of *facebook official* concern private affairs like relationships and pregnancies.

(86) I've been itching to get over here & write this post, but couldn't, because I've been keeping a secret! And, I SUCK at keeping secrets! So, anyway, now everyone knows and I can make it "blog & *Facebook official*"! Yep, you got it, Luke's going to be a big brother! We're *pregnant*! (general personal blog, December 2010)[257]

(87) Everyone thinks we're together. My parents, probably H (he's good at that, you know. He predicted Tuck and KFab before they were '*facebook official*'), Melvin or whatever his name is won't leave us alone about it. (general personal blog, January 2011)[258]

(88) Don't get me wrong, I'd love to get married some day, have kids that whole bit, but I've just never been the type to spend endless nights doing the dinner and a movie

257 teachinauntie.blogspot.com/2010/12/merry-christmas-by-way-im-pregnant.html.
258 lettersillneversend.com/id-need-a-cipher-to-read-you-darling.html.

> thing with a new guy every night. Nor have I ever had a *Facebook official relationship* (Ok once, but that was probably a mistake. So I don't count it.). (general personal blog, December 2010)[259]

Of the 59 tokens of *facebook official*, which is the only word-form in the sample, four are used with reference to babies or pregnancies, as in (86) and 34 with respect to relationships. It is important to note, as illustrated by examples (86) and (87) that the adjective is frequently used predicatively: *it is* or *it's* precedes in 33 instances. Three sources also use *facebook official* in connection with the ex-boyfriend of Sarah Palin's daughter announcing his new relationship on Facebook. This news did not spark a topicality peak, probably because the persons involved are of secondary newsworthiness.

The neologisms sample contains a further type of syntagmatic usage patterns that does not achieve the significance of collocational networks, but provides cotextual usage clues like the semantically specified head nouns addressed above. In the case of *bromosexual*, however, these clues are not semantic, but grammatical-syntactic in nature, yielding what could be called lexico-pragmatic usage constructions. Rather than supporting and/or assisting in transferring the individual semantic meaning of the novel lexeme, such lexico-pragmatic constructions instantiate specific types of usage in context. The example of *bromosexual* will illustrate this. At the time of coinage, *bromosexual*, a blend of *bro(ther)* and *homosexual*, was the latest addition to the *bro* family (with *bromance* being the most popular and *brogrammer* a more recent addition at the time of writing[260]) and first appeared on a discussion forum thread replacing parts of titles and famous people's names with *bro*-derivatives, e.g. *Bromeo and Juliet, David Browie* and *Broget's Thesaurus*[261]. Although the extensive contemporary use of *bro* might seem a rather recent phenomenon, the clipped form of *brother* goes back to 1660, as listed in OED quotation in the *bro* entry. Nevertheless, partially due to popular TV series like *How I Met Your Mother* and films playing with the word and the underlying concept, *bro* coinages have become part and parcel of colloquial English, frequently as the subject of a never-ending stream humorous word plays and satirical comments. The first two attestations that provide a meaning, albeit vaguely, for *bromosexual* are listed in (89) and (90). The former furthermore contains related

259 tuneintol.blogspot.com/2010/12/im-cool-being-single-got-it.html.

260 "A male programmer who eschews the stereotypical nerdy characteristics associated with programming culture." (WordSpy entry, March 2012, wordspy.com)

261 Unfortunately, due to a technical error, the original URL cannot be retrieved.

coinages and illustrates the morpho-semantic playfulness with which members of the speech community develop novel *bro* coinages and concepts. An example of the current meaning 'two males that are close to each other without being homosexual' is found in (91).

(89) Although "bromosapien" may seem like an all-encompassing term, the species is a diverse circle of subsets with, oftentimes, very slight similarities to differentiate the various sterebrotypes. [...]. Genus: The *Bromosexual.* Looks exactly like the Brotype, but would never be caught dead in ripped Joe Boxer underpants. Watches college football as foreplay. (September 2004, general personal blog)[262]

(90) [...] So whenever non-asexual people look at people that are "nice looking, kind, have a sexy attitude" they want to have sex with them? I used to have a crush on this guy but I just wanted to spend time with him and talk to him. [Reply:] This topic makes my stomach queasy, so I'm a *bromosexual.* (September 2006, sports discussion forum)[263]

(91) What's up bromosexual?!! I have the worst effing cold ever, that's why I've yet to be back... It's killin me softly with it's song. haha.New digits, I'll text ya from it. (June 2010, social network MySpace post)[264]

In terms of diffusion, *bromosexual* mostly occurs in informal types of source: 34% of the pages are discussion fora, 22% from social networks and a further 17% from personal blogs. Not until the release of *Pineapple Express*, a movie on bromances, in August 2008 did the lexeme appear in two newspapers and on some portals and only with explicit reference to it. The event caused *bromosexual* to become topical and fueled its further increase in frequency, as shown in Figure 48 on the next page, mostly limited to informal discourse. If the different fields of discourse are considered, *bromosexual* is predominantly found in non-specific, general topics (56%) as well as typically male domains like GAMING (11%) and SPORTS (7%). Although the lexeme seems to be restricted to colloquial English, the high overall frequency indicates that progress towards establishment has taken place, which might still swap over to the speech community at large. Further evidence is found in occurrences from user profiles (18 distinct mentions), user names and even on T-shirt prints that can be purchased.

262 orbitalocularit.livejournal.com.

263 wrongplanet.net/postt17626.html.

264 myspace.com/twintattoos.

*Fig. 48: New and cumulative pages per month of* bromosexual

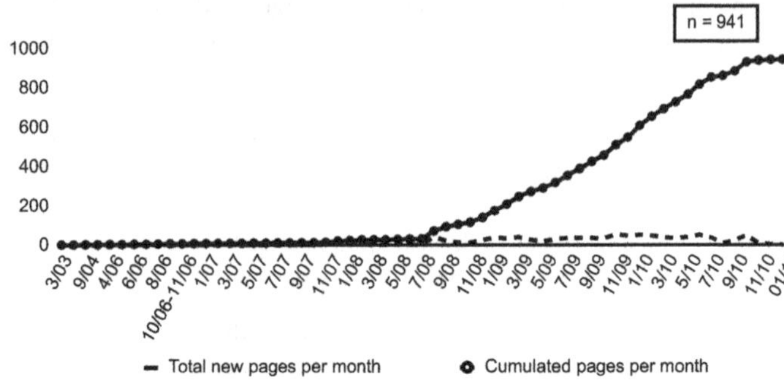


An analysis of the syntagmatic cotext reveals two distinct uses. Firstly, from a pragmatic perspective, *bromosexual* is frequently used as a form of address for other people in real or virtual social interactions. Since such forms of address are found in a variety of linguistic realizations and often involve grammatical collexemes and word order strategies, quantitative evidence does not appear very compelling[265]. Table 17 lists the lexemes directly preceding *bromosexual* in the data from the typically interactive DISCUSSION FORUM and SOCIAL NETWORK types of source.

*Table 17: Lexemes preceding* bromosexual *in the DISCUSSION FORUM and SOCIAL NETWORKS categories*

| Word-Form | Amount of tokens | Collocate 1L | T-score (raw F) |
|---|---|---|---|
| *bromosexual* | 437 | *thanks*<br>*my*<br>*up*<br>*sup*<br>*hey*<br>*you* | 5.32 (15)<br>5.00 (28)<br>3.72 (15)<br>2.23 (5)<br>3.35 (6)<br>2.91 (13) |
| *bromosexuals* | 243 | *my*<br>*you*<br>*up*<br>*sup*<br>*thanks*<br>*hey*<br>*u* | 4.22 (21)<br>2.89 (11)<br>2.71 (8)<br>2.23 (5)<br>2.20 (5)<br>1.65 (3)<br>1.65 (3) |

265 Although a T-score of less than 2 is not significant (cf. above), they are listed here to illustrate the flexibility with which *bromosexual* occurs as a form of address.

| | | | |
|---|---|---|---|
| *bromo-sexual* | 7 | *up*<br>*my*<br>*sup*<br>*care*<br>*you* | 1.38 (2)<br>1.35 (2)<br>0.99 (1)<br>0.99 (1)<br>0.99 (1) |

The linguistic flexibility of such pragmatic patterns of address can be nicely illustrated with the tokens of *bromo-sexual*. Six of the seven occurrences in the sample are listed in (92).

(92) *what up bromo-sexual!* happy birthday, i would have called but my phone got stolen
*yo my bromo-sexual*
*Whats up bromo-sexual?* Ha ha. Just thought I`d stop by and leave a mark
*Take care bromo-sexual* come down soon
*I LOVE YOU BROMO-SEXUAL!!!!!!!!!!!!!*
*sup bromo-sexual?*

More examples from the form of address usage pattern are *you need to chillax* (blend of *chill* and *relax*), *bromosexual, get on you crazy bromosexual, […] is the cooliest, bromosexual, whats up my bromosexual, for all you bromosexuals, totally awesome my bromosexuals, any of u bromosexuals, rest of you bromosexuals, whats goin' on bromosexuals*. In addition, various greetings like *hey* and *yo* are found.

A second syntagmatic pattern that crystallizes in the data is syntactic in nature. A closer look at the occurrences in which *bromosexual* is directly preceded by *my* shows that not all of them are used as greetings. Of the 28 tokens of this kind in the DISCUSSION FORUM and SOCIAL NETWORKS categories in the sample, *my bromosexual* functions as a subject complement in almost half of the occurrences. For the plural forms, the same proportion is found. Two examples are given in (93) and (94).

(93) Showing feelings showing feelings of an almost human nature. Mohawk_ming is my *bromosexual*. (November 2009, gaming discussion forum)[266]

(94) Operation Jacob wrote: SAY JAY AND JACOB ARE MY BROMOSEXUALS. (August 2008, entertainment discussion forum)[267]

266 gamefaqs.com/boards/959185-jak-and-daxter-the-lost-frontier/52140088.
267 snazztastic.com/filmcow/forums/viewtopic.php?p=906489&sid=52870b2dd66e00 8cc98fb41c9eac059b.

Thus, a tendency was found for the neologism to feature in a subject complement construction with morphological forms of the verb paradigm of *to be* (*X was/be/been/wanna be*), in which a male person is designated as the speaker or other conversation participant's *bromosexual*.

Finally, I will discuss one instance of a novel idiom that became rapidly established because it appeared in an episode of the popular *Simpsons* series. The blended noun *frogurt* (or *froghurt*) was coined by a New England-based company in the 1970s as a brand name for frozen yogurt. Despite huge popularity in the '80s, the product was deemed "too tart" and "never really caught on" (Mike Harlington, "Learn more about Fro-Yo", December 2010[268]) until it re-appeared in society and as a consequence, also in language. The first attestation in the data culled from the Internet dates from April 2004, presented in (95). As shown in Figure 49, the frequency did not increase significantly until 2010, when several celebrities including actress Anna Paquin and singer Britney Spears were photographed while enjoying a *frogurt* with their children. An example of *frogurt* used in this context is given in (96). Another extralinguistic event slightly fueling the diffusion took place in November 2010, as can be inferred from the dotted peak in Figure 49 on the next page. In a *Playboy* interview, Conan O'Brien talked about his return to the TV screen and said about his former *Tonight Show*: "So this was good, this was bad, this was ugly, this was beautiful, this was f*cked-up, this was sublime. It was cherry, it was vanilla, it was *frogurt*, it was mocha chocolate chip."[269].

(95) So Giblets goes down to the Pottery Barn and I go after him to try to get him to stop and to maybe get something at the *frogurt* stand which is a couple stores down and Giblets starts by picking up a glass bowl and says "oops" and dropping it. (general personal blog)[270]

(96) Stephen Moyer & Anna Paquin Take His Daughter Out For *Frogurt*. (April 2010, headline on a professional blog dedicated to celebrities)[271]

Despite these extralinguistic events, the overall frequency of 211 pages for *frogurt* indicates only tentative conventionalization in objectlinguistic use, i.e. not related to shop or brand names that were excluded from the sample, or definitions.

---

268 morefreeinformation.com/Art/126032/88/Learn-More-About-Fro-Yo.html.

269 conanchristoperobrien.com.

270 fafblog.blogspot.com/2004/04/lost-weekend-in-pottery-barn-of-soul.html.

271 celebritygossiptalk.com/tag/celeb-sightings/page/262/.

*Fig. 49: New and cumulative pages per year of* frogurt

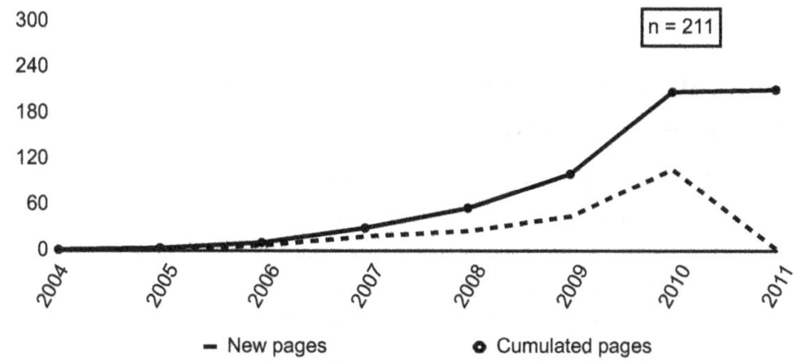


However, the quantitative picture needs to be differentiated further. An additional 84 pages containing *frogurt* were retrieved by the NeoCrawler. These are not included in the diffusion figures, because they do not contain purely objectlinguistic uses, but literal reiterations of a dialogue in which *frogurt* is used from a *Simpsons* episode. In the scene Homer Simpson purchases a cursed Krusty doll for Bart's birthday. The shopkeeper tells Homer that the doll, though cursed, comes with a free frogurt, which is also cursed[272]. Although the "Treehouse of Horror III" episode was first broadcasted in 1992, Internet users regularly quote the *frogurt* dialogue. These instances of direct copy-pasting have given rise to the idiom *the frogurt is cursed* also appearing outside of the *Simpsons* context. Admittedly, a mere five occurrences were found, often as a negative afterthought after a positive message similar to the *Simpsons* use. They nevertheless show that a neologism or novel lexical unit originally strongly linked to a particular meaning and context of usage can become detached and acquire a new, non-literal meaning in a different socio-pragmatic context. Since the common background knowledge presupposes familiarity with the original scene in order to understand the speaker's intentions, the idiom does not stand a very good chance of successfully diffusing in isolation.

Save for the minor case of idioms, all of the types of syntagmatic patterns discussed in this section provide explanations regarding the meaning and usage of neologisms to various degrees. This explanatory function is realized by means of periphrastic syntagmas, semantic preferences for referents and syntactic and pragmatic specifications of usage. In the following section I will discuss the linguistic and cognitive origins of the collocational networks and their explicatory

272 See, for instance, imdb.com/title/tt0758368/quotes.

potential as well as present statistical evidence of their fostering role during conventionalization.

## 5.3. Collocations as cotextual anchoring points during conventionalization

As mentioned above, collocational networks facilitate lexical retrieval because of their expectancy and predictability of co-occurrence. Moreover, they are vital for comprehension on the part of the hearer because they add semantic and pragmatic content to the lexeme. With regard to neologisms, both the cognitive potential of easy activation and the semantic potential of meaning retrieval are of utmost importance. Since the former aspect needs extensive psycholinguistic testing, the remainder of the section will investigate the linguistic origins of collocates for novel lexemes and thus provide an answer to the question of how collocates fulfill their semantic potential and function as cotextual clues during comprehension and promote conventionalization.

The first kind of cotextual support arises from morpho-semantic, semantic or lexical compatibility with the base lexeme. Neologisms inherit morphological, semantic and conceptual information from their base in the form of semi-identical adjacent collocates, which cognitively and linguistically embed the novel lexeme into the existing language structure. On the one hand, on-line comprehension benefits from these overt (morpho-)lexical or (morpho-)semantic anchoring points and simultaneously associative links in long-term memory are activated, which enhance (partial) entrenchment. In 5.2.1 I presented *little* as the most significant collocate for *bloglet*[1]. In terms of morphology, *little* is a periphrastic reiteration of the diminutive suffix. In order to investigate the cotextual, explanatory utility of this reiteration, I analyzed the collocates for a selection of other *-let* derivations and the base *blog* in the OEC, the results of which are shown in Table 18.

*Table 18: Collocates for morpho-lexical associates of* bloglet[1] *in the OEC*

| **Collocation node** | **Collocates** | | |
|---|---|---|---|
| | **little** | **humble** | **short** |
| **a) Morphological associates** | | | |
| *booklet* | 11.54 | – | 3.93 |
| *leaflet* | 4.03 | – | – |
| *piglet* | 4.23 | – | – |
| **b) Morpho-lexical associate** | | | |
| *blog* | 8.33 | 6.00 | - |

From a morphological perspective, *booklet, leaflet* and *piglet* are all used to varying degrees with *little*. Thus, it is not unusual for *-let* derivations to be accompanied by a lexically free morpheme duplicating the meaning. When a novel lexeme is coined on the basis of this schema, it seems to inherit the same morpho-lexically compatible collocate(s). However, the results for *booklet*, which is conceptually the most contiguous, reveal a further interesting pattern. Although the concept of a succinct written passage can also be captured by means of *short*, both *booklet* and *bloglet*[1] prefer *little*; *short* is not even present as a collocate in the NeoCrawler sample of the former. A second inheritance pattern, morpho-semantic in nature, reinforces the morpho-lexical carry-over. The base *blog* in the OEC is preceded both by *little* and *humble*, which is reduplicated in the findings for *bloglet*[1]. As discussed in 5.2.1, especially during the early stages of conventionalization, *humble* frequently co-occurs with *bloglet*[1]. *Little* only gradually gains significance when *bloglet*[1] diffuses. Although *-let* derivations belong to the class of more transparent word-formation processes and accordingly would not need explicit semantic reduplication in order to ensure comprehension, their collocational network is passed on to subsequent novel coinages. Simultaneously, by means of the same collocate, *bloglet*[1] is also lexico-semantically linked to the base lexeme. As a result, *bloglet*[1] becomes embedded in the morpho-lexical network set up by its associates, which significantly aid semantic comprehension.

In the example of *hyperlocal*, the wide range of possible referents is narrowed down with the help of collocates passed down from the morpho-lexical relative *local*. Although the inheritance effect is less compelling than in the case of *bloglet*[1] due to the semantic versatility of the base lexeme, an investigation of the most significant collocates for *local* in the OEC yields many lexemes that belong to the lexical field of media. *Media* itself for instance ranks the highest with a T-score of 62.44, closely followed by *newspaper* (62.40) and *news* (56.05). It is therefore not surprising that a novel coinage in the same lexico-semantic domain selects an already established lexeme and modifies it by prefixation to reflect a new related concept rather than resort to morphologically distinct creations like *neighborhood* or *community news*. It seems that the existing links within morphological, lexical and semantic networks are not only a facilitatory strategy during comprehension, but also constitute a supportive foundation during production.

Morpho-lexically- and lexico-semantically-motivated cotextual anchors are also found in novel blends. In section 5.2.2 I presented evidence that *intexticated* diffused as part of the phrase *driving while intexticated*. An analysis of collocates for *intoxicated*, one of the blended elements, in the OEC yields an identical pattern. In the OEC, *intoxicated* is frequently preceded by *driving while* to the extent that they constitute the most frequent collocates: *while* achieves a T-score of 15.95, *driving* 14.81. In addition, the attributive instances reveal the same lexico-semantic preferences: *driving* (21.60), *driver* (6.45) and *drivers* (5.63) are the three most significant collocates and constitute the same lexical set as found for *intexticated*. Since *intexticated* is more opaque than *bloglet*[1] and *hyperlocal*, these lexico-semantic anchoring points are deemed of particular importance, because they call up an already established pattern, i.e. *driving while*, and substitute the familiar and expected lexeme with a morpho-semantically compatible, but novel one. The hearer or reader is able to benefit from these existing links in the lexicon and disentangle the intended meaning with less effort.

Iterations of existing syntagmatic co-occurrences are also found on the syntactic-pragmatic level. As mentioned in 5.2.3, the blend *bromosexual* is claimed to be used in two characteristic constructions: as a pragmatically-motivated, lexico-syntactically realized form of address in instances like *hey bromosexual* and as a subject complement surfacing through word order. Results from the OEC confirm that *bro*, the clipped form of *brother*, too is frequently used as a form of address. Again, the specific pragmatic patterns are manifold and cannot be easily captured by a mere T-score. Therefore, only the most conspicuous lexical instances are listed in Table 19. Further examples from the OEC include *geez, bro, you know, bro, don't worry bro, get real, bro, no way bro, she'll never fall for it, bro, hey, little bro!* and nicely illustrate the multifarious linguistic realizations.

*Table 19: Collocational profile for* bro *in the OEC*

| **Collocation node** | **Collocates** | | | | |
|---|---|---|---|---|---|
| | *hey* | *you/u* | *thanks* | *shit* | *sorry* |
| *bro* (1874 tokens) | 7.12 | 5.21/2.40 | 4.80 | 3.15 | 2.42 |

One of the most frequent and significant collocates in a technical sense was a preceding comma, accounting for 399 instances. A manual analysis of these instances shows that 394 of them are found as forms of address. Since *bro* is predominantly used in non-standard and informal language (68% in the OEC), in which punctuation is not always a primary concern on the part of the language user, the actual numbers might be even higher, substantiating the claim that *bromosexual* represents a further case of cotextual inheritance.

All of the neologisms discussed so far are characterized by a high degree of semantic similarity to the base lexeme. A *bloglet* is a small blog, *hyperlocal* an intensification of local, *intexticated* an undesirable form of behavior behind the wheel and *bromosexual* an intense relationship not unlike the intimacy between siblings. In two cases of novel collocation formation from the sample, the new meanings are still contiguous with the base, but express a semantic contrast. As a corollary, the established collocates in the lexico-semantic network of the base cannot be readily reduplicated. Semantically, not all of these collocates would be compatible with the neologisms, which reflect certain conceptual differences that will also appear in their syntagmatic lexical choices. As mentioned above, an *encore career* is a second career-like occupation after retirement, dedicated to more socially-oriented, non-profit causes. The compound modifier *encore* does not highlight this semantic specification of the head noun, but captures the temporal aspect, rendering the entire compound less transparent. These conceptual and semantic differences are embedded in the preceding cotext. The results of the collocation analysis for *encore career* in the NeoCrawler sample and *career* in the OEC[273] are presented in Table 20. Only the most frequent collocates are listed; the substantial differences in T-score are due to the differences in frequency in the two corpora and are therefore not entirely comparable.

*Table 20: A comparison of the collocates for* encore career *and* career

**a) Collocates for *encore career* in the NeoCrawler sample**

| | ***encore career* (1633 tokens)** | | ***encore careers* (749 tokens)** | |
|---|---|---|---|---|
| **Collocation span** | **Collocate** | **T-score** | **Collocate** | **T-score** |
| 1L | *emerging*<br>*meaningful*<br>*fulfilling* | 6.84<br>5.44<br>4.22 | *want* | 4.51 |
| 5L | *green* | 5.03 | *boomers*<br>*baby*<br>*want*<br>*boomer* | 7.83<br>5.09<br>4.73<br>3.82 |
| 1R | *opportunities*<br>*starter*<br>*paths*<br>*coach*<br>*initiative* | 8.42<br>5.47<br>4.98<br>4.65<br>3.58 | *campaign*<br>*combining* | 4.09<br>4.23 |

273 It should be noted that *encore career* also occurs five times in the OEC, but predominantly in metalinguistic use. All of them belong to American English, mostly from formal sources in 2008.

| | *encore career* (1633 tokens) | | *encore careers* (749 tokens) | |
|---|---|---|---|---|
| **Collocation span** | **Collocate** | **T-score** | **Collocate** | **T-score** |
| 5R | *opportunities*<br>*retirement*<br>*women*<br>*green* | 8.53<br>6.33<br>5.97<br>5.13 | - | - |

**b) Collocates for *career* in the OEC**

| | *career* (243485 tokens) | | *careers* (33474 tokens) | |
|---|---|---|---|---|
| **Collocation span** | **Collocate** | **T-score** | **Collocate** | **T-score** |
| 1L | *political*<br>*successful*<br>*professional*<br>...<br>*fulfilling*<br>*meaningful* | 67.42<br>44.67<br>43.48<br><br>9.62<br>10.40 | *political*<br>*professional*<br>*successful* | 20.65<br>20.27<br>20.00 |
| 5L | [no mention of *green*] | | [no mention of *boomers* etc.] | - |
| 1R | *starts*<br>*opportunities*<br>*paths*<br>*counseling*<br>*guidance* | 65.64<br>35.49<br>29.76<br>15.10<br>17.74 | [no mention of *campaign* etc.] | - |
| 5R | *opportunities*<br>*retirement*<br>*women* | 39.28<br>10.42<br>7.09 | - | - |

The semantic specialization contributed by *encore* is evident from the collocating lexemes preceding the compound. Firstly, they characterize the entire concept as novel by means of *emerging*. Secondly, in the case of *fulfilling* and *meaningful*, they foreground the conceptual attributes of 'non-profit, charitable'. Traditional careers are most typically, at least on the basis of the collocational profile from the OEC, *political, professional* and *successful*. Nevertheless, *fulfilling* and *meaningful* do appear in the *career* list, but in comparison to the other lexemes, they are of minor significance. Another conceptual difference between *encore career* and *career* is evident in the premodifying lexemes for the plural forms. While the collocates for the latter are identical to those in the singular, the collocates for the former again contain cotextual clues. These encore careers are said to be a phenomenon typical of the baby boomer generation, who are still in good enough health to continue working, but at the same time also more concerned with social causes. Thus, references to *baby boomer* appear in premodifying position in order to anticipate the new concept, which is not entirely transparent with regard to meaning and use. In spite of these collocational differences in premodifying position, patterns of lexical consistency with the compound head emerge in the postmodifying slots. Save for the appearance of *green* in the extended cotext of *encore career*, highlighting the semantic specification of socially-responsible work fields, the collocates that follow the node *career* are semantically homogenous. Both the neologism and the established head noun are found to recur in combination with *opportunities*, *paths* and *retirement*. In addition, lexemes referring to guidance appear, *coach* with *encore career*, *counseling* and *guidance* with *career*. These results indicate that neologisms expressing semantic contrasts in relation to a base or head lexeme benefit both from different collocating premodifiers, which anticipate the novel concept and lexeme and linguistically highlight or clarify these differences, and semantically homogenous or even identical postmodifiers, which transfer the established syntagmatic patterns of the morpho-lexical identical head noun.

To a lesser degree of significance, the differences between the collocational profile of *Eurofascist(s)* and *fascist* is akin to the case of *encore career*. In the NeoCrawler, the neologism is mainly followed by *groups* and *conference* (T-scores 4.24). In the OEC, however, the most significant collocates of *fascist* are *regime, state, dictatorship, dictator, movement* and *Italy*. These deviations are not surprising, since none of these Eurofascist groups hold power in any of the affected countries. Moreover, while no premodifying collocates are found for the neologism, the base is frequently preceded by *Italian* (T-score 7.23) in singular instances and *Islamic, Italian, British* and *German* in the plural forms. On the one hand, *Islamic* would not accord with *Eurofascist(s)*, because in Europe, such parties do not belong to the traditional political establishment. On the other hand, the *Euro-* prefix already expresses the idea that these fascist groups are found across Europe, which makes a lexical repetition in the form of adjectives denoting nationality rather redundant.

In sum, the collocational profiles for the neologisms are to a greater or lesser extent linguistically compatible with their bases or reflect a contrast. I argue that these morpho-lexical, morpho-semantic and syntactic-pragmatic reiterations in the syntagmatic cotext are the result of schematic inheritance from the lexical network from the base, because they function as cotextual and conceptual anchoring points. When a novel formation enters the language, it may be, by definition, linguistically naked. It has only feeble connections and associations to other lexemes in the lexicon, since these links become activated and strengthened through frequent recurrence. Depending on the initial occurrences, i.e. in flexible or in semi-fixed phrases, these lexical links will develop into more permanent and robust ties and have the potential to yield collocations of various degrees of strength. The language user benefits from these syntagmatic connections in two ways. Firstly, they provide vital comprehension aids. They embed the previously unfamiliar neologism in a known cotext, which contains lexico-semantic clues that are required for comprehension. In premodifying position, such lexemes semantically and conceptually anticipate the encounter with a novel word and prime the hearer or reader to the extent that the information necessary for comprehension is recalled from the corresponding established lexical and conceptual network, made available during processing. Komlósi and Knipf remark that this reiteration produces "special effects evoked and activated by different types of encoded information - phonological, phonotactic, morphological, morpho-syntactic, syntactic, semantic, conceptual, contextual and pragmatic" and that "these special effects prompt meaning assignment via active meaning construction, meaning extension and conceptual integration" (cf. 2005: 266). Secondly, collocations not only facilitate cognitive processing during the first encounter, but also enhance subsequent retrieval from memory, because the supportive cotext is predictable and functions as a mnemonic device. Since neologisms with firm collocations are integrated better in the mental lexicon, by virtue of their strong ties to other entries, and are thus partially entrenched, they stand a better chance of diffusing into the language and the speech community. The strong effect estimate factor of 15.35 mentioned in 4.2.6 reflects this beneficiary role of syntagmatic lexical networks during the conventionalization process.

Figure 50 graphically represents the distribution of the presence of collocations for the neologisms in the sample. The overall frequency for each of the neologisms is shown on the Y-axis. On the X-axis, the presence of collocations is marked by '1', the absence by '0'. The figure shows that the frequency range of the neologisms that are embedded in syntagmatic lexical networks is broader, with overall figures roughly between 200 and 2000. Moreover, the median of the left boxplot, marked as the thick black bar, confirms the linguistically-guided assumption that collocations are a factor promoting conventionalization, being located higher along the frequency axis. As discussed in the previous chapter, this result is statistically significant and its significance is held upright when other variables are included in the model.

*Fig. 50: Boxplot for the variable 'collocation'*

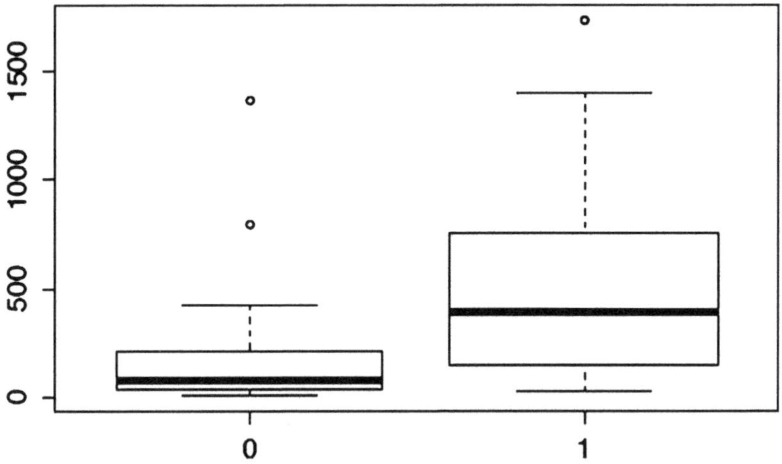


The results of the analysis of the emergence of syntagmatic lexical networks, their function and origin conclude the empirical investigation that forms the core of the present study. The final chapter will summarize the main findings in 6.1 and discuss the theoretical implications in 6.2.

# 6. Summary and conclusion

## 6.1. Summary of the results

The aim of the present study was twofold. Firstly, I aimed to provide the first systematic, empirical study of a selection of alleged conventionalization-promoting or -inhibiting factors by closely monitoring the social and linguistic diffusion behavior of 44 English neologisms in the online speech community. Secondly, I aimed to investigate the emergence of syntagmatic lexical networks during the conventionalization process, again based on longitudinal data retrieved from the Internet. In order to pursue these aims, I claimed it was necessary to establish a finer definition of *conventionalization* and provide a set of quantitative-qualitative criteria differentiating between the various stages along the continuum. Before discussing the theoretical implications for the existing theories regarding the diffusion of linguistic innovations and their viability for modeling lexical innovation in 6.2, I will summarize the main findings of the present study, starting with the operationalization of conventionalization as presented in 4.1.

Chapter 4.1.1 began at the lower end of the conventionalization continuum by presenting several cases of *non-conventionalization* at the time of writing. Based on the available evidence, I define non-conventionalization as low overall frequency in objectlinguistic mode of usage in less than two types of source and fields of discourse. Since precise information on the total amount of words on the Internet, which served as the source corpus for extraction, is unavailable it was not deemed feasible to fix a frequency threshold in relation to this unknown number, but proportionally to the frequency numbers for the most conventionalized cases in the data. As a result, low overall frequency in the present study corresponds to less than 150 retrieved pages during the entire monitoring period, which roughly equals ten percent of the averaged overall frequency of the three most frequent neologisms in the sample (*hyperlocal*, *robosigning* and *slacktivism*). The two additional socio-pragmatic criteria, the number of different types of source and fields of discourse a neologism appeared in, were operationalized according to the mathematical-statistical principle of random distribution. In short, a specific type of source was assumed to be significantly represented if the neologism occurrences exceeded 1/9 of the overall frequency, given that there are nine types of source in the socio-pragmatic classification scheme. Due to the stronger conceptual-semantic associations between the meaning of a given neologism and the 13 fields of discourse in the present study it can be used in, the threshold was fixed at 2/13, i.e. the double of the expectations under the random distribution hypothesis. I illustrated these criteria with the help of *roofvertising* (six occurrences), *preghead* (14 occurrences), *mesofact* (80 occurrences) and *bloglet*[2] (26 occurrences).

In 4.1.2 the term *topical* or *transitional conventionalization* was introduced to describe the sudden increase in overall frequency in multiple types of source. Many cases of transitional conventionalization, often found as *fashion* or *vogue words* in the literature, were explained as the result of a momentary topicality period of the coiner such as the transitory media hype regarding Heidi Montag's cosmetic surgeries triggering the short-lived extensive use of her creation *back scooping,* or the underlying concept or event in society, as in the controversy regarding burquinis being banned from public pools in France, Italy and Britain in the case of *burquini.* Frequently, these topically conventionalized neologisms are found in metalinguistically-used occurrences, highlighting the meaning, use and coinage context, often even continuing long after the extralinguistic topicality period without concomitant objectlinguistic usage. I moreover argued that the degree of permanent conventionalization of such topically-established lexemes depends on the intensity of the topicality period.

Sometimes, a succession of multiple periods of topicality occurs, related to the events in the speech community. *Recurrent semi-conventionalization*, as I have labeled this phenomenon in 4.1.3, is characterized by a series of sudden increases in overall frequency in multiple types of source of a given neologism. Several processes yield patterns of recurrent semi-conventionalization. Firstly, recurrent semi-conventionalization can be caused by the topical recurrence of the underlying concept, which I illustrated by the seasonal use of *cherpumple.* Secondly, it can also arise as the result of a linguistic cause, i.e. the morphosemantic schematicity of the neological form. As shown by means of the example *Boobgate*, certain word-forms operate as generic placeholders for detailed meanings and conceptualizations that surface whenever extralinguistic events that are perceived as similar by the speakers need linguistic coding in a particular situational-communicative context. In the case of *Boobgate*, the general meaning 'a scandal involving a breast-related event' is filled with specific detail according to the kind of issue involved, i.e. showing too much cleavage and accidental exposure of parts of the breast among others. Similar to the cases of transitional conventionalization, the intensity of the topicality periods as well as the frequency of recurrence will determine the degree of subsequent conventionalization in the speech community and entrenchment in the individual minds of the speakers.

The final stage distinguished along the conventionalization continuum on the basis of the available data is represented by *advanced conventionalization*. Advanced conventionalization is described as high overall frequency during an extended period in multiple types of source and/or fields of discourse in chapter 4.1.4. The lower threshold in the present study was placed at 50% of the averaged total number of occurrences, measured as retrieved pages, of the three most conventionalized neologisms in the sample as mentioned above, which corresponds to 750 occurrences. However, these frequency thresholds should not be interpreted in the strictest sense; on the basis of the available qualitative evidence *globesity* and *encore career* are found among the better conventionalized neologisms in the present study despite their overall frequency of 681 and 724 respectively not reaching the lower limit. The most advanced examples of conventionalization from the sample are *robosigning* (1735 occurrences), *hyperlocal* (1399 occurrences) and *slacktivism* (1366 occurrences). Further evidence of advanced conventionalization is presented by the existence of a full inflectional paradigm for verbs and the emergence of lexico-morphological derivations, illustrated, for instance, by *robosigner* and *robosignature* in the case of *robosigning*. Moreover, neologisms in advanced stages of conventonialization are also found on SELF-REFERENTIAL pages, indicating that the concept and the lexeme reflect a degree of establishment strong enough to spark the creation of texts and webpages dedicated to the topic.

Chapter 4.2 systematically presented the results of the statistical and linguistic analysis of the six assumed diffusion-promoting and -inhibiting factors introduced in 1.2. Although attempts were made to include both overall frequency of occurrence and relative frequency in the various types of source as the dependent variables in the regression model, because I claim that both measures are necessary to capture the degree of conventionalization, only overall frequency was used in the present regression model. Furthermore, statistical evaluation of the potential influence of the nameworthiness of a neologism on the conventionalization process was omitted due to the incompleteness of the experiment-based results. In general, the quantitative results should be interpreted with caution, since, in statistical terms at least, the number of investigated neologisms is low, possibly too low to allow substantiated generalizations. This word of caution not only applies to the results for the factors tested in isolation, but in particular to the outcome regarding interactions between the individual factors. A summary of the degree of influence of all factors, as well as the interactions tested is listed in Table 21, with factors > 1 acting as diffusion-promoting factors and factors between 0 and 1 acting as diffusion-inhibiting factors during the conventionalization process.

*Table 21: Summary of the factor-of-influence analysis*

| Factors | Effect estimate factor | p-value |
|---|---|---|
| (Intercept) | 0.77 | 0.315078 |
| a) IN ISOLATION | | |
| Coiner status celebrity | 33.69 | 4.41e-05 *** |
| Coiner status professional | 3.65 | 0.000387 *** |
| Collocations | 15.35 | 1.52e-11 *** |
| Type of source NEWS (measured in percentage) | 1.11 | 0.041267 * |
| Metalinguistic usage (measured in percentage) | 1.01 | 0.032851 * |
| (Semantic ambiguity | 0.87 | 0.717754) |
| b) INTERACTIONS | | |
| Semantic ambiguity X coiner status professional | 0.11 | 0.003160 ** |
| Collocations X coiner status celebrity | 0.05 | 0.017417 * |
| Collocations X metalinguistic usage | 0.95 | 0.000323 *** |

AIC corrected: 645.86

As the table shows, the strongest fueling effect with an effect estimate factor of 33.69, which is also statistically highly significant, is found for those neologisms that were coined by celebrities, most notably *back scooping* and *cherpumple*. Lexemes coined by professionals too, stand a better chance of diffusing, yielding an effect estimate factor of 3.65 in the present model. These promoting effects corroborate earlier claims made that the prestige of the coiner and early users act as positively-evaluated associations a speaker possesses and reacts to during communication and accommodation (cf. below). If the more speculative interactions are included, the positive effect of a famous or knowledgeable coiner is overridden, leading to a slightly inhibiting effect for semantically ambiguous neologisms that were coined by professionals and neologisms with collocations coined by professionals. However, since both interactions are based on one single observation, further research is necessary to determine the precise extent. At present, the results of the interactions were merely included for reasons of completeness and cannot be interpreted as firm evidence.

The second strongest diffusion-promoting factor, with an effect estimate factor of 15.35, again highly statistically significant, in the present model is the presence of collocations. If a neologism forms part of a syntagmatic lexical network in language in which it is frequently and recurrently accompanied by one or more collocates, its diffusion process is propelled forward. I assume the positive effect to arise firstly from the continuous recurrence of stable lexeme pairs increasing the degree of entrenchment, which speeds up consequent retrieval along the lines of the well-known Hebbian principle 'what fires together, wires together' and reduces the processing load. Secondly, collocates act as comprehension-aiding cotextual anchors, which are beneficiary to the reader-hearer confronted with a novel lexeme without firm traces in the mental lexicon, in turn again facilitating cognitive processing. The results of the collocation analysis with AntConc and supplemented by evidence from the OEC reveal a remarkable and interesting pattern regarding the precise nature of cotextual anchoring. The collocates accompanying the neologisms frequently show a high degree of linguistic compatibility with the morpho-lexical base lexeme, leading to the conclusion that such collocational profiles are inherited from those of the bases, which are already established. The explicatory and comprehension-facilitating role of collocations as cotextual anchors therefore arises from morphological, lexical and semantic network correspondences to those of the conventionalized relative. In 5.3 I showed that the collocation *little bloglet*[1] is a continuation and reiteration of the established collocations *little booklet* and *little blog*. Since not all neologisms are semantically compatible with their bases or morphological relatives, collocates also function as carriers of semantic contrast in order to support the semantic deviations from established relatives. The example of *encore career* illustrated this pattern of contrast. Particularly the premodifiers of the lexeme differed from those of *career* in order to anticipate the semantic contrast, because an *encore career* is not merely a second or subsequent career, but one that takes place after retirement and is situated in more social or charitable branches of the labor market. This semantic component is reflected in the significant presence of *green*, *meaningful* and *fulfilling* as the top three preceding collocates of *encore career*, whereas the three most frequent premodifiers for *career* in the OEC are *political*, *successful* and *professional*.

Returning to Table 21 on p. 230, frequent occurrence in the formal type of source NEWS exerts a minor positive influence, reflected in the effect estimate factor of 1.11. No effect was observed for the PORTAL type of source category, which represented the formal text types together with the NEWS category. The quantitative results were mirrored by evidence from the socio-pragmatic analysis, which did not yield any obvious causal increase in frequency concomitant to or after increased frequency in the NEWS and PORTAL categories. It was assumed that frequent occurrences in such formal types of source would promote diffusion for two reasons. Firstly, these categories are the closest virtual counterparts to the traditional formal text types, in which language is used with an authoritative and normifying force. Similar to the prestige and expertise of the coiner, speakers are sensitive to such associations when engaging in communicative exchanges. Secondly, these formal categories are typically characterized by reaching large audiences, establishing a broader basis for potential diffusion in comparison to more informal, less popular types of source. The perhaps surprising results regarding the minimal degree of influence can be explained by the complexity of the Internet as a medium. Given the frequent popularity of blogs, many of which have become professional modes of information exchange not unlike newssites and portals, one could argue for inclusion of the PROFESSIONAL BLOG category into the model. Such considerations indicate a more fundamental problem with the application of the classic concept of stylistic formality in CMD as the prime medium of linguistic innovation and in itself innovating linguistic norms. I argue that the traditional role of newspapers as channels of diffusion is complemented, perhaps even substituted by the rapid mode of exchange of information within social networks many Internet users form part of with increasing creativity and flexibility.

Considering now the role of the linguistic variables in the current model, Table 21 on p. 230 reveals a slight diffusion-promoting effect, effect estimate factor 1.01, for frequent metalinguistic use. Metalinguistic usage refers to the linguistic practice of embedding a word in an explanatory cotext commenting on the use, behavior or appearance of the lexeme. Such instances are therefore not used in referential mode, i.e. pointing to an extralinguistic referent, but to the lexeme itself. The observed fueling effect refutes H1, which assumed frequent metalinguistic usage to be an inhibiting factor. The positive influence is presumed to arise from a combination of social processes of salience in the speech community and cognitive processing aspects in the individual mental lexicon. Given the novelty of the neologisms, in the present study both regarding their forms and meanings, users will benefit from explicit comprehension clues, which are present in the form of explanations, paraphrases and definitions in metalinguistic occurrences. As a result, meaning construction is facilitated and storage also enhanced, following the metalinguistic awareness skills that have been observed in language learning. Moreover, metalinguistic usage is frequently linked to topicality periods in society, during which the concept and its linguistic form receive a great deal of attention from the media, word-watchers, lexicographers etc., for instance, around the annual Word of the Year elections of he various dictionaries and linguistic societies. Such salience in society can also be assumed to have an effect on the cognitive salience of the lexeme, setting it apart from the continuous stream of others pouring into the brain, and thus increases the traces necessary for reproduction and diffusion. Further evidence is needed to investigate the interplay between social and cognitive salience.

The final aspect considered in detail as a factor of influence from a statistical perspective concerns semantic ambiguity. The association between one word-form and multiple novel meanings was assumed to inhibit conventionalization because of an increased processing load. In contrast to established polysemous and homonymous lexemes, speakers cannot benefit from existing underlying representations in lexical memory, but are required to assemble the meaning on-line. If no sufficiently informative cotext is present in the form of explicit explanations or collocations, comprehension of ambiguous neologisms can be challenging. In isolation, the ambiguity factor did not produce any significant effect in the statistical model, as shown by the p-value in Table 21 on p. 230. Its inhibiting influence could only be glimpsed at on the basis of its interaction with professional coiner status. Due to the relatively low number of observations, however, the extent of this negative influence should be interpreted with caution. A further linguistic factor that was assumed to inhibit conventionalization included in the present model was synonymy. However, no effect could be observed, which explains the omission of the factor in Table 21.

As described at the outset of chapter 4.2 the factor nameworthiness did not feed into the regression model due to the incomplete data. Despite the absence of any quantitative evidence regarding the potential degree and direction of influence, some remarkable evidence on the psychological reality of the theoretical notion of nameworthiness was presented in 4.2.4. I discussed in detail (some of) the principles informants apply when responding to the perceived usefulness of linguistic items. The nameworthiness experiment, conducted in order to investigate the influence of the usefulness of the concept expressed by the neologism, has yielded further evidence on the subjectivity with which novel meanings are gauged. Three broad types of communication-driven utility have been identified. Firstly, the subjects expressed personal concerns. They assigned nameworthiness scores according to the salience and usefulness of a given meaning in their individual lives. Thus, most informants deemed *tynonym* not nameworthy, because they do not frequently write short messages, have a Blackberry without T9 or disable the predictive texting device.

Secondly, the salience in society influenced people's responses. Societal utility emerges when a concept becomes topical and needs to be communicated about on the level of the speech community. The meanings of *globesity* and *halfalogue*, for instance, were felt to be useful, because they conceptualize currently pervasive phenomena the speakers from the study have encountered. Similarly, some subjects found *tube-free* useless, claiming that all toilet paper is wrapped around a tube. Lastly, the aptness of unified cognitive representation or categorization provided a motivation for accepting or rejecting a particular meaning in the study. Holistic utility surfaced when the informants judged the descriptive potential or clarity and specificity of the meaning and indicated that a corresponding lexeme in the lexicon would be helpful, e.g. *Boobgate*. However, some of the results did not correlate with the degree of diffusion. The meaning of *sodcasting*, for instance, elicited a high nameworthiness score, but has not diffused widely in terms of frequency. Aberrations of this kind are attributed to the onomasiological design of the experiment and the potential interplay with other factors such as morphological transparency. Since subjects were presented with the meaning, their judgements were informed by semantic and conceptual input. It should be assumed that the linguistic word-form, which is an intrinsic component of the neologism in natural language, and the degree of transparency between form and meaning also affect speakers' perceptions of naming need. As mentioned above, the precise extent of the influence of nameworthiness could not be statistically tested within the model due to the small sample size. Further experiments are required to investigate the effect of nameworthiness and the role of morphological make-up and transparency.

The second aim of the study was to closely monitor the emergence of syntagmatic lexical networks for each of the 44 neologisms. Several kinds of syntagmatic lexical network relations were discussed in 5.2. The first kind are collocations in the narrowest sense, defined in the traditional sense as frequently recurring co-occurrences of two directly adjacent lexemes. Examples from the sample include *little bloglet* and *hyperlocal news*. Secondly, as discussed in 5.2.3, neologisms are also often syntagmatically embedded in explicit explanatory phrases, particularly in metalinguistic usage. I showed that the cotext of *halfalogue*, for instance, frequently contained lexical flags such as *overheard*, *cell phone* and *conversation*, explicitly describing the meaning. Patterns of this kind appear in variable degrees during the conventionalization process. Due to the decreasing need of explicit cotextual anchoring once the neologism has become more established, such explicit explanations can also be reduced. A third pattern arising from the data are lexico-pragmatic and lexico-syntactic usage constructions. I illustrated such usage constructions with the help of *bromosexual*. *Bromosexual* is found in two specific patterns: as a form of address used for close friends and as a subject complement, similar to possessive constructions. The former use consists of the neologisms being preceded by various greetings and address-related formulae such as *hey*, *what's up* and *yo*. The lexico-syntactic pattern surfaces as the *X-to be-my-bromosexual(s)* construction. The collocation analysis for *bro*, which constitutes one of the sources for the blend, in the OEC revealed that these patterns mirror those of *bro*, consistent with the re-iterative inheritance patterns observed for true collocations mentioned above. Finally, a single and perhaps rare case of idioms, *the frogurt is cursed*, was presented. The idiom was adopted from a *Simpsons* episode and only occasionally used in novel, non-*Simpsons*-related contexts.

Chapter 5.2. also discussed the emergence patterns I observed in the data. The collocation analysis yielded two patterns of emergence, discussed in detail in 5.2.1 and 5.2.2. On the one hand, collocations were observed to crystallize from a set of preselected lexical choices that frequently, but to varying degrees, co-occurred with the neologism in its initial stages of conventionalization. Concomitantly with the increase in frequency, one or more of these preferred lexical companions develop into strong collocations. Collocations of this type are *little bloglet* and *hyperlocal news*. On the other hand, collocations also seem to appear instantaneously. Thus, during the initial stages of diffusion, *intexticated* was almost exclusively found in co-occurrence with *driving while*. Afterwards, the meaning of *driving while* gradually became incorporated in *intexticated*, which subsequently emancipated itself from the initial collocational cotext and connected to other lexemes. These examples again illustrate the cotextual anchoring function of collocates accompanying neologisms and provide an explanation for their fostering role during the conventionalization process, which concluded chapter 5. The very final chapter will now take up on these results and incorporate them into the proposed EC-model, occasionally also referring to the evolutionary selection model addressed in 2.3.

## 6.2. Towards a sociocognitive model of the conventionalization process of English neologisms

At the beginning of this book in chapter 2.3 I introduced the socio-cognitive *entrenchment-and-conventionalization* framework (Schmid 2014), which supplants the lexical theory of institutionalization as a necessary means to explain the potential establishment process of English neologisms. Rather than merely describing whether a novel lexeme has become an addition to the lexicon, the entrenchment-and-conventionalization model attempts to explain the language system as a dynamic process embedded in and influenced by social and cognitive processes in the minds of the individual speakers and the speech community at large. A final question that needs to be addressed in the present work concerns the viability of the EC-model, or more precisely its conventionalization pole, regarding lexical innovation.

The results from the factor-of-influence investigation confirm the assumption that the diffusion of neologisms is fueled or inhibited not only by social and socio-pragmatic aspects, but also by comprehension and storage processes in the mental lexicon. On the basis of the evidence presented in the previous chapters both Trudgill's view on accommodation as an exclusively frequency-driven and socially-insensitive process (cf. 2004, 2008) and the evolutionary models as propagated by Baxter, Blythe and colleagues (cf. Baxter et al. 2008) in which the selection and replication of linguistic variants is essentially socially determined fall short of explaining the conventionalization process of lexical innovation. Lexical innovation seems to be more accurately explained by the EC-model, which despite its current vagueness regarding the precise nature of diffusion mechanisms, contains the important integration of social and cognitive aspects of linguistic behavior into one usage-based, dynamic model.

Turning to the individual factors tested, among the social set of conventionalization factors, the positive effects of coiner status and formal type of source are attributed to accommodation. When speakers encounter a novel lexeme coined by a professional or celebrity, their readiness to adopt the word is triggered by the social prestige and professional authority, probably more aptly labeled as "social success" by Keller (1994: 84), of the coiner and early adopters such as newspaper journalists. As a result of its appearance in more formal media such as newspapers, the neologism also gains exposure and reaches a wide audience, which has the potential to continue the diffusion, sometimes simply by copy-pasting the relevant passages. Thus, accommodation is both a matter of speaker attitude, characterized by a flexible set of social norms, associations and values with respect to the members speech community and its code, and frequency of exposure.

Since every exposure instance increases the degree of entrenchment, reducing the processing load (see 2.2.2) and facilitating subsequent use, it is apparent that the social and cognitive planes of diffusion are interwoven in multifarious ways. However, large-scale exposure does not guarantee permanent adoption into the language, as evidenced by the low effect estimate value for the NEWS category. As discussed in 4.1, transitional conventionalization in language might arise due to a concomitant period of extralinguistic salience, but does not necessarily lead to advanced conventionalization. Moreover, the sample contains evidence that in addition to audience size, its social make-up might be of considerable importance and needs to be incorporated as a factor of influence. Neologisms such as *bromosexual* and *bloglet*[1], which were neither coined by a professional or celebrity nor frequently occur in formal types of source, are progressing towards establishment in specific virtual communities. These online communities, as found in social networks or discussion fora, it is assumed, constitute a significant diffusion-promoting factor, since they represent micro-societies of a potentially innovating and innovation-propagating core surrounded by predominantly weak ties, which have been since long acknowledged as strong channels of diffusion (cf. Labov 1972; the work by the Milroys; Granovetter 1973; Eckert 2000; Fagyal et al. 2010; Paradowski and Jonak 2012). I have argued that the flexibility with which these communities emerge and develop in cyber-reality provides a complementary platform for peer group-driven accommodation processes.

Although accommodation is an inter-individual process taking place as a series of small-scale processes, I have necessarily generalized and discussed some of its mechanisms and effects on the level of the speech community. This abstraction does not imply that all speakers will conform to the same degree. As noted in 2.3 and 4.2.2, the threshold of adoption varies for the individual speaker (cf. Granovetter 1978).

The two other promoting factors, metalinguistic usage and presence of collocations, are assumed to result from comprehension and processing facilitation and reflect cognitive mechanisms feeding into the conventionalization process. As mentioned above, the second strongest positive effect is observed for collocations. Collocations adorn a neologism with lexical companions that represent cotextual anchors aiding the interpretation of a novel meaning and possibly become stored together in the course of advancing conventionalization and entrenchment. These lexical companions contain morpho-lexical and/or lexico-semantic iterations, specifications or contrasts, or are expressed in pragmatic-syntactic patterns that serve as linguistic clues on which the unfamiliar speaker can rely in their comprehension process. A similar promoting effect of a supportive cotext was observed for frequent metalinguistic usage, which is considered as a less prototypical type of relation within the lexical network. However, the effect proved to be relatively weak. Some neologisms are advancing towards conventionalization without much supportive metalinguistic discourse, whereas others do not seem to become established in spite of frequent metalinguistic occurrences. As mentioned above, a monthly frequency analysis might shed light on the precise interaction between metalinguistic usage and diffusion development. In sum, I have shown that conventionalization straddles and emerges from the dynamic interaction between social and cognitive process of accommodation and processing, although the precise mechanisms and extent of interaction between the various aspects require further study within the EC-framework.

The present work has also introduced a novel methodological framework for the study of linguistic innovation and change. The monthly retrieval of data from the Internet has enabled a detailed investigation of the socio-pragmatic behavior of English neologisms in order to answer some long-standing questions in lexical theory. In addition to a quantitative and qualitative analysis of six hypotheses, I also introduced descriptive criteria for the various stages in the conventionalization process as summarized in detail in 6.1.1. It is important to note that any of these stages can become the endpoint of the process. Thus, the diffusion of a neologism can progress towards permanent establishment or become arrested at a particular stage. Moreover, the various stages do not necessarily affect every neologism to the same degree. Topicality, for instance, can be sudden and short-lived (e.g. *burquini, back scooping, tynonym* or *kindergarchy*), recurrent (e.g. *cherpumple*) or long-term (e.g. *bromosexual, globesity*). The diffusion curve of *hyperlocal*, on the other hand, does not display any indication of topicality, but shows a slanting, continuing increase in frequency. Although it has been claimed that transitional conventionalization arises from extralinguistic salience, such a direct correlation between frequency and pervasiveness did not always materialize. As illustrated in the case study of *detweet*, where earlier expectations were disconfirmed on the basis of recent frequency developments, firm and conclusive decisions regarding the conventionalization status of a given neologism require a longer period of perpetual monitoring than could be conducted within the framework of the present study.

In addition to long-term tracking, any statements regarding conventionalization need to complement evidence from overall frequency with relative frequency in types of source and fields of discourse as well as a variety of other factors. Since conventionalization is concerned with diffusion and establishment in the speech community at large, i.e. in different socio-pragmatic contexts and cotexts, overall frequency regarded in isolation does not always represent the ongoing process accurately. On the basis of the 515 occurrences of *bloglet*[1], one might argue that it belongs to a more advanced stage of conventionalization. However, 491 of these pages are personal blogs. Therefore, *bloglet*[1] might be on its way to becoming established in the blog community, but it cannot be claimed that it is in the process of becoming an established lexeme in the entire speech community. Such subcommunity-specific processes can be defined as instances of micro-conventionalization, if one is to introduce a new term for them.

Low overall frequency, on the other hand, does not necessarily indicate a lower degree of conventionalization. *E-tivity*, for instance, was attested on merely 51 pages, but was frequently used as a tag or a category, implying familiarity among the users. Similarly, some neologisms feature as website or domain names, e.g. mesofacts.org. In order to capture such instances, it was necessary to introduce a new classification category SELF-REFERENTIAL. This kind of usage seems to provide a hint that hypostatization has taken place, which in turn has been assumed to indicate progressing establishment. These examples illustrate the need for a careful and detailed interpretation of overall and relative frequency. Therefore, I have explicitly refrained from assigning frequency thresholds to the individual stages all too strictly, because the number of words on the Internet is elusive. The number of pages changes daily and the content is continually modified, which renders frequency counts virtually impossible. Any conclusions regarding the conventionalization stage and status cannot be based exclusively on frequency as reflected in an arbitrary threshold that needs to be exceeded. Any kind of model describing language and language change based on frequency data should therefore always be careful in operationalizing and applying the measure.

Despite drawbacks of this kind in data retrieved from the Internet, I hope I have shown that it is precisely the Internet that has allowed me to conduct such a detailed investigation of the conventionalization process of English neologisms. The two components of the NeoCrawler offer the opportunity to identify and observe lexical innovation in online discourse in almost realtime-like fashion. While the Discoverer automatically extracts novel grapheme strings and assesses the likelihood of their instantiating new words, the multifunctional Observer tracks the relevant neologisms, downloads the pages and prepares them for linguistic analysis. In addition to automatic page clean-up and tokenization, the Observer's in-built socio-pragmatic classification system has greatly contributed to the fine-grained study of diffusion. The classification options on three levels of data structure have uncovered further indicators of conventionalization, such as the token position in tags and categories and the conceptual hypostatization in self-referential texts and domains. Furthermore, the present type of source classification represents a compact toolkit to distinguish between various Internet genres on the basis of their most salient features. Particularly the possibility of observing linguistic phenomena in close-knit and socio-economically diverse online communities has raised important questions as to how they contribute to the diffusion of innovation. Although a cautious approach to analysis and interpretation of online data is certainly warranted in the light of its non-representativity and lack of balancedness, the Internet provides access to the dynamics of communities and their languages that frequently remain off-limits in reality.

New words will continue to behave like casting show winners. Some will have a short-lived career, leaving minimal traces in the language before being consigned to oblivion. Others will not leave any trace at all. However, those that reveal tentative signs of advancing conventionalization have been shown to do so because of an interplay of social and cognitive factors postulated in the EC model. Data-driven approaches to lexical innovation cannot always raise universally-valid claims of exhaustiveness since words often tend to behave idiosyncratically in language and society. I do hope I have shown, however, that a number of general socio-cognitive mechanisms take effect in the conventionalization process of English neologisms and contribute to or inhibit their establishment as everyday English words.

# Appendices

## Appendix 1: List of nonce-formations in alphabetical order

| Lexeme | Word class | Gloss | Word-formation process |
|---|---|---|---|
| A | | | |
| ***affiliopinion*** | n. (count.) | a subjective opinion expressed on the Internet by affiliate members of websites and their products | blend |
| ***agile business continuity*** | n (uncount.) | <unclear> | compound |
| ***to anagramise*** | v. | to make an anagram | suffixation |
| B | | | |
| ***blubdate*** | n. (count.) | a blog update | blend |
| ***businessosphere*** | n. (uncount.) | the realm of business | suffixation |
| C | | | |
| ***carbohydritis*** | n. (uncount.) | a lack of carbohydrates in food, which allegedly causes weight gain | suffixation |
| ***carpie*** | n. (uncount.) | a dirty kind of sloshy snow | <unclear> |
| ***chinsumer*** | n. (count.) | a Chinese consumer | blend |
| ***crapaging*** | n. (uncount.) | bad-quality packaging | blend |
| D | | | |
| ***deprofitizing*** | n. (uncount.) | the act of not raising money with a particular activity or product | prefixation + suffixation |
| ***to detweetify*** | v. (intrans.) | to analyze sales trends of a company without regarding their advertising or marketing strategies on Twitter | prefixation + suffixation |

| Lexeme | Word class | Gloss | Word-formation process |
|---|---|---|---|
| ***dext*** | n. (count.) | a text written or sent when drunk | blend |
| ***digital plebeian*** | n. (count.) | | compound |
| ***dualers*** | n. (pl.) | a group of people who believe Obama's presidency is against the constitution because of his alleged dual citizenship | suufixation |
| **E** | | | |
| ***e-ther*** | n. (uncount.) | Internet broadcasting space | blend |
| ***evangerealist*** | n. (count.) | modern evangelists operating through the Internet | blend |
| **F** | | | |
| ***floodite*** | n. (count.) | an old-fashioned peon who just discovered e-mail and is making up for lost time by filling your inbox with ancient jokes and dubious petitions | suffixation |
| ***funcontrollable*** | adj. | referring to something uncontrollable and funny | blend |
| **G** | | | |
| ***giddyupidness*** | n. (uncount.) | nonce meaning | <unclear> |
| **H** | | | |
| ***half-ican*** | n. (count.) | a person with multiple ethnic backgrounds | <unclear> |
| ***hearitable*** | adj. | referring to an irritating sound | blend |
| ***herbal tea bagger*** | n. (count.) | <unclear> | compound + suffixation |
| ***hillbilly airbag*** | n. (count.) | a child sitting on the lap of the driver | compound |
| **I** | | | |
| ***ideocentrism*** | n. (uncount.) | the inability to view the world from a different ideological perspective | prefixation |

| | | | |
|---|---|---|---|
| ***idiosynchronize*** | v. (trans.) | to synchronize supply and demand in a business effectively | prefixation |
| ***infidelitexting*** | adj | to commit adultery by means of text messages | blend |
| ***instamatically*** | adj | referring to an activity a person does instantly and automatically without further delay | blend |
| ***iPadable*** | adj. | compatible with an iPad | suffixation |
| ***iPod league*** | n. (count.) | of the same level of quality as the iPod | compound |
| ***iPodlian*** | n. (count.) | iPod user | suffixation |
| **N** | | | |
| ***neoboomers*** | n. (pl.) | a class of wealthy people that remain active after retirement | prefixation (+ back-formation) |
| ***nymskull*** | n. (count.) | a person anonymously posting provocative messages on the Internet | compound |
| **O** | | | |
| ***obesogens*** | n. (pl.) | obesity-causing gens | blend |
| ***old girls' network*** | n. (count.) | a network managed by women | compound |
| ***open services infrastructure*** | n. (count.) | a form of centralized service platforms with the help of communication technology | compound |
| **P** | | | |
| ***permabstinent*** | adj. | referring to the feeling of never having to have sex anymore because you can't even remember the last time it happened | blend |
| ***photobituary*** | n. (count.) | an obituary in photos | blend |
| ***Pippi Longcrotching*** | n. (count.) | trousers for men that are wide at the crotch | pun on Longstocking |
| ***polargeists*** | n. (pl.) | a new class of Democrats and Republicans that will polarize further | borrowing with semantic change |

| Lexeme | Word class | Gloss | Word-formation process |
|---|---|---|---|
| ***publiclairing*** | n. (uncount.) | the act of voicing a complaint in public | blend |
| **R** | | | |
| ***reperbation*** | n. (uncount.) | <unclear> | <unclear> |
| ***runner's hair*** | n. (uncount.) | the sloppy look of a person's hair after running | compound |
| **S** | | | |
| ***selfish tiger disease*** | n. (count.) | a condition of putting yourself over everything | compound |
| ***simianification*** | n. (uncount.) | the historical, dehumanizing treatment of the Irish by the British | suffixation |
| ***sleepcation*** | n. (uncount.) | holidays spent sleeping a lot | blend |
| ***social venting incident*** | n. (count.) | the public ventilation of strong emotions regarding a particular topic/event by a group of people | compound |
| ***superbness*** | n. (uncount.) | the state of being excellent | suffixation |
| ***surf rescue technician*** | n. (count.) | advanced lifeguard | compound |
| ***surfing beach facilitator*** | n. (count.) | advanced lifeguard | compound |
| ***survey knowledge*** | n. (uncount.) | overall knowledge of a hypermedia system | compound |
| ***synaptic branding*** | n. (uncount.) | <unclear> | compound |
| ***syncredent*** | n. | <unclear> | <unclear> |
| **T** | | | |
| ***telapathy*** | n. (uncount.) | a psychic's lack of interest in or concern for things that others find moving or exciting | orthographic pun |
| ***tenderpreneurship*** | n. (uncount.) | a form of business obtained through government tenders (South Africa) | blend |

| | | | |
|---|---|---|---|
| ***tigerism*** | n. (uncount.) | the religion, culture, and mindset describing the forces of righteousness | suffixation |
| **U** | | | |
| ***un-reality*** | n. (uncount.) | reality being harsh | prefixation |
| **V** | | | |
| ***virginality*** | n. (uncount.) | virginity | suffixation |
| **W** | | | |
| ***wreckconciliation*** | n. (uncount.) | "Wreckconciliation Sunday", the day America as a republic died, because the government took over healthcare | blend |

# Appendix 2: List of neologisms in alphabetical order

| Lexeme | Word class | Gloss | Word-formation process |
|---|---|---|---|
| A | | | |
| ***administrativia*** | n. (uncount.) | trivial administrative issues | blend |
| B | | | |
| ***back scooping*** | n. (count.) | a small liposuction around the hips and flanks to narrow the waist | compound + suffixation (metaphorical 2nd element) |
| ***bloglet*** | n. (count.) | 1. a short blog entry<br>2. a form of address to to fellow bloggers<br>3. blog update notification system | suffixation |
| ***Boobgate*** | n. (uncount.) | 1. a scandal involving a famous person (in)adver-tedly showing too much cleavage<br>2. the scandal surrounding Sarah Palin's alleged breast augmentation | suffixation |
| ***bromosexual*** | n. (count.) | a straight man who is very close to another man without being homosexual. | blend |
| ***burquini*** | n. (count.) | a bathing suit which covers arms, legs and hair for Muslim women | blend |
| C | | | |
| ***cherpumple*** | n. (count.) | a cake consisting of three layers of pie: cherry, pumpkin and apple | blend |
| ***crapget*** | n. (count.) | an alleged gadget which proves to be useless | blend |

| | | | |
|---|---|---|---|
| ***cyberchondriac*** | n. (count.) | a person who imagines they have a particular disease because their symptoms match those listed on an Internet health site | blend |
| ***cyberdisinhibition*** | n. (uncount.) | the temporary loss of inhibition while online, which causes people to divulge more personal information than they would in real-life interaction | prefixation |
| **D** | | | |
| ***decycling***<br>***to decycle*** | n. (uncount.)<br>v. (trans.) | the act of anti-recycling<br>to anti-recycle | back-formation + prefixation |
| ***to detweet*** | 1. v. (trans.)<br>2. v. (intrans.)<br>3. v. (trans.)<br>4. v. (trans.)<br>5. v. (trans.)<br>6. v. (trans.) | 1. to delete a tweet on Twitter<br>2. to sign off<br>3. to unfollow<br>4. to pass on a tweet with disapproval; opposite of *retweet*<br>5. to suspend a Twitter account by the Twitter authorities | prefixation |
| ***diabesity*** | n. (uncount.) | type 2 diabetes caused by obesity | blend |
| **E** | | | |
| ***e-tivity*** | n. (count.) | an online exercise or learning activity | prefixation (with base modification) |
| ***encore career*** | n. (count.) | a second career after retirement or resignation, usually more socially oriented | compound (with a borrowed 1st element) |
| ***Eurofascists*** | n. (count.) | modern form of extreme right in Europe | prefixation |

| Lexeme | Word class | Gloss | Word-formation process |
|---|---|---|---|
| F | | | |
| ***facebook official*** | adj. | an event, mainly a relationship, that is awarded official status because it is marked accordingly on Facebook | compound |
| ***floordrobe*** | n. (count.) | a pile of discarded clothes on the floor | blend |
| ***friendsourcing*** | n. (uncount.) | the use of the Internet for gathering information and feedback from friends | blend |
| ***froghurt*** | n. (count.) | frozen yoghurt | blend |
| G | | | |
| ***ganky*** | adj. | uncool, strange, old, not normal, disgusting | |
| ***ghost surgery*** | n. (count.) | a surgery performed by an unauthorized substitute surgeon | compound (with a metaphorical first element) |
| ***globesity*** | n. (uncount.) | the idea that obesity has become a global problem | blend |
| ***grawlix*** | n. (count.) | a string of typographical symbols (e.g. "@#$%&!") used (especially in comic strips) to represent an obscenity or swearword. | |
| H | | | |
| ***half-false*** | adj. | quasi-false; not entirely true, not entirely false | prefixation |
| ***halfalogue*** | n. (count.) | part of a conversation bystanders hear when someone is talking on the phone in a public place | blend |

| | | | |
|---|---|---|---|
| ***hyperlocal*** | adj. | referring to the immediate surroundings; mainly used for referring to new | prefixation |
| **I** | | | |
| ***intexticated*** | adj. | busy reading or writing text messages, especially while driving | blend |
| ***iPad friendly*** | adj. | a device/format/website which can be used on an iPad | compound |
| **K** | | | |
| ***kindergarchy*** | n. (uncount.) | rule or domination by children; the belief that children's needs and preferences take precedence over those of their parents or other adults. | blend |
| **M** | | | |
| ***meaniac*** | n. (count.) | a person who is both mean and a maniac | blend |
| ***mesofact*** | n. (count.) | a fact that changes over time (like earth's population) | prefixation |
| **P** | | | |
| ***Politerati*** | n. (uncount.) | political decision-makers in Washington | blend |
| ***preghead*** | n. (count.) | a pregnant woman who forgets more than usually | blend |
| **R** | | | |
| ***radiculous*** | adj. | referring to something that is so rad it becomes ridiculous | blend |
| ***recombobulation area*** | n. (count.) | an area at the airport where passengers can collect their belongings and clothes after the security check | compound |

| Lexeme | Word class | Gloss | Word-formation process |
|---|---|---|---|
| ***robosigning*** <br> ***to robosign*** | n. (uncount.) <br> v. (trans.) | the act of automatically signing official documents without manual check | compound |
| ***roofvertising*** | n. (uncount.) | the use of roofs and high buildings to make advertisement | blend |
| **S** | | | |
| ***slacktivism*** | n. (uncount.) | a type of activism that seeks projects and causes that require the least amount of effort. | blend |
| ***sodcasting*** | n. (uncount.) | the act of playing loud music on a phone or loudspeaker in public | suffixation |
| **T** | | | |
| ***tynonym*** | n. (count.) | a word that you get as a suggestion on your mobile phone when you spell a word using the spelling aid device T9 | compound |
| ***tube-free (toiletpaper)*** | adj. | toiletpaper not wrapped around a tube | compound |
| **W** | | | |
| ***wellderly*** | n. (uncount.) | a group of elder people who are in good health | blend |
| **Y** | | | |
| ***yaka-wow*** | interjection | referring to something yuck and wow | misheard blend |

# Appendix 3: Questionnaires for the nameworthiness experiment

Questionnaire design:

1) Sex: M F

2) Age group: 18-25 26-46 46-66 66+

3) Highest educational level completed: secondary
university (degree:__________________)

Occupation: ____________________________________

TASK: Please read the following definitions and answer the questions:
(1 = not useful at all, 2= not so useful, 3= not sure, 4= useful, 5= very useful)

**< DEFINITION>**

a) How useful is this meaning? 1 2 3 4 5
b) Why/Why not? ______________________________
c) Did you ever encounter this meaning? Yes No
d) What is the word for it or might the word for it be? __________________

Definition sets in alphabetical order

| Target (T) & Control (C) | Definition | Lemma |
|---|---|---|
| T | a short blog entry | ***bloglet***[1] |
| C | a small book | *booklet* |
| T | a scandal involving a famous person (in) advertedly showing too much cleavage | ***Boobgate*** |
| C | a scandal involving a famous person (in) advertedly showing her uncovered genitals | (made up) |
| T | a straight man who is very close to another man without being homosexual | ***bromosexual*** |
| C | a straight man who is very interested in fashion and the way he looks without being gay. | *metrosexual* |
| T | a cake consisting of three layers of pie: cherry, pumpkin and apple | ***cherpumple*** |
| C | a cake consisting of rum and raisins | *rum cake* |

| Target (T) & Control (C) | Definition | Lemma |
|---|---|---|
| T | the temporary loss of inhibition while online | ***cyberdisinihibition*** |
| C | the act of sharing more information online than one would do in face-to-face interactions | *oversharing* |
| T | to log off from Twitter | ***detweet*** |
| C | to pass on a tweet on Twitter | *retweet* |
| T | to anti-recycle; the act of not recycling | ***decycling*** |
| C | to re-use used products and materials | *recycling* |
| T | a second career after retirement | ***encore career*** |
| C | a professional occupation while being a student | (made up) |
| T | the use of the Internet to gather information and feedback from friends | ***friendsourcing*** |
| C | the use of the Internet to collect money from people to fund a project | *crowdfunding* |
| T | the idea that obesity has become a global problem | ***globesity*** |
| C | the idea that the earth is warming up | *global warming* |
| C | the idea that anorexia has become a global problem | (made up) |
| T | part of a conversation bystanders hear when someone is talking on the phone in a public place | ***halfalogue*** |
| C | a conversation between two people | *dialogue* |
| T | referring to the immediate surroundings; mainly used for referring to news | ***hyperlocal*** |
| C | referring to the surroundings; often used for referring to news | *local* |
| T | busy reading or writing text messages, especially while driving | ***intexticated*** |
| C | busy reading or writing text messages, especially while in class | (made up) |
| T | rule or domination by children; the belief that children's needs and preferences take precedence over those of their parents or other adults. | ***kindergarchy*** |
| C | rule or domination by a handful or influential people; the belief that their needs and preferences precedence over those of the other people | *oligarchy* |

| | | |
|---|---|---|
| T | a pregnant woman who forgets more than usually | ***preghead*** |
| C | a person who forgets more than usually or than other persons | *forgetful person* |
| C | a pregnant women who behaves more stupidly than usually | (made up) |
| T | an area at the airport where passengers can collect their belongings and clothes after the security check | ***recombobulation area*** |
| C | the area at the airport where passengers have to take off their clothes/shoes and empty their hand luggage to have them checked by security | *security area* |
| T | a type of activism that seeks projects and causes that require the least amount of effort. | ***slacktivism*** |
| C | a type of activism that seeks projects and causes that do not cost a lot of money to contribute to. | (made up) |
| T | the act of playing loud music on a phone or loudspeaker in public | ***sodacsting*** |
| C | the act of talking loudly in public | (made up) |
| T | a word that you get as a suggestion on your mobile phone when you spell a word using the spelling aid device T9 | ***tynonym*** |
| C | a word/symbol you add in a phone/chat message to express your emotions (e.g. LOL) | *emoticon* |
| T | toilet paper not wrapped around a tube | ***tube-free*** |
| T | a group of elder people in good health | ***wellderly*** |
| C | a group of elder people over 70. | *septuagenerians* |
| C | a group of elder people in bad health | (made up) |

# Appendix 4: Frequency distribution of word-forms and morpho-lexical relatives of *robosigning*

4.1. Objectlinguistic usage

| Word-form/ Morpho-lexical relative | N | V | Adj | Total |
|---|---|---|---|---|
| *robo-signing* | 1689 | 6 | | 1695 |
| *robosigning* | 697 | 1 | | 698 |
| *robo signing* | 249 | - | | 249 |
| *robo-signed* | – | 41 | 319 | 360 |
| *robosigned* | – | 55 | 57 | 112 |
| *robo signed* | – | 51 | 31 | 82 |
| *robo-sign* | 51 | 47 | – | 98 |
| *robosign* | 4 | 19 | – | 23 |
| *robo sign* | 2 | 16 | – | 18 |
| *robo-signs* | – | 2 | – | 2 |
| *robosign* | – | – | – | 0 |
| *robo signs* | – | – | – | 0 |
| *robo-signature* | 2 | – | – | 2 |
| *robo-signatures* | 34 | – | – | 34 |
| *robosignature* | 2 | – | – | 2 |
| *robosignatures* | 9 | – | – | 9 |
| *robo signature* | 24 | – | – | 24 |
| *robo signatures* | 32 | – | – | 32 |
| *robo-signer* | 257 | – | – | 257 |
| *robo-signers* | 364 | – | – | 364 |
| *robosigner* | 79 | – | – | 79 |
| *robosigners* | 114 | – | – | 114 |
| *robo signer* | 34 | – | – | 34 |
| *robo signers* | 105 | – | – | 105 |
| *Robogate* | 2 | – | – | 2 |
| *Robo gate* | 3 | – | – | 3 |
| *Robo-gate* | 7 | – | – | 7 |
| *Foreclosuregate* | 173 | – | – | 173 |

| | | | | |
|---|---|---|---|---|
| *Foreclosre gate* | 19 | – | – | 19 |
| *Foreclosure-gate* | 91 | – | – | 91 |

## 4.2. Metalinguistic usage

| | N | V | Adj | Total |
|---|---|---|---|---|
| *robo-signing* | 37 | – | – | 37 |
| *robosigning* | 47 | – | – | 47 |
| *robo signing* | 2 | – | – | 2 |
| *robo-signed* | 4 | – | – | 4 |
| *robosigned* | 2 | – | – | 2 |
| *robo signed* | – | – | – | – |
| *robo-sign* | – | – | – | – |
| *robosign* | 4 | – | – | 4 |
| *robo sign* | – | – | – | – |
| *robo-signs* | – | – | – | – |
| *robosigns* | – | – | – | – |
| *robo signs* | – | – | – | – |
| *robo-signature* | 1 | – | – | 1 |
| *robo-signatures* | – | – | – | – |
| *robosignature* | – | – | – | – |
| *robosignatures* | – | – | – | – |
| *robo signature* | – | – | – | – |
| *robo signatures* | – | – | – | – |
| *robo-signer* | 10 | – | – | 10 |
| *robo-signers* | 42 | – | – | 42 |
| *robosigner* | 3 | – | – | 3 |
| *robosigners* | 6 | – | – | 6 |
| *robo signer* | 1 | – | – | 1 |
| *robo signers* | 1 | – | – | 1 |
| *Robogate* | – | – | – | – |
| *Robo gate* | – | – | – | – |
| *Robo-gate* | – | – | – | – |
| *Foreclosuregate* | 7 | – | – | 7 |

| | N | V | Adj | Total |
|---|---|---|---|---|
| *Foreclosre gate* | – | – | – | – |
| *Foreclosure-gate* | 1 | – | – | 1 |

# Appendix 5: Type of source frequency distribution in objectlinguistic use

| Neologism | Frequency | Type of source | | | | | | | | |
|---|---|---|---|---|---|---|---|---|---|---|
| | | Academic | Private blog | Prof. blog | Discussion forum | Filesharing | Micro-blogging | News | Portal | Social networks |
| *administrativia* | 41 | 0 | 5 | 3 | 5 | 10 | 1 | 0 | 16 | 0 |
| *back scooping* | 148 | 0 | 11 | **28** | 2 | 10 | 2 | 16 | **73** | 6 |
| *bloglet*[1] | 515 | 0 | **491** | 0 | 13 | 0 | 1 | 0 | 0 | 0 |
| *bloglet*[2] | 26 | 0 | **26** | 0 | 0 | 0 | 0 | 0 | 0 | 0 |
| *Boobgate* | 121 | 0 | **24** | 23 | 4 | 4 | 8 | **15** | **41** | 2 |
| *bromosexual* | 941 | 0 | **163** | 31 | **309** | 37 | 56 | 5 | 96 | **201** |
| *burquini* | 392 | 0 | **72** | 51 | **73** | 5 | 1 | **59** | **124** | 0 |
| *cherpumple* | 387 | 0 | **168** | 108 | 12 | 8 | 8 | 2 | 77 | 1 |
| *crapget* | 17 | 0 | 1 | 1 | **9** | 0 | **2** | 0 | 1 | **2** |
| *cyberchondriac* | 794 | 0 | 159 | 119 | 46 | 26 | 18 | 42 | **222** | 3 |
| *cyberdisinhibition* | 111 | 1 | 12 | 21 | 3 | 4 | 0 | 0 | **49** | 0 |
| *decycling* | 20 | 0 | 5 | 4 | 1 | 3 | 1 | 0 | **4** | 0 |
| *to detweet*[1] | 47 | 0 | 3 | 1 | 1 | 0 | **34** | 0 | 1 | 0 |
| *to detweet*[2] | 41 | 0 | 2 | 1 | 2 | 0 | **17** | 1 | 3 | 0 |
| *to detweet*[3] | 19 | 0 | 2 | 0 | 2 | 0 | **14** | 0 | 0 | 0 |
| *to detweet*[4] | 20 | 0 | 1 | **4** | 0 | 0 | **4** | 0 | **4** | 0 |
| to detweet[5] | 7 | 0 | **1** | 0 | 0 | 0 | 5 | 0 | **1** | 0 |
| *diabesity* | 785 | 167 | 58 | **192** | 20 | 46 | 12 | **46** | 202 | 10 |
| *e-tivity* | 51 | 18 | 10 | **17** | 0 | 1 | 2 | 0 | 3 | 0 |

| Neologism | Frequency | Type of source | | | | | | | | |
|---|---|---|---|---|---|---|---|---|---|---|
| | | Academic | Private blog | Prof. blog | Discussion forum | Filesharing | Micro-blogging | News | Portal | Social networks |
| *encore career* | 724 | 0 | 33 | **313** | 2 | 37 | 39 | **81** | **197** | 15 |
| *Eurofascists* | 324 | 7 | 53 | **134** | 33 | 27 | 1 | 20 | **49** | 0 |
| *facebook-official* | 51 | 0 | **31** | 8 | 1 | 0 | 1 | 0 | **9** | 1 |
| *floordrobe* | 291 | 0 | **68** | 5 | **57** | 13 | 25 | 5 | 29 | **36** |
| *friendsourcing* | 212 | 2 | 22 | **89** | 1 | 23 | **27** | 3 | **24** | 9 |
| *frogurt* | 211 | 0 | **82** | 42 | 2 | 3 | 0 | 5 | **54** | 3 |
| *ganky* | 92 | 0 | **37** | 20 | **13** | 1 | 0 | 0 | **20** | 1 |
| *ghost surgery* | 48 | 11 | 2 | **9** | 0 | 0 | 0 | 2 | **6** | 0 |
| *globesity* | 681 | 125 | 42 | **87** | 17 | 32 | 13 | 71 | **151** | 6 |
| *grawlix* | 427 | 0 | 13 | 11 | 4 | 0 | 4 | 3 | 12 | 1 |
| *half-false* | 58 | 0 | **18** | 7 | **9** | 1 | 0 | 5 | **14** | 4 |
| *halfalogue* | 164 | 0 | 2 | 0 | 0 | 0 | 0 | 0 | 0 | 0 |
| *hyperlocal* | 1399 | 0 | 102 | **714** | 15 | 27 | 21 | 60 | **445** | 1 |
| *intexticated* | 913 | 0 | **143** | 103 | 18 | 32 | 20 | 41 | **135** | 13 |
| *iPad friendly* | 146 | 0 | 11 | **90** | 4 | 10 | 2 | 0 | **29** | 0 |
| *kindergarchy* | 178 | 0 | **72** | 23 | 17 | 10 | 1 | 12 | 8 | 0 |
| *meaniac* | 41 | 0 | **13** | 6 | **9** | 0 | 1 | 0 | 3 | 0 |
| *mesofact* | 80 | 0 | 15 | **17** | 0 | 0 | 2 | 1 | 7 | 0 |
| *politerati* | 51 | 0 | 2 | **11** | 0 | 1 | 0 | 4 | **33** | 0 |

| | | | | | | | | | | |
|---|---|---|---|---|---|---|---|---|---|---|
| *preghead* | 14 | 0 | **6** | 3 | 1 | 0 | 0 | 0 | **4** | 0 |
| *radiculous* | 211 | 0 | 29 | **30** | **54** | 8 | 6 | 5 | **54** | 21 |
| *recombobulation area* | 231 | 0 | **69** | 8 | 11 | 27 | **30** | **29** | 15 | 1 |
| *robosigning* | 1735 | 0 | 61 | **1106** | 25 | 33 | 2 | 48 | **424** | 0 |
| *roofvertising* | 6 | 0 | **5** | 0 | 0 | 0 | 0 | 0 | 0 | 0 |
| *slacktivism* | 1366 | 0 | 251 | **282** | 31 | 39 | 87 | 46 | **218** | 25 |
| *sodcasting* | 76 | 0 | **14** | 9 | 2 | 5 | 7 | 5 | 8 | 0 |
| *tynonym* | 104 | 0 | 2 | 0 | 0 | 1 | 3 | 0 | 1 | 0 |
| *tube-free* | 161 | 0 | 7 | **72** | 5 | 5 | 3 | 5 | **63** | 0 |
| *wellderly* | 608 | 15 | 3 | **156** | 18 | 11 | 15 | 59 | **173** | 2 |
| *yaka-wow* | 78 | 0 | 3 | 3 | 0 | 5 | **17** | 1 | 4 | 1 |

# Bibliography

Adelman, James S., Gordon D.A. Brown and José F. Quesada. 2006. "Contextual diversity, not word frequency determines word-naming and lexical decision times". *Psychological Science* 17. 814-823.

Aitchison, Jean. 1991. *Language Change: Progress or Decay?* Cambridge: Cambridge UP. Second edition.

Aitchison, Jean and Diana Lewis. 1995. "How to handle wimps: Incorporating new lexical items as an adult". *Folia Linguistica* 29. 7-20.

Alaoui, Khalid. 2003. "Petite histoire de la néologie: approche conceptuelle et idéologique (XVIe - XIXe siècle)". In: Sablayrolles. 149-180.

Alegre, Maria and Peter Gordon. 1999. "Frequency effects and the representational status of regular inflections". *Journal of Memory and Language* 40. 41-61.

Algeo, John. 1993. "Desuetude among new English words". *International Journal of Lexicography* 6. 281-293.

Algeo, John. 1991. (Ed.). *Fifty Years among the New Words. A Dictionary of Neologisms, 1941-1991.* Cambridge: Cambridge UP.

Andrés, Louis, David Cuberes, Mame Astou Diouf and Tomás Serebrisky. 2007. "Diffusion of the Internet: A Cross-Country Analysis". *World Bank Policy Research Paper WPS4420.*

Auer, Peter and Frans Hinskens. 2005. "The role of interpersonal accommodation in a theory of language change". In: Auer, Peter, Frans Hinskens and Paul Kerswill. (Eds.). *Dialect Change.* Canbridge: Cambridge UP. 335-357.

Autenrieth, Ulla P. and Jana Herwig. 2011. "Zwischen begrenzten Mitteln und komplexen Strukturen: Gemeinschaftsorientierte Kommunikation und Interaktion auf Microblogging-Plattformen am Beispiel Twitter". In: Neumann-Braun, Klaus and Ulla P. Autenrieth, Ulla. (Eds.). *Freundschaft und Gemeinschaft im Social Web. Bildbezogenes Handeln und Peergroup-Kommunikation auf Facebook und Co.* Baden-Baden: Nomos. 211-232.

Baayen, R. Harald and Antoinette Renouf. 1996. "Chronicling the Times: Productive lexical innovations in an English newspaper". *Language* 72. 69-96.

Baayen, R. Harald and Anneke Neijt. 1997. "Productivity in context: A case study of a Dutch suffix". *Linguistics* 35. 565-587.

Baker, Paul. 2006. *Using Corpora in Discourse Analysis*. London: Continuum.

Barnhart, Robert K., Sol Steinmetz and Clarence L. Barnhart. (Eds.). [3]1990. *Third Barnhart Dictionary of New English*. New York: Wilson. First edition 1973.

Barnhart, David K. 2007. "A calculus for new words". *Journal of the Dictionary Society of North America* 28. 132-138.

Baroni, Marco and Silvia Bernardini. 2004. "BootCaT: bootstrapping corpora and terms from the web". *Proceedings of the 4th International Conference on Language Resources and Evaluation*. Lisbon.

Baroni, Marco and Silvia Bernardini. (Eds.). 2006. *Wacky! Working Papers on the Web as Corpus*. Bologna: GEDIT.

Baroni, Marco, Silvia Bernardini, Adriano Ferraresi and Eros Zanchetta. 2009. "The WaCky Wide Web: A Collection of Very Large Linguistically Processed Web-Crawled Corpora". *Language Resources and Evaluation* 43(3): 209-226.

Bartsch, Sabine. 2004. *Structural and Functional Properties of Collocations in English*. Tübingen: Narr.

Barz, Irmhild. 1998. "Neologie und Wortbildung. Zum Neuheitseffekt von Wortneubildungen". In: Teubert, Wolfgang. (Ed.). *Neologie und Korpus*. Tübingen: Günter Narr. 11-30.

Bauer, Laurie. 1983. *English Word-Formation*. Cambridge: Cambridge UP.

Bauer, Laurie. 2001. *Morphological Productivity*. Cambridge: Cambridge UP.

Baugh, Albert C. and Thomas Cable. [5]2002. *A History of the English Language*. London: Routledge. Fifth edition.

Baxter, Gareth J., Richard A. Blythe, William Croft and Alan J. Mckane. 2006. "Utterance selection model of language change". *Physical Review* 73. 1-21.

Baxter, Gareth. J., Richard A. Blythe and Alan J. McKane. 2007. "Exact solution of the multi-allelic diffusion model". *Mathematical Biosciences* 209. 124–70.

Baxter, Gareth J., Richard A. Blythe, William Croft and Alan J. Mckane. 2009. "Modeling language change: An evaluation of Trudgill's theory of the emergence of New Zealand English". *Language Variation and Change* 21. 257–96.

Beaugrande, Robert-Alain and Wolfgang Dressler. 1981. *Introduction to Text Linguistics*. London: Longman.

Beciri, Hélène. 2003. "Néologie et transmission des connaissances". In: Sablayrolles. 59-78.

Berg, Donna Lee. 1993. *A Guide to the OED*. Oxford: Oxford UP.

Biber, Douglas. 1988. *Variation across Speech and Writing*. Cambridge: Cambridge UP.

Biber, Douglas. 1989. "A typology of English texts". *Linguistics* 27. 3–43.

Biber, Douglas. 1995. *Dimensions of Register Variation*. Cambridge: Cambridge UP.

Biber, Douglas and Jerry Kurjian. 2007. "Towards a taxonomy of web registers and text types: a multi-dimensional analysis". In: Hundt, Nesselhauf and Biewer. 109-131.

Biber, Douglas. 2006. *University Language: A Corpus-based Study of Spoken and Written Registers*. Amsterdam: John Benjamins.

Biber, Douglas and Susan Conrad. 2009. *Register, Genre, and Style*. Cambridge: Cambridge UP.

Blank, Andreas. 2001. "Pathways of lexicalization". In: Haspelmath, Martin, Ekkehard König, Wuld Oesterreicher and Wolfgang Raible. (Eds.). *Language Typology and Language Universals/ La Typologie des Langues et les Universeaux Linguistiques/ Sprachtypologie und Sprachliche Universalien. An International Handbook/Manuel International/Ein Internationales Handbuch*. Vol. 2. Berlin: Mouton de Gruyter. 1596-1608.

Blythe, Richard A. and William A. Croft. 2009. "The speech community in evolutionary language dynamics". *Language Learning* 59. 47-63.

Blythe, Richard A. and William A. Croft. 2009. "S-Curves and the mechanisms of propagation in language change". *Language* 88:2. 269-304.

Boulanger, Valerie Michele. 1997. *What Makes a Coinage Successful? The Factors Influencing the Adoption of English New Words*. Unpublished PhD dissertation, University of Georgia.

Brinton, Laurel J. and Elizabeth Closs Traugott. 2005a. *Lexicalization and Language Change*. Cambridge: Cambridge UP.

Brinton, Laurel J. and Elizabeth Closs Traugott. 2005b. "Lexicalization and grammaticalization all over again". In: Salmons, Joseph C. and Shannon Dubenion-Smith. (Eds.). *Historical Linguistics*. Amsterdam: John Benjamins. 3-19.

Bruce, Ian. 2010. "Evolving genres in online domains: The hybrid genre of the participatory news article". In: Mehler et al. 323-350.

Buchstaller, Isabelle, John R. Rickford, Elizabeth Closs Traugott, Thomas Wasow and Arnold Zwicky. 2010. "The sociolinguistics of a short-lived innovation: tracing the development of quotative *all* across spoken and internet newsgroup data". *Language Variation and Change* 22. 191–219.

Burchfield, Robert W. (Ed.) 1972. *A Supplement to the Oxford English Dictionary. Volume 1 A-G*. Oxford: Clarendon Press.

Bybee, Joan. 1985. *Morphology: A Study in the Relation between Meaning and Form*. Amsterdam: John Benjamins.

Bybee, Joan. 2007. "Introduction". In: Bybee, Joan. (Ed.). *Frequency of Use and the Organization of Language*. Oxford: Oxford UP. 5-22.

Bybee, Joan and Dan Slobin. 2007. "Rules and schemas in the development and use of the English past tense". In: Bybee, Joan. (Ed.). *Frequency of Use and the Organization of Language*. Oxford: Oxford UP. 101-126.

Cabré, Maria-Teresa, Meritxell Domènech, Rosa Estapà, Judit Freixa and Élisabet Solé. 2003. "L'Observatoire de néologie: Conception, méthodologie, résultats et nouveaux travaux": In: Sablayrolles. 125-147.

Chaffin, Roger, Robin K. Morris and Rachel E. Seely. 2001. "Learning new word meaning from context. A case study of eye movements". *Journal of Experimental Psychology* 27. 225-235.

Chambers, Jack K. 1992. "Dialect acquisition". *Language* 68. 673-705.

Church, Kenneth W. and Patrick Hanks. 1990. "Word association norms, mutual information and lexicography". *Computational Linguistics* 16. 22-29.

Clark, Herbert H. 1996. *Using Language*. Cambridge: Cambridge UP.

Clark Eve and Herbert H. Clark. 1979. "When nouns surface as verbs". *Language* 55. 767-811.

Clauzure, Émilie. 2003. "Le terme *neologism* dans le monde anglo-saxon: origine et évolution". In: Sablayrolles. 207-223.

Clear, Jeremy. 1993. "From Firth principles: Computational tools for the study of collocation". In: Baker, Mona, Gill Francis and Elena Tognini-Bonelli. (Eds.). *Text and Technology. In Honour of John Sinclair*. Amsterdam: John Benjamins. 271-292.

Coltheart Max, Kathleen Rastle, Conrad Perry, Robyn Landon and Johannes Ziegler. 2001. "DRC: A dual route cascaded model of visual word recognition and reading aloud". *Psychological Review* 108. 204-256.

Costello, Fintan J. and Mark T. Keane. 2005. "Compositionality and the pragmatics of conceptual combination". In: Machery, Edouard, Markus Werning and Gerhard Schurz. (Eds.). *The Compositionality of Meaning and Content. Vol. II: Applications to Linguistics, Psychology and Neuroscience*. Heusenstamm: Ontos. 203-216.

Croft, William A. 2000. *Explaining Language Change*. Harlow: Longman.

Crystal, David. 1995. *The Cambridge Encyclopedia of the English Language*. Cambridge: Cambridge UP.

Crystal, David. 2006. *Language and the Internet*. Second edition. Cambridge: Cambridge UP.

Davies, Mark. (2011-). *Google Books (American English) Corpus (155 billion words, 1810-2009)*. Available online at googlebooks.byu.edu/.

Davis, Matt H., Anna Maria Di Betta, Mark J. E. Macdonald and M. Gareth Gaskell. 2009. "Learning and consolidation of novel spoken words". *Journal of Cognitive Neuroscience* 21. 803–820.

de Kunder, Maurice. 2007. *Geschatte Grootte van het Geïndexeerde World Wide Web*. Unpublished MA thesis at Tilburg university. Available via dekunder.nl. Last accessed Agust 2, 2014.

de Saussure, Ferdinand. 1916. *Cours de la Linguistique Générale*. Paris: Payot.

Deterding, Sebastian. 2009. "Virtual communities". In: Hitzler, Ronald, Anne Honer and Michaela Pfadenhauer. (Eds.). *Posttraditionale Gemeinschaften. Theoretische und Ethnografische Erkundungen*. Wiesbaden: Verlag für Sozialwissenschaften. 115-131.

de Vaan, Laura, Robert Schreuder and Harald R. Baayen. 2007. "Regular morphologically complex neologisms leave detectable traces in the mental lexicon". *The Mental Lexicon* 2. 1-24.

Downing, Pamela. 1977. "On the creation and use of English compound nouns". *Language* 53. 810-842.

Dumay, Nicolas, M. Gareth Gaskell and Xiaojia Feng. 2004. "A day in the life of a spoken word". *Proceedings of the Twenty-Sixth Annual Conference of the Cognitive Science Society*. Mahwah: Lawrence Erlbaum Associates. 339-344.

Dunbar, George. 2005. "The Goldilocks scenario: Is noun-noun compounding compositional?". In: Werning, Markus, Édouard Machery and Gerhard Schurz. (Eds.). *The Compositionality of Meaning and Content. Vol. 2*. Heusenstamm: Ontos. 217-228.

Dunning, Ted. 1993. "Accurate methods for the statistics of surprise and coincidence". *Computational Linguistics* 19. 61-74.

EAGLES. 1996. *Preliminary Recommendations on Text Typology*. Available via ilc.cnr.it/EAGLES96/texttyp/texttyp.html.

Eckert, Penelope. 2000. *Linguistic Variation as Social Practice*. Malden: Blackwell.

Encyclopaedia Britannica.

Evans, Vyvyan and Melanie Green. 2006. *Cognitive Linguistics*. Edinburgh: Edinburgh UP.

Evert, Stefan. 2008. "Corpora and collocations". In: Lüdeling, Anke and Merja Kytö. (Eds.). *Corpus Linguistics. An International Handbook*. Berlin: Mouton de Gruyter. 1212-1248.

Fairon, Cédrick, Kévin Macé and Hubert Naets. 2008. "GlossaNet 2: a linguistic search engine for RSS-based corpora". In: Evert, Stefan, Adam Kilgarriff and Serge Sharoff. (Eds.) *Proceedings of the 4th Web as Corpus Workshop (WAC-4) – Can we beat Google?* Marrakech, 1 June 2008. Available via cental.fltr.ucl.ac.be/team/~ced/papers/2008-wac4-glossanet.pdf. Last accessed October 18, 2011.

Fagyal, Zsuzsanna, Samarth Swarup, Anna María Escobar, Les Gasser and Kiran Lakkaraju. 2010. "Centers and peripheries: Network roles in language change". *Lingua* 120. 2061-2079.

Ferraresi, Adriano. 2007. *Building a very large corpus of English obtained by Web crawling: ukWaC*. Master Thesis, University of Bologna. Available via wacky.sslmit.unibo.it/lib/exe/fetch.php?media=a_ferraresi_thesis.pdf. Last accessed on October 18, 2011.

Ferraresi, Adriano, Eros Zanchetta, Marco Baroni and Silvia Bernardini. 2008. "Introducing and evaluating ukWaC, a very large web-derived corpus of English". In: Evert, Stefan, Adam Kilgarriff and Serge Sharoff. (Eds.) *Proceedings of the 4th Web as Corpus Workshop (WAC-4) – Can we beat Google?* Marrakech, 1 June 2008.

Firth, John R. 1951/1957. "Modes of meaning". In: Firth, John R. *Papers in Linguistics 1934-1951*. London: Oxford UP. 190-215.

Fischer, Roswitha. 1998. *Lexical Change in Present-Day English. A Corpus-Based Study of the Motivation, Institutionalization, and Productivity of Creative Neologisms*. Tübingen: Narr.

Fletcher, William. 2001. "Concordancing the Web with KWiCFinder". *American Association for Applied Corpus Linguistics. Third North American Symposium on Corpus Linguistics and Language Teaching*. Boston, MA, 23-25 March 2001. Available via kwicfinder.com/FletcherCLLT2001.pdf. Last accessed October 18, 2011.

Fletcher, William. 2007. "Concordancing the web: promise and problems, tools and techniques". In: Hundt, Nesselhauf and Biewer. 25-45.

Flexner, Stuart Berg. (Ed.). [2]1993. *Random House Unabridged Dictionary*. Second revised edition. New York: Random House. First edition 1966.

Folch, Helka, Serge Heiden, Benoît Habert, Serge Fleur, Gabriel Illouz, Pierre Lafon, Julien Nioche and Sophie Prévost. 2000. "TypTex: Inductive typological text classification by multivariate statistical analysis for NLP systems tuning/evaluation". In: Gavrilidou, Maria, George Carayannis, Stella Markantonatou, Stelios Piperidis, Gregory Stainhaour. (Eds.). *Proceedings of the Second Language Resources and Evaluation Conference.*

Forster, Kenneth I. 2007. "Visual word recognition: Problems and issues". In: Jarema, Gonia and Gary Libben. (Eds.). *The Mental Lexicon: Core Perspectives.* Amsterdam: Elsevier. 31-54.

Fowler, Henry W. and Francis G. Fowler. [3]1954. *The King's English.* Oxford: Clarendon Press. First edition published 1906.

Friemel, Thomas N. 2010. "Diffusionsforschung". In: Stegbauer, Christian and Roger Häussling. (Eds.). *Handbuch Netzwerkforschung*. Wiesbaden: Verlag für Sozialwissenschaften. 825-833.

Giles, Howard. 1973. "Accent mobility: A model and some data". *Anthropological Linguistics* 15. 87-105.

Giles, Howard, Nikolas Coupland and Justine Coupland. 1991. "Accommodation theory: Communication, context, and consequence". In: Giles, Howard, Nikolas Coupland and Justine Coupland. (Eds.). *Contexts of Accommodation. Developments in Applied Sociolinguistics*. Cambridge: Cambridge UP. 1-68.

Giltrow, Janet and Dieter Stein. 2009. "Genres in the Internet: Innovation, evolution, and genre theory". In: *Genres in the Internet: Issues in the Theory of Genre*. Giltrow, Janet and Dieter Stein.(Eds.). Amsterdam: John Benjamins. 1–26.

Gleick, James. 2006. "Cyber-Neologoliferation. The Oxford English Dictionary meets cyberpace". *New York Times Magazine* 5. (November 2006).

Gove, Philip B. and Noah Webster. (Eds.). 1976. *Webster's Third New International Dictionary of the English Language Unabridged. Volume 4*. Springfield: Merriam-Webster.

Granovetter 1973. "The strength of weak ties". *The American Journal of Sociology* 78. 1360-1380.

Granovetter 1978. "Threshold models of collective behavior". *The American Journal of Sociology* 83. 1420-1443.

Grieve, Jack, Douglas Biber, Eric Frinigal and Tatiana Nekrasova. 2010. "Variation among blogs: A multi-dimensional approach". In: Mehler et al. 303-322.

Große, Rudolf and Albrecht Neubert. 1982. "Soziolinguistische Aspekte der Theorie des Sprachwandels". *Sitzungsberichte der Akademie der Wissenschaften der DDR* 10. 5-14.

Gulli, Antonio and Alessio Signorini. 2005. "The indexable web is more than 11.5 billion pages". *Proceedings WWW '05 special interest tracks and posters of the 14th international conference on World Wide Web*. New York: ACM.

Halliday, Michael and Rugaiya Hasan. 1976. *Cohesion in English*. London: Longman.

Hamblin, Robert L., Jerry L. Miller and D. Eugene Saxton. 1979. "Modeling diffusion". *Social Forces* 57. 799-811.

Harder, Peter. 2010. *Meaning in Mind and Society. A Functional Contribution to the Social Turn in Cognitive Linguistics*. Berlin: Mouton de Gruyter.

Hargraves, Orin. 2007. "Taming the wild beast". *Journal of the Dictionary Society of North America* 28. 139-141.

Herberg, Dieter. 1988. "Neologismen – lexikologisch und lexikographisch betrachtet". *Sprachpflege* 37. 109-112.

Herbst, Thomas. 1996. "What are collocations: Sandy beaches or false teeth?". *English Studies* 4. 379-393.

Herring, Susan C. 2007. "A faceted classification scheme for Computer-Mediated Discourse". *Language@internet* 4. www.languageatinternet.de/articles/2007/761/. Last accessed November 1, 2011.

Hoey, Michael. 2005. *Lexical Priming: A New Theory of Words and Language*. London: Routledge.

Hoffmann, Sebastian. 2007. "From webpage to mega-corpus: the CNN transcripts". In: Hundt, Nesselhauf and Biewer. 69-86.

Hoffmann, Sebastian, Stefan Evert, Nicholas Smith, David Lee and Ylva Berglung-Prytz. 2008. *Corpus Linguistics with BNCweb: A Practical Guide*. Frankfurt am Main: Peter Lang.

Hohenhaus, Peter. 1996. *Ad-hoc-Wortbildung. Terminologie, Typologie und Theorie kreativer Wortbildung im Englischen*. Frankfurt am Main: Peter Lang.

Hohenhaus, Peter. 2005. "Lexicalization and institutionalization". In: Stekauer, Pavol and Rochelle Lieber. (Eds.). *Handbook of Word-Formation*. Dordrecht: Springer. 353-373.

Hohenhaus, Peter. 2006. "Bouncebackability. A web-as-corpus-based study of a new formation, its interpretation, generalization/spread and subsequent decline". *SKASE Journal of Theoretical Linguistics* 3. 17-27.

Hohenhaus, Peter. 2007. "How to do (even more) things with nonce words (other than naming)". In: Munat, Judith. (Ed.). *Lexical Creativity, Texts and Contexts*. Amsterdam: John Benjamins. 15-38.

Holcomb, Phillip J. and Helen J. Neville. 1990. "Auditory and visual semantic priming in lexical decision: A comparison using event-related brain potentials". *Language and Cognitive Processes* 5. 281-312.

Holmes, Janet. 2008. *An Introduction to Sociolinguistics*. Third edition. London: Pearson Longman.

Hopper, Paul J. 1994. "Phonogenesis". In: Pagliuca, William. (Ed.). *Perspectives on Grammaticalization*. Amsterdam: John Benjamins. 29-45.

Hruschka, Daniel J., Morten H. Christiansen, Richard A. Blythe, William Croft, Paul Heggarty, Salikoko S. Mufwene, Janet B. Pierrehumbert and Shana Poplack. 2009. "Building social cognitive models of language change". *Trends in Cognitive Sciences* 13. 464-469.

Hundt, Marianne, Nadja Nesselhauf and Carolin Biewer. (Eds.). *Corpus Linguistics and the Web*. Amsterdam: Rodopi.

Hunston, Susan. 2002. *Corpora in Applied Linguistics*. Cambridge: Cambridge UP.

Hymes, Dell. 1974. *Foundations in Sociolinguistics: An Ethnographic Approach*. Philadelphia: University of Pennsylvania Press.

Irvine, Alexander H. (Ed.). 1975. *Collins English Dictionary*. London: Collins.

Itkonen, Esa. 2008. "The central role of normativity in language and linguistics". In: Zlatev, Jordan, Timothy P. Racine, Chris Sinha and Esa Itkonen. (Eds.) *The Shared Mind. Perspectives on Intersubjectivity*. Amsterdam: John Benjamins. 279-306.

Jakobs, Eva-Maria. 2003. "Hypertextsorten". *Zeitschrift für Germanistische Linguistik* 31. 232-252.

Johanson, Lars. 2008. "Remodelling grammar: Copying, conventionalization, grammaticalization". In: Siemund, Peter and Noemi Kintana. (Eds.). *Language Contact and Contact Languages*. Amsterdam: John Benjamins. 61-79.

Johnson-Laird, Philip N. 1983. *Mental Models*. Cambridge (MA): Harvard UP.

Joseph, Brian D. and Richard D. Janda. 1988. "The how and why of diachronic morphologization and demorphologization". In: Hammond, Michael T. (Ed.). *Theoretical Morphology*. 193-210.

Kamhi, Alan G. and Linda A. Koenig. 1985. "Metalinguistic awareness in normal and language-disordered children". *Language, Speech, and Hearing Services in Schools* 16. 199-210.

Kastovsky, Dieter, 1982. *Wortbildung und Semantik*. Düsseldorf: Schwann-Bagel.

Katamba, Francis. 1994. *English Words*. London: Routledge.

Kehoe, Andrew and Antoinette Renouf. 2002. "WebCorp: Applying the Web to Linguistics and Linguistics to the Web". WWW2002 Conference, Honolulu, Hawaii. Available via 2002.org/CDROM/poster/67/. Last accessed October 24, 2011.

Keil, Frank. 1979. *Semantic and conceptual development: An ontological Perspective*. Cambridge (MA): Harvard UP.

Keil, Frank. 1981. "Constraints on knowledge and cognitive development". *Psychological Review* 88. 197-227.

Keller, Rudi. 1990. *Sprachwandel. Von der Unsichtbaren Hand in der Sprache*. Tübingen: Francke.

Keller, Rudi. 1998. *Zeichentheorie*. Tübingen: Francke.

Kemmer, Suzanne. 2003. "Schemas and lexical blends". In: Cuyckens, Hubert, Thomas Berg, René Dirven and Klaus-Uwe Panther. (Eds.). *Motivation in Language: Studies in Honor of Günter Radden*. Amsterdam: John Benjamins. 69-97.

Kerremans, Daphné, Susanne Stegmayr and Hans-Jörg Schmid. 2012. "The NeoCrawler: identifying and retrieving neologisms from the Internet and monitoring on-going change". In: Allan, Kathryn and Justyna Robinson. (Eds.). *Current Methods in Historical Semantics*. Berlin: Mouton de Gruyter. 59-96.

Kilgarriff, Adam. 2003. "Linguistic Search Engine". In: *Proceedings of the Shallow Processing of Large Corpora Workshop (SProLaC 2003) Corpus Linguistics 2003*. Lancaster University. Available via kilgarriff.co.uk/Publications/2003-K-LSEsprolac.pdf. Last accessed October 19, 2011.

Kim, Yunhyong and Seamus Ross. 2010. "Formulating representative features with respect to genre classification". In: Mehler et al. 129-148.

Kjellmer, Göran. 1982. "Some problems relating to the study of collocations in the Brown Corpus". In: Johansson, Stig. (Ed.). *Computer Corpora in English*

*Language Research 1975-1981*. Bergen: Norwegian Computer Centre for the Humanities. 25-33.

Kjellmer, Göran. 2000. "Potential words". *Word* 51. 205-228.

Kneidinger, Bernadette. 2010. *Facebook und Co: eine soziologische Analyse von Interaktionsformen in Online Social Networks*. Wiesbaden: Verlag für Sozialwissenschaften.

Komlósi, László I. and Elisabeth Knipf. "A contrastive analysis of entrenchment and collocational force in variable-sized lexical units". In: Butler, Christoper S. (Ed.). *The Dynamics of Language Use*. Amsterdam: John Benjamins. 243-268.

Kristiansen, Gitte. 2008. "Style-shifting and shifting styles: A socio-cognitive approach to lectal variation". In: Kristiansen, Gitte and René Dirven. (Eds.) *Cognitive Sociolinguistics*. Berlin: Mouton de Gruyter. 45-90.

Kroch, Anthony, S. 1989. "Reflexes of grammar in patterns of language change". *Language Variation and Change* 1. 199-244.

Labov, William. 1972. *Language in the Inner City: Studies in Black English Vernacular.* Philadelphia: University of Philadelphia Press.

Labov, William. 1980. "The social origins of sound change". In Labov, William. (Ed.). *Locating Language in Time and Space*. New York: Academic Press. 251-266.

Labov, William. 1994. *Principles of Linguistic Change. Volume 1: Internal Factors.* Oxford: Basil Blackwell.

Labov, William. 2001. *Principles of Linguistic change. Volume II: Social Factors.* Oxford: Blackwell.

Landauer, Thomas K. and Susan T. Dumais. 1997. "A solution to Plato's problem: The latent semantic analysis theory of acquisition, induction, and representation of knowledge". *Psychological Review* 104. 211-240.

Langacker, Ronald W. 1987. *Foundations of Cognitive Grammar. Vol. 1: Theoretical Prerequisites*. Stanford: Stanford UP:

Langacker, Ronald W. 1991. *Foundations of Cognitive Grammar. Vol. 2: Descriptive Application*. Stanford: Stanford UP.

Lawrence Steve and C. Lee Giles. 1999. "Accessibility of information on the web". *Nature* 400: July 1999. 107-109.

Leech, Geoffrey. 1974. *Semantics. The study of meaning.* Harmondsworth: Penguin.

Leech, Geoffrey, Marianne Hundt, Christian Mair and Nicolas Smith. 2009. *Change in Contemporary English: A Grammatical Study*. Cambridge: Cambridge UP.

Lehrer, Adrienne. 1996. "Identifying and interpreting blends: An experimental approach". *Cognitive Linguistics* 7. 359-390.

Lewandowski, Dirk. 2008a. "A three-year study on the freshness of web search engine databases". *Journal of Information Science* 34:6. 817-831.

Lewandowski, Dirk. 2008b. "The retrieval effectiveness of web search engines considering results descriptions" *Journal of Documentation* 64: 6. 817-831.

Lewis, David. 1969. *Convention*. Cambridge: Cambridge UP.

Libben, Gary, Martha Gibson, Yeo Bom Yoon and Dominiek Sandra. 2003. "Compound fracture: The role of semantic transparency and morphological headedness". *Brain and Language* 84. 50-64.

Libben, Gary. 2006. "Why study compound processing? An overview of the issues". In: Libben, Gary and Gonia Jarema. (Eds.). *The Representation and Processing of Compound Words*. Oxford: Oxford UP. 1-22.

Lipka, Leonhard. 1977. "Lexikalisierung, Idiomatisierung und Hypostasierung als Probleme einer synchronischen Wortbildungslehre." In: H.E. Brekle and D. Kastovsky (eds.), *Perspektiven der Wortbildungsforschung. Beiträge zum Wuppertaler Wortbildungskolloquium vom 9.-10. Juli 1976 anläßlich des 70. Geburtstags von Hans Marchand am 1. Oktober 1977*. Bonn: Bouvier Verlag Herbert Grundmann, 155-164.

Lipka, Leonhard. 1992a. "Lexicalization and Institutionalization in English and German." *Linguistica Pragensia* 1. 1-13.

Lipka, Leonhard. 1992b. "Lexicalization and institutionalization in English and German. Or: Piefke, Wendehals, smog, perestroika, AIDS etc." *Zeitschrift für Anglistik und Amerikanistik* 40. 101-111.

Lipka, Leonhard. 1999. "*Blairites*, *Teletubbies*, *Spice Girls*, and *Wheelie Bins* – Neologisms, the Word of the Year, and the Nomination Function of 'Words'." In: Carls, Uwe. (Ed.). *Form, Function, and Variation in English*. Studies in Honour of Klaus Hansen. Frankfurt am Main: Peter Lang, 41-48.

Lipka, Leonhard. 2002a. *English Lexicology: Lexical Structure, Word Semantics and Word-Formation*. Tübingen: Narr.

Lipka, Leonhard, Susanne Handl and Wolfgang Falkner. 2004. "Lexicalization and institutionalization. The state of the art in 2004". *SKASE Journal of Theoretical Linguistics* 1. 2-19.

Lüdeling, Anke, Stefan Evert and Marco Baroni. 2007. "Using web data for linguistic purposes". In: Hundt, Nesselhauf and Biewer. 7-24.

Luhn, Hans Peter. 1958. "The automatic creation of literature abstracts". *IBM Journal of Research Development* 2: 2. 159-165.

Lyons, John. 1977. *Semantics*. 2vols. Cambridge: Cambridge UP.

Mair, Christian. 2006. *Twentieth-Century English: History, Variation and Standardization*. Cambridge: Cambridge UP.

McEnery, Tony, Richard Xiao and Yukio Tono. 2006. *Corpus-based Language Studies: An Advanced Resource Book*. London: Routledge.

McEnery, Tony and Andrew Hardie. 2012. *Corpus Linguistics*. Cambridge: Cambridge UP.

Mehler, Alexander, Serge Sharoff and Marina Santini. (Eds.). 2010. *Genres on the Web. Computational Models and Empirical Studies*. Dordrecht: Springer.

Metcalf, Allan. 2002. *Predicting New Words*. Boston: Houghton Mifflin.

Miller, Carolyn R. and Dawn Shepherd. 2004. "Blogging as social action: A genre analysis of the weblog". *Into the Blogosphere: Rhetoric, Community, and Culture of Weblogs*. Gurak, Laura J., Smiljana Antonijevic, Laurie Johnson, Clancy Ratliff, and Jessica Reyman. (Eds.). Available via blog.lib.umn.edu/blogosphere/blogging_as_social_action_a_genre_analysis_of_the_weblog.html. Last accessed November 15, 2011.

Milroy, James. 1992. *Linguistic Variation and Change*. Oxford: Oxford UP.

Milroy, Lesley. 1989. *Language and Social Networks*. Oxford: Blackwell. Reprint of the second edition 1987.

Milroy, James and Lesley Milroy. 1985. "Linguistic change, social network and speaker innovation". *Journal of Linguistics* 21. 339-384.

Morris, Merrill and Christine Ogan. 1996. "The Internet as mass medium". *Journal of Communication 46*. 39-50. Available via jcmc.indiana.edu/vol1/issue4/morris.html. Last accessed November 16, 2011.

Murray, Wayne S. and Kenneth I. Forster. 2004. "Serial mechanisms in lexical access: The rank hypothesis". *Psychological Review* 111. 721-756.

Nagy, William, Patricia A. Herman and Richard C. Anderson. 1985. "Learning new words from context". *Reading Research Quarterly* 20. 233-253.

Nagy, William E., Richard C. Anderson and Patricia A. Herman. 1987. "Learning new word meanings from context during normal reading". *American Educational Research Journal* 24. 237-270.

Nagy, William E. and Dedre Gentner. 1990. “Semantic constraints on lexical categories”. *Language and Cognitive Processes* 5. 169-201.

Nagy, William E. and Richard C. Anderson. 1995. “Metalinguistic awareness and literacy acquisition in different languages”. Center for reading at the University of Illinois technical report 618. Available via ideals.illinois.edu/bitstream/handle/2142/17594/ctrstreadtechrepv01995i00618_opt.pdf?sequence=1. Last accessed on March 25, 2012.

Nagy, William E. 2007. “Metalinguistic awareness and the vocabulary- comprehension connection”. In: Wagner, Richard K., Andrea E. Muse and Kendra R. Tannenbaum. (Eds.). *Vocabulary Acquisition: Implications for Reading Comprehension.* New York: Guilford Press. 52-77.

Nevalainen, Terttu and Helena Raumolin-Brunberg. 1996. “Corpus of Early English”. In: Nevalainen, Terttu and Helena Raumolin-Brunberg. (Eds.). *Sociolinguistics and Language History*. Amsterdam: Rodopi. 39-56.

Nevalainen, Terttu and Helena Raumolin-Brunberg. 2003. *Historical Sociolinguistics*. London: Longman.

Ntoulas, Alexandros, Junghoo Cho and Christopher Olson. 2004. “What’s new on the Web? The Evolution of the Web from a Search Engine Perspective”. Available via cs.cmu.edu/~olston/publications/webstudy.pdf. Last accessed November 1, 2011.

Oakes, Michael P. 1998. *Statistics for Corpus Linguistics*. Edinburgh: Edinburgh UP.

*Oxford English Corpus*. Oxford: Oxford UP.

OED *online*. Simpson, John A. and Edmund S.C. Weiner. (Eds.). ³2000. *The Oxford English Dictionary*. Oxford: Oxford UP. oed.com.

Odlyzko, Andrew. 2003. “Internet growth: Myth and reality, use and abuse. In: SPIE – Optical Transmission Systems and Equipment WDM Networking II, 2003, vol. 5247, pp. 1–15.

Paradowski, Michal B. and Lukasz Jonak. 2012. “Diffusion of linguistic innovation as social coordination”. *Psychology of Language and Communication* 16. 53-64.

Pinker, Steven and Michael J. Ullman. 2002. “The past and future of the past tense”. *Trends in Cognitive Science* 6. 456-463.

Plag, Ingo. 2003. *Word Formation in English*. Cambridge: Cambridge UP.

Plaut, David C., James L. McClelland, Mark S. Seidenberg and Karalyn Patterson. 1996. “Understanding normal and impaired reading: Computational principles in quasi-regular domains”. *Psychological Review* 103. 56-115.

Raumolin-Brunberg, Helena. 2006. "Leaders of linguistic change in early modern England". In: Facchinetti, Roberta and Matti Rissanen. (Eds.). *Corpus-based Studies of Diachronic English*. Frankfurt am Main: Peter Lang. 115-134

Renouf, Antoinette. (Ed.). 1998. *Explorations in Corpus Linguistics*. Amsterdam: Rodopi.

Renouf, Antoinette and Laurie Bauer. 2000. "Contextual clues to word-meaning". *International Journal of Corpus Linguistics* 5. 231-258.

Renouf, Antoinette, Andrew Kehoe and Jay Banerjee. 2005. "The WebCorp Search Engine. A holistic approach to web text search". In: *Electronic Proceedings of CL2005*. University of Birmingham. Available via webcorp.org.uk/publications.html. Last accessed October 19, 2011.

RDUES (Research and Development Unit for English Studies, Birmingham City University). 1999. *WebCorp*. Available via webcorp.org.uk/live/. Last accessed October 19, 2011.

Resnik, Philip and Aaron Elkiss. 2005. "The Linguist's Search Engine: An Overview". *Proceedings of ACL 2005*. Available via acl.ldc.upenn.edu/P/P05/P05-3009.pdf. Last accessed October 19, 2011.

Rheingold, Howard. 1994. *The Virtual Community*. London: Secker and Warburg.

Rogers, Everett M. 1962. *Diffusion of Innovations*. New York: The Free Press.

Rogers, Everett M. and Floyd F. Shoemaker $^{2}$1971. *Communication of Innovations: A Cross-Cultural Approach*. New York: The Free Press.

Rumšienė, Goda. 2006. "Neologisms of Internet English: Sociolinguistic aspects of development". *Kalbotyra: Germanų ir Romanų Studijos* 56. 114-121.

Sablayrolles, Jean-François. 2000. *La Néologie en Français Contemporain. Examen du Concept et Analyse de Productions Néologiques Récentes*. Paris: Honoré Champion Éditeur.

Sablayrolles, Jean-François. (Ed.). 2003. *L'Innovation Lexicale*. Paris: Honoré Champion Éditeur.

Sandra, Dominiek. 1990. "On the representation and processing of compound words: Automatic access to constituent morphemes does not occur". *Quarterly Journal of Experimental Psychology* 42. 529-567.

Santini, Marina. 2010. "Cross-testing a genre classification model for the Web". In: Mehler et al. 87-128.

Schippan, Thea. 2001. "Neologismen und Archaismen. Fallstudien". In: Cruse, Alan D, Franz Hundsnurscher, Michael Job and Peter Rolf Lukevier. (Eds.).

*Lexicology/Lexikologie. An International Handbook on the Nature and Structure of Words and Vocabularies/Ein Internationales Handbuch zur Natur und Struktur von Wörtern und Wortschätzen*. Berlin: Mouton de Gruyter. Vol. II. 1373-1380.

Schmid, Hans-Jörg. 2003. "Collocation: hard to pin down, but bloody useful". *Zeitschrift für Anglistik und Amerikanistik* 3. 235-258.

Schmid, Hans-Jörg. 2005. *Englische Morphologie und Wortbildung*. Berlin: Erich Schmidt Verlag.

Schmid, Hans-Jörg. 2007. "Entrenchment, salience and basic levels". In: Geeraerts, Dirk and Hubert Cuyckens. (Eds). *The Oxford Handbook of Cognitive Linguistics*. Oxford: Oxford UP. 117-138.

Schmid, Hans-Jörg. 2008. "New words in the mind: concept-formation and entrenchment of neologisms". *Anglia. Zeitschrift für Englische Philologie* 126: 1. 1-36.

Schmid, Hans-Jörg. 2010. "Does frequency in text really instantiate entrenchment in the cognitive system?". In: Dylan Glynn and Kerstin Fischer. (Eds.). *Quantitative methods in cognitive semantics: Corpus-driven approaches*. Berlin: Mouton de Gruyter. 101-133.

Schmid, Hans-Jörg. 2011a. *English Morphology and Word-Formation*. Berlin: Erich Schmidt Verlag. Second revised and translated edition.

Schmid, Hans-Jörg. 2011b. "Tracing paths of conventionalization from the Bible to the BNC: A concise corpus-based history of the *not that* construction". In: Bauer, Renate and Ulrike Krischke. (Eds.). *More than Words. Essays presented to Hans Sauer on the occasion of his 65th birthday*. Frankfurt: Peter Lang. 199-316.

Schmid, Hans-Jörg. 2014. "Lexico-grammatical patterns, pragmatic associations and discourse frequency". In: Herbst, Thomas, Hans-Jörg Schmid and Susen Faulhaber. (Eds.). *Constructions. Collocations and Patterns*. Berlin: Mouton de Gruyter. 239-293.

Seidenberg, Mark S. and James L. McClelland. 1989. "A distributed, developmental model of word recognition and naming". *Psychological Review* 96. 523-568.

Sinclair, John. 1991. *Corpus, Concordance, Collocations*. Oxford: Oxford UP.

Sinclair, John. 1996. "Corpus typology". EAGLES Preliminary Recommendations on Corpus Typology. Available via ilc.cnr.it/EAGLES/pub/eagles/corpora/corpustyp.ps.gz. Last accessed October 19, 2011.

Soanes, Catherine and Angus Stevenson. (Eds.). [11]2008. *Concise Oxford English Dictionary*. Oxford: Oxford UP.

Sommant, Micheline. 2003. "Innovation lexicale: Sources des néologismes, normalisation et intégration dans les nomenclatures des dictionaries de langue française". In: Sablayrolles. 247-260.

Sommers. Fred. 1963. "Types and ontology". *Philosophical Review* 72. 327-363.

Stahl, Steven A. 1991. "Beyond the instrumentalist hypothesis: Some relationships between word meanings and comprehension". In: Schwanenflugel, Paula J. (Ed.). *The Psychology of Word Meanings*. Hillsdale: Erlbaum. 157-186.

Stefanowitsch, Anatol and Stefan Th. Gries. 2003. "Collostructions: Investigating the interaction of words and constructions". *International Journal of Corpus Linguistics* 8. 209-243.

Stein, Gabriele. 1973. *English Word-Formation over Two Centuries*. Tübingen: Narr.

Štekauer, Pavol. 2005. "On the theory of neologisms and nonce-formations". *Australian Journal of Linguistics* 22:1. 97-112.

Sternberg, Robert J. 1987. "Most vocabulary acquisition is learned from context". In: McKeown, Margaret G. and Mary E. Curtis. (Eds.). *The Nature of Vocabulary Acquisition*. Hillsdale: Erlbaum. 89-105.

Stubbs, Michael. 1995. "Collocations and semantic profiles. On the cause of the trouble with quantitative studies". *Functions in Language* 2. 23-55.

Taylor, John R. 2003. "Polysemy's paradoxes". *Language Sciences* 25. 637-665.

Teubert, Wolfgang. 1998. "Korpus und Neologie". In: Teubert, Wolfgang. (Ed.). *Neologie und Korpus*. Tübingen: Narr. 129-170.

Tomasello, Michael. 2003. *Constructing a Language. A usage-based Theory of Language Acquisition*. Cambridge: Harvard UP.

Tournier, Jean. 1985. *Introduction Descriptive à la Lexicogénétique de l'Anglais Contemporain*. Paris: Champion-Slatkine.

Trudgill, Peter. 2004. *New-Dialect Formation: The Inevitability of Colonial Englishes*. Edinburgh: Edinburgh UP.

Trudgill, Peter. 2008. "Colonial dialect contact in the history of European languages: On the irrelevance of identity in new-dialect formation". *Language in Society* 37. 241-280.

Tuggy, David, 1993. "Ambiguity, polysemy, and vagueness". *Cognitive Linguistics* 4. 273-290.

Tuggy, David. 2005. "Cognitive approach to word-formation". In: Štekauer, Pavol and Rochelle Lieber. (Eds.). *Handbook of Word-Formation*. Dordrecht: Springer. 233-265.

Tuggy, David. 2006. "Schematic network". In: Geeraerts, Dirk. (Ed.). *Cognitive Linguistics*. Berlin: Mouton de Gruyter. 167-184.

Tyler, Andrea and Vyvan Evans, 2001. "Reconsidering prepositional polysemy networks. The case of *over*." *Language* 77. 724-765.

Uyar, A. 2009. "Investigation of the accuracy of search engine hit counts." *Journal of Information Science* 35.4. 469-480.

Verhagen, Arie. 2011. "Conventionality in an evolutionary perspective". Shanghai, 9 July 2011. Available via arieverhagen.nl.

Verkoeijen, Peter P.J.L., Remy M. J.P. Rikers and Henk Schmidt. 2004. "Detrimental influence of contextual change on spacing effects in free recall". *Journal of Experimental Psychology: Learning, Memory, and Cognition* 30. 796–800.

Werlich, Egon. 1976. *A Text Grammar of English*. Heidelberg: Quelle and Meyer.

Wilso, Wolfram. 1985. "Zur Produktion und Rezeption von Wortbildungserscheinungen". *Zeitschrift für Germanistische Linguistik* 13. 278-294.

Wilso, Wolfram. 1992. "Schematheorie und Wortbildung". *Deutsch als Fremdsprache* 29. 230-234.

Zorzi Marco, George Houghton and Brian Butterworth. 1998. "Two routes or one in reading aloud? A connectionist dual-route model". *Journal of Experimental Psychology: Human Perception and Performance* 24. 1131-1161.

Zwisterlood, Pienie. 1994. "The role of semantic transparency in the processing and representation of Dutch compounds". *Language and Cognitive Processes* 9. 341-368.

**English Corpus Linguistics**

Edited by Thomas Kohnen and Joybrato Mukherjee

Vol. 1 Roberta Facchinetti / Frank Palmer (eds.): English Modality in Perspective. Genre Analysis and Contrastive Studies. 2004.

Vol. 2 Grace Y. W. Tse: A Corpus-based Study of Proper Names in Present-day English. Aspects of Gradience and Article Usage. 2005.

Vol. 3 Sabine Braun / Kurt Kohn / Joybrato Mukherjee (eds.): Corpus Technology and Language Pedagogy. New Resources, New Tools, New Methods. 2006.

Vol. 4 Clemens W. A. Fritz: From English in Australia to Australian English. 1788–1900. 2007.

Vol. 5 Christiane Brand: Lexical Processes in Scientific Discourse Popularisation. A corpus-linguistic study of the SARS coverage. 2008.

Vol. 6 Sebastian Hoffmann / Stefan Evert / Nicholas Smith / David Lee / Ylva Berglund Prytz: Corpus Linguistics with *BNCweb* – a Practical Guide. 2008.

Vol. 7 Lars M. Blöhdorn: Postmodifying Attributive Adjectives in English. An Integrated Corpus-Based Approach. 2009.

Vol. 8 Uta Katharina Elisabeth Schäpers: Nominal versus Clausal Complexity in Spoken and Written English. Theory and Description. 2009.

Vol. 9 Ulrike Gut: Non-native Speech. A Corpus-based Analysis of Phonological and Phonetic Properties of L2 English and German. 2009.

Vol. 10 Sandra Boggel: Metadiscourse in Middle English and Early Modern English Religious Texts. A corpus-based study. 2009.

Vol. 11 Donald Sims MacQueen: The Integration of MILLION into the English System of Number Words. A Diachronic Study. 2010.

Vol. 12 Tanja Rütten: How to Do Things with Texts. Patterns of Instruction in Religious Discourse 1350–1700. 2011.

Vol. 13 Yvonne Alexandra Breyer: Corpora in Language Teaching and Learning. Potential, Evaluation, Challenges. 2011.

Vol. 14 Kirsten Gather: Syntactic Dislocation in English Congregational Song between 1500 and 1900. A Corpus-based Study. 2014.

Vol. 15 Daphné Kerremans: A Web of New Words. A Corpus-Based Study of the Conventionalization Process of English Neologisms. 2015.

www.peterlang.com